Transforming Emoti
Psychotherapy

Emotion-focused therapy is a research-informed psychological therapy that to date has mainly been studied in the context of depression, trauma, and couple distress. The evidence suggests that this therapy has a lasting and transformative effect. **Ladislav Timulak** presents EFT as a particular therapeutic approach that addresses psychological human suffering, offering a view that puts more emphasis on attending to the distress, rather than avoiding or suppressing it.

Focusing on the latest developments in EFT, *Transforming Emotional Pain in Psychotherapy* presents a theory of human suffering and a model of therapy that addresses that suffering. The model of suffering assumes that the experienced emotional pain is a response to an injury that prevents or violates the fulfilment of the basic human needs of being loved, safe, and acknowledged. This book focuses on a particular way of transforming emotional pain in psychotherapy through: helping the client to tolerate the pain; assisting the client to identify the core of the difficult emotional experiences; identifying the needs connected to the core pain which are unmet or being violated, and responding (with compassion and protective anger) to the underlying needs of the client that transforms the original pain.

Transforming Emotional Pain in Psychotherapy provides an account of how emotional pain can be conceptualised and how it can be addressed in therapy. It provides practical tips for therapists working with emotional pain and shows how it can then be made more bearable and transformed allowing the client to be more sensitive to the pain of others, and to seek support when needed. This book will be essential reading for clinical and counselling psychologists, psychotherapists and counsellors in practice and training, as well as for fully qualified professionals undergoing further training in EFT.

Ladislav Timulak is Course Director of the Doctorate in Counselling Psychology at Trinity College Dublin. He is the author of several books, and a number of book chapters and research papers. He is involved in the training of psychologists and psychotherapists, and maintains a part-time private practice.

'With this book Ladislav Timulak shows his insightfulness into the therapeutic change process and has made an original contribution, demonstrating how people transform emotional pain.'
—Leslie S. Greenberg, PhD, Distinguished Research Professor Emeritus, Department of Psychology, York University, Toronto, Canada

'This book provides a concise, clear, lively, compassionate, and personal introduction to contemporary emotion-focused therapy, touching on the latest theory, practice and research. Timulak has developed an elegant, readable and useful formulation of the nature and transformation of human emotional suffering. Highly recommended.'
—Robert Elliott, PhD, Professor of Counselling, University of Strathclyde, Scotland, Professor Emeritus of Psychology, University of Toledo, USA

'A bold new development in emotion focused therapy. This book is a rich reflection on how human suffering is transformed. Delivered as an accessible guide that leaves plenty of room for contemplation, Timulak distills a complex theory of change which therapists will recognize from their practice.'
—Antonio Pascual-Leone, PhD, Associate Professor, Director of the Psychological Services and Research Centre, Department of Psychology, University of Windsor, Windsor, Canada

'This is a book that … offers a coherent and research-informed theoretical framework, practical principles and procedures for conducting therapy, and a wealth of vividly-described case examples … I warmly recommend this book to all students and practitioners of counselling and psychotherapy …'
—John McLeod, PhD, Emeritus Professor Counselling, University of Abertay, Scotland, Adjunct Professor of Psychology, University of Oslo, Norway

Transforming Emotional Pain in Psychotherapy

An emotion-focused approach

Ladislav Timulak

Routledge
Taylor & Francis Group
LONDON AND NEW YORK

First published 2015
by Routledge
27 Church Road, Hove, East Sussex, BN3 2FA

And by Routledge
711 Third Avenue, New York, NY 10017

Routledge is an imprint of the Taylor & Francis Group, an informa business

British Library Cataloguing in Publication Data
A catalogue record for this book is available from the British Library

Library of Congress Cataloging in Publication Data

Timulak, Ladislav, author.
Transforming emotional pain in psychotherapy : an emotion-focused approach / Ladislav Timulak.
p. ; cm.
Includes bibliographical references.
I. Title.
[DNLM: 1. Psychotherapy—methods. 2. Emotions. 3. Stress, Psychological—therapy. WM 420]
BF636.6
158.3—dc23 2014043693

ISBN: 978-1-138-79016-2 (hbk)
ISBN: 978-1-138-79018-6 (pbk)
ISBN: 978-1-315-76065-0 (ebk)

Typeset in Times New Roman
by codeMantra

Dedicated to my parents, and to Katka, Adam, Dominika, and Natalia.

Contents

Acknowledgment ix
Foreword xi

1 Introduction 1

Part I
Theoretical conceptualisation

2 Emotional pain 11

3 Transforming emotional pain 33

Part II
Practical application

4 Therapeutic relationship promoting emotional transformation 47

5 Conceptualising core emotional pain 58

6 Strategy for therapy—accessing core emotional pain 85

7 Strategy for therapy—transforming core emotional pain 112

8 Overall treatment strategy and working with difficulties in therapeutic process 143

Afterword 167
References 169
Index 177

Acknowledgments

This book would not be possible without the generous contribution of many people around me. I would like to thank Les Greenberg for the many excellent opportunities he has afforded me to learn about the theory and practice of emotion-focused therapy (EFT). I would like to thank Robert Elliott from whom I learned to take my first steps in EFT, and whose work I continue to find stimulating and inspiring. I would like to thank Antonio Pascual-Leone whose work has greatly influenced my own thinking about EFT, but also, the many other EFT theorists, therapists, and researchers who have shared their learning and understanding of the therapeutic process.

I would like to thank all the clients and research collaborators who contributed to my own learning and to the ideas presented in this book. Ongoing collaboration with my students (now colleagues) has greatly contributed to the shaping of my thinking with regards to the therapeutic process. Specifically, a large number of research projects investigating the process of emotion transformation have directly contributed to the ideas outlined in this book (thanks to Jim McElvaney, Ciara Keogh, Casey O'Brien, Siobhan McNally, Andrew Dillon, Katie O'Brien, Niall Crowley, Daragh Keogh, Sam Hughes, Jen Murphy, and Lucy Rowell). I would like to thank those students and colleagues with whom I continue to collaborate on other, related, EFT research projects. It is hoped that these studies will lead to new publications in the near future. I would also like to thank my colleagues on the Counselling Psychology programme in Trinity College Dublin for their continuing support and for creating an excellent working environment.

My thanks also go to Daragh Keogh and Anne Davis for initial proofreading of my 'Slovakian' English manuscript. I would like to thank the team in Routledge (Joanne Forshaw, Kirsten Buchanan, Sioned Jones, and codeMantra). The work on this book was also supported by the funding awarded by the Irish Health Research Board (H01388-HRA POR/2010/7) to a related project.

Finally, I would like to thank my family, my parents, my sister, and especially my wife, Katka, for all the support they have given me over the years.

Foreword

It is with great pleasure that I write a preface to this volume on *Transforming Emotional Pain in Psychotherapy: An Emotion-Focused Approach.* Emotion-focused therapy is based on the notion that "I feel, therefore I am", and that emotions are not simply secondary to cognition. Rather emotions provide both colour and meaning to life and are the constant companions of our lives, governing much of what we do. As Vincent van Gogh (1889) wrote to his brother, "Don't let's forget that the little emotions are the great captains of our lives, and that we obey them without knowing it".

With the advent of a view of emotion as an adaptive resource and a meaning system, rather than as something that needs to be gotten rid of cathartically, modified, down-regulated or corrected by reason, the understanding of emotion's role in human relationships and psychotherapy has produced a sea change in psychotherapy. This "new look" has begun to set a new agenda for psychotherapy research—to determine how we can best facilitate change in emotions, treating emotions as independent variables that exist as such, rather than being secondary to cognition. Key issues for clinicians now are how best to promote access to and awareness of emotion and how to help the transformation of maladaptive emotion. This book helps to improve understanding of how to facilitate this kind of emotional change.

As the work in this book demonstrates, there is a duality in working with emotions. This occurs because primary emotions are both carriers of knowledge and givers of pleasure-pain. Feelings often provide us with immediate, intimate, personally meaningful knowledge about ourselves and others in an unmediated and personally specific manner. These feelings need attention and *articulation in language* to sharpen and clarify what is felt and promote self-understanding. But there comes a point when feelings as a result of past trauma or neglect can become too painful to bear, and they then lose their meaning giving function and can become overwhelming, destructive experiences. These feelings carry suffering and pain at intensities that cannot be tolerated and can become a source of threat. Then they produce intolerable experiences and can be a danger to psychological existence. In these cases they need to be transformed or regulated to preserve a sense of self-coherence.

Building on the basic tenet of the primacy of emotion and the importance of its acceptance, EFT, over the past decades, has developed to stress the importance of emotional transformation, suggesting that the best way to change emotion is with another emotion (Greenberg 2002, 2010). Ladislav Timulak, as a second generation emotion-focused therapist, theorist, trainer, and researcher, has been in an excellent position to expand and develop the approach as he has done in this book. This book makes a significant contribution to understanding the process of emotional change in psychotherapy.

This book will enhance the practice of EFT and add to the training which is taking place all over the world. In addition to the training program in Ireland developed by Ladislav in which these ideas are implemented, there now are many training programs in Europe, Asia, and the Americas. In these training programs people learn that emotional suffering cannot be understood simply as caused by or changed by cognitive or behavioural difficulties and that rather pain comes from deep in the soul from implicit sources. They learn that people benefit by facing avoided pain, transforming it and creating new meaning to change narratives.

With this book Ladislav Timulak shows his insightfulness into the therapeutic change process and has made an original contribution, demonstrating how people transform emotional pain.

Leslie Greenberg
Toronto
September 2014

1 Introduction

This book focuses on emotional pain and its transformation in psychotherapy from the theoretical framework represented by emotion-focused therapy (EFT; Elliott, Watson, Goldman, and Greenberg, 2004; Greenberg, 2002; Greenberg and Johnson, 1988; Greenberg, Rice, and Elliott, 1993). While there are a number of books, chapters, and papers written on the use of emotion-focused therapy with a variety of client presenting issues, this book provides a unique framework that builds on the model of emotional transformation first presented by Pascual-Leone and Greenberg (2007; Pascual-Leone, 2009; see also work of Pascual-Leone and his colleagues: Pascual-Leone, 2005; Kramer, Pascual-Leone, Despland & de Roten, in press; Paivio and Pascual-Leone, 2010) and then further developed in the research group I run in Trinity College Dublin (e.g., Crowley, Timulak, and McElvaney, 2013; Dillon, Timulak, and Greenberg, 2014; Keogh, Timulak, and McElvaney, 2013; Keogh, O'Brien, Timulak, and McElvaney, 2011; McNally, Timulak, and Greenberg, 2014; O'Brien, Timulak, McElvaney and Greenberg, 2012; Timulak, Dillon, McNally, and Greenberg, 2012), and finally in the collaborative work of Timulak and Pascual-Leone (2014). The emotion transformation model is used as a framework, organising a theory of psychopathology and theory of psychotherapy (i.e., case conceptualisation and strategy for therapy).

Emotion-focused therapy (EFT; Greenberg et al., 1993; Greenberg, 2002; Greenberg and Johnson, 1988) is a research-informed psychological therapy that to date has mainly been studied in the context of depression, trauma, and couple distress (Elliott, Greenberg, Watson, Timulak, and Freire, 2013). There are also new developments in this therapy for a variety of client difficulties such as eating disorders (Lafrance Robinson, Dolhanty, and Greenberg, 2013), social anxiety (Elliott, 2013, Shahar, 2013), or generalised anxiety disorder (Timulak, McElvaney, Martin, and Greenberg, 2014). The evidence suggests that this therapy has a lasting and transformative effect (Elliott et al., 2013), and its popularity is growing apace, particularly in North America. This is evidenced, for instance, by the huge growth in published books on EFT such as Elliott et al. (2004), Greenberg (2002; 2011), Greenberg et al. (1993), Greenberg and Goldman (2008), Greenberg and Johnson (1988), Greenberg and Paivio (1997), Greenberg and Watson (2006), Johnson (2004), Paivio and Pascual-Leone (2010), and Watson, Goldman, and Greenberg (2007). The approach has a strong research base, some of which will be presented in this book.

This book presents a theory of human suffering (psychopathology in more traditional terms) and a model of therapy that addresses that suffering. The model of suffering assumes that the experienced *emotional pain* is a response to an injury that *prevents or violates the fulfilment of the basic human needs of being loved, safe, and acknowledged.* The book is written for trainees in professional training programmes (clinical and counselling psychology, counselling and psychotherapy) as well as for fully qualified professionals undergoing further training in EFT or having an interest in this approach. This book is most helpful for those people who already have some background in EFT.

HUMAN SUFFERING—EMOTIONAL PAIN

As will be postulated later in the book, some psychotherapy research suggests that the motivation which underlies the psychological world of clients is characterised by a longing for safety, belonging, and creative actualisation. One can easily see the parallels to the arguments suggested by a neuroscientist Damasio (2011), who argues that motivational force in all living creatures is to flourish and to live to its full potential and argues that this principle can be seen on a biological as well as cultural and societal level.

On a psychological level, it has been shown that there is a correlation between a fulfilment of internal needs and personal well-being, fulfilment, and contribution to society (cf. also Deci and Ryan, 2000 on fulfilment of inner needs). However, human experience is full of real and potential adversities that do not allow fulfilment of our core fundamental needs and strivings and thus bring experiences of psychological (emotional) pain. The human experience can bring both joy and suffering. Joy comes when our fundamental needs are fulfilled, and suffering comes when they are violated or not fulfilled. Some of us are luckier and encounter less pain and suffering than others, but to encounter pain is inevitable. This book will focus on psychological pain, often described as emotional (Greenberg, 2002), or more recently, social pain (MacDonald and Jensen-Campbell, 2011) and its transformation in psychotherapy. It will focus on how psychological pain develops, how it is experienced, and how it can be transformed, leading to a fuller and more mature living.

The psychological (emotional) pain can be defined as an unpleasant, overwhelming, upsetting internal experience. It often presents itself in the form of general distress, physiological tension in the middle part of the body (e.g., head, throat, neck, shoulders, solar plexus, stomach), and a mixture of upsetting emotions and thoughts. Psychological pain also shows itself in the form of symptoms of anxiety and depression. People can be tormented by worries or obsessions that do not allow them to sleep or tense and tire them during the day. They may have panic attacks with unpleasant bodily symptoms, or they can feel hopelessness and helplessness that shut them off from others and stop their joy in living.

It seems likely that both emotional and physical pain share a neural circuitry, which is why we use the same word to describe the unpleasant consequences of distress in either the psychological or physical aspects of our being (Eisenberg, 2011). For instance, Eisenberg, in a review of her own and her colleagues' studies, suggests that individuals who are more sensitive to physical pain are also more sensitive to social rejection. Additionally, she points out that pharmacological studies have shown that regulating physical pain also regulates social pain.

Emotional pain also has physiological aspects that are uncomfortable and bring a tangible, bodily experienced pain. The emotional pain impacts our breathing, our muscular tensions, our digestion, our thinking (which may be narrower and ruminative), our sleep, levels of tiredness, appetite, and physical aches (probably linked to the muscle tension). The emotional pain also expresses itself through changes in the cardiovascular, neuroendocrine, and immune systems that initially mobilise and alert the organism, but from a longer-term perspective have negative effect on our overall health (e.g., levels of cortisol) (Dickerson, 2011). In its more extreme form, the emotional pain can be characterised by a strong emotion dysregulation (Bradley et al., 2011).

On the other hand, there are some significant dissimilarities between emotional and physical pain. For example, the memories of emotional pain are more upsetting than the memories of physical pain, and the anticipation of emotional pain is more easily pre-lived than the anticipation of physical pain (Chen & Williams, 2011). For instance, if we experienced humiliation, the memory of it will make us cringe. Similarly, if I am to deliver a talk in a hostile environment, I will be nervous and anxious, expecting rejection and fearing humiliation. My body will make me feel this anxiety, and I will be able to imagine felt experience of shame in the face of being criticised or ridiculed.

The scientific disciplines of medicine (psychiatry) and psychology often do not speak about the emotional pain. When trying to capture psychological suffering, these disciplines focus on the description of common symptoms such as anxiety, behavioural avoidance, negative thinking, sleeplessness, irritation, muscular tension, negative view of the future, obsessive thoughts, compulsory behaviour, and so on. They classify people according to the clusters of symptoms, and the presence of some symptoms in the absence of some other symptoms serves as a basis for a particular diagnosis. At the same time many of those symptoms such as depression and apprehensive anxiety (focusing on potential triggers that may bring or worsen the experienced pain) are often secondary to more primary feelings (Greenberg, 2002), which can be present in the form of discreet emotions such as loneliness and loss, shame, and a sense of being judged (Dickerson, 2011; Greenberg and Watson, 2006; MacDonald, Borsook, and Spielman, 2011) and as upsetting trauma, dread, and terror (Ford, 2009).

The mainstream diagnostic classifications, such as the DSM (American Psychiatric Association, 2013), take very little account of the impact on these symptoms of the individual's response to 'stressors' that may be involved in either the present life situation or have historically been implicated in the formation of specific symptoms. These classifications lack an emphasis for understanding the presenting symptoms in the context of the suffering person's life situation, life history, and biological and developmentally shaped predispositions. Rather, the DSM-5 focuses on answering the question of whether the psychological presentation of the person is more or less normative and whether it causes impairment in everyday functioning. The classification systems do not try to understand how the suffering relates to the person's overall sense of the self (including the biological level of functioning such as tiredness, irritability, bodily pain expression, and tolerance), the person's sense of the self in the community, and the sense of self in the context of close family or intimate relationships. The mainstream classifications do not try to understand the psychological suffering in the context of the person's life project, in the context of the person's life history, or in the context of the person's needs and wishes.

To understand human suffering fully, however, we need to understand what people strive for in their life. Along with psychology, many of the philosophical, scientific, and theological theories and approaches have attempted to provide answers to this question. The question of what people strive for thus becomes metaphysical, and various conceptualisations are provided. These conceptualisations are often shaped by personal persuasions, worldviews, and the preferences of scientists, psychologists, and so on.. As a result, there has been much disagreement both within and between the various disciplines as they are loaded with values and their consequences. Most of the concepts are set *a priori*, on the basis of the theoretician's persuasions.

Each therapist is a theoretician, trying to understand what needs are not being met when people are suffering and experiencing psychological and emotional pain. Thus, considering what needs are unmet is a crucial part of the therapist's work. Whilst it is not possible to know fully what people strive for in their lives, we can observe the principles that appear to capture the directions of these strivings.

RESPONDING TO EMOTIONAL PAIN

For centuries people have sought and offered both informal and formal help in responding to emotional pain. Family members or caretakers in childhood, friends and acquaintances, as well as formally trained doctors, priests, teachers, elders, and more recently psychologists, counsellors, and psychotherapists were or are the ones who offer this help. Caring others provided attentive presence and listening as well as more active guidance. However, during the twentieth century, with the development of psychology along with counselling and psychotherapy research, we have developed a more scientific understanding of various forms of help through psychological means. For instance, the recent neuroscientific evidence suggests that the caring and empathic presence of the other has an analgesic impact on the pain centres in the brain (Panksepp, 2011). A further line of research suggests that providing social support increases the threshold of physical pain (Eisenberg, 2011; Master et al., 2009) or decreases the experience of threat as detected on a neural basis (Coan et al., 2006). Much research evidence exists which documents the positive role of social support (in its various forms) in increasing the capacity to bear physical as well as emotional pain (see e.g., Brown, Sheffield, Leary, and Robinson, 2003; Eisenberger, Taylor, Gable, Hilmert, and Lieberman, 2007).

Nevertheless, despite the positive role of social support and our advancing understanding of how this social support alleviates (and sometimes transforms) emotional pain, there are clear limitations to our capability of addressing emotional pain. Although a lot of emotional suffering is transformed through informal social help or through formal counselling or psychotherapy into safer, more sensitive, connected, and more creative lives, it is also the case that a lot of suffering is not transformed due to its complexity, the personal history of the suffering person, the level of adversity the person experienced, along with possible genetic and biological predispositions that may influence the biological resilience of the organism, and so on.

Psychotherapy research is attempting to distil and nuance the processes responsible for transformation of emotional pain. We know quite a lot about what is helpful, but we want to know more about which actual psychological processes may optimally respond to emotional processing. We want to understand what type of emotional pain can be transformed through what kind of intervention processes (Castonguay and Beutler, 2006). There are an infinite number of helping approaches to emotional human suffering. These approaches are often similar or complementary, although occasionally they are following exactly the opposite steps.

This book is another contribution to the debate on how to address psychological human suffering. It offers a view that places more emphasis on attending to the distress, rather than avoiding or suppressing it. It focuses on the underlying pain that informs the person about their unfulfilled needs. It focuses on responding to those needs by generating an emotional response from the self as well as from the other(s). This approach does not assume that people have irrational thoughts as some approaches suggest, nor does it focus on an interpretation of how unresolved conflicts are unconsciously and unsuccessfully played out in everyday functioning. Nonetheless, this approach agrees that people may not always fully understand their own experiences and the resulting action tendencies.

The approach presented here assumes that there are strong genetic and environmentally caused biological vulnerabilities (e.g., influencing neural substrate reactivity; Caspi and Moffitt, 2006) that influence the level of human psychological suffering. Indeed, a genetic predisposition may explain why some people are more sensitive to physical as well as psychological pain (Way and Taylor, 2011). It may even predispose some people to react to a social injury (in the form of rejection) with more irritability and aggression (Way and Taylor, 2011). However, the research also suggests (e.g., Ford, 2009) that it is the experience of emotional injuries, particularly if they are chronic in nature, that contributes to an enduring emotional pain and further vulnerability and sensitivity to experiencing hurt. The experienced *emotional pain* is then a response to an injury that *prevents or violates the fulfilment of the basic human needs, such as being loved, safe, and acknowledged.*

The (interpersonal) injury may come in the form of exclusion, rejection,[1] or a psychological and/or physical trauma/intrusive attack. All these forms of injury are fundamental, direct, or indirect threats to healthy living and ultimately survival. For instance, the experience of a negative judgement may increase the cortisol levels, which burdens the organism and so may contribute to a variety of physical health problems (Dickerson, 2011). Exclusion leads to a psychological withdrawal, but also physiological resignation (DeWall, Pond, and Deckam, 2011). Traumatic attack brings an upsetting, uncontrollable experience that has an immediate, as well as post-traumatic, effect (Ford, 2009).

Experienced emotional pain is always a result of the interaction of a harmful trigger and the person's need in the given situation. Indeed, any emotional reaction is a reaction to a trigger in the context of the need related to the trigger (Greenberg, 2011). We constantly appraise situations, whether they are meeting our needs, and the result of that appraisal is present in our emotional experiences. Each trigger is contextually specific, as is the need and thus also the resulting emotional reaction. I will feel let down (emotional reaction) if my wife appears unresponsive (trigger) to my need for comfort (need) while the unresponsiveness of somebody who is not that emotionally relevant to me may be much less salient.

Our psychotherapy studies examining the emotional pain of clients with depression and anxiety problems (e.g., Crowley, Timulak, and McElvaney, 2013; Keogh, Timulak, and McElvaney, 2013; Keogh, O'Brien, Timulak, and McElvaney, 2011; McNally, Timulak, & Greenberg, 2014; O'Brien, Timulak, McElvaney, and Greenberg, 2012; Timulak, Dillon, McNally, and Greenberg, 2012) suggest that the psychological needs that are *violated or not responded to* and thus bring an experience of emotional pain cluster around (1) the need to be loved, understood, and connected, (2) the need to be respected, acknowledged, appreciated, and validated in what the person does and who they are, and (3) the need for safety and security. These appear to be the needs which, if not met or are violated, result in the experiences of emotional pain that bring clients to therapy. These needs seem to be connected to discreet clusters of emotions (emotional experiences) that are at the core of emotional pain. These clusters involve: (1) The *loneliness and loss*-(sadness) related cluster connected to the need to be loved and connected, (2) the *shame*-related cluster connected to the need to be acknowledged as valuable, and (3) *terror/fear*-related cluster that is connected to the need to be safe.

I would argue that conceptualisation of human distress in those underlying emotional experiences is more meaningful than its conceptualisation in terms of surface-level psychopathology, such as depression and anxiety. In EFT, these symptoms are traditionally considered to be secondary emotional experiences (Greenberg, 2011) as they are in general secondary to the underlying pain. If I feel excluded or invalidated, I will not only feel sadness or shame, but if my need in the sadness and shame, which is to be included and supported, is not responded to, secondary hopelessness, helplessness, and depression will ensue. If I feel profoundly alone and my need for being loved and close to somebody is not fulfilled, I may resign myself to these feelings with no expectation that it will ever change. With the resignation of my needs never being met comes overall depression, withdrawal, sometimes also irritation and dismissal of my own attempts for closeness and the attempts of others to approach me. A distressing picture of unhappiness, despair, hopelessness, helplessness, and perhaps irritation with the self or others is then presented around me; I may employ strategies in an attempt to avoid others. Hopelessness, helplessness, and depression will then be secondary to my primary sense of abandonment or shame.

Similarly, since the trauma (terror), exclusion, and rejection are painful, it is no wonder that I will feel debilitating apprehensive anxiety and fear that I may be a subject of such adverse experiences again. The anxiety is experienced as an uncomfortable emotion with an action tendency to flee. It focuses the person to anticipate danger and thus keeps that person alert and mobilised, which from a short-term perspective enhances the person's response but from a longer-term perspective has negative mental and physical health consequences. The anxiety of further pain is uncomfortable on its own and thus mobilises a variety of avoidance strategies that restrict the person's functioning and restricts the fulfilment of the basic psychological needs. Avoidance may be either behavioural or emotional. In behavioural, we try to avoid any potential triggers of anxiety; for instance we may avoid situations in which we could be evaluated or rejected. An extreme of such behaviour would be agoraphobic behaviour that leads the person to avoid practically all situations. Emotional avoidance is characterised by strategies through which we try not to feel the anxiety and especially the underlying painful emotions.

We employ many strategies in order to avoid pain. For instance, to avoid the emotional pain of shame, abandonment, and terror, people may numb themselves, dissociate, or overlook what they experience. Alternatively, they may lash out in rage, attacking the source of pain and thus covering their underlying pain. Other times the avoidance may be more deliberate, and people may attempt to use a quick remedy such as numbness and relaxation induced by drugs or alcohol. We also prepare ourselves for the impact of threat by worrying and imagining all types of potentially dangerous scenarios. We may also overdo things in order to minimise any potential threat.

This book focuses on particular ways of transforming emotional pain in psychotherapy. Pain can be transformed by (1) helping to tolerate it and differentiate its narrative and emotional components; (2) identifying the core of the pain; (3) identifying the needs connected to the emotional pain that are not being met or are violated; and (4) subsequent emotional response to those underlying needs. The suffering, while still painful and sad, is then more tolerable for the individual; it can inform the future life experience in a way that allows the person to be more sensitive to the pain of others and enables him or her to provide a caring presence. Additionally, the person is better able to seek support when needed and is more able to stand up for his or her rights and those of vulnerable others. Paradoxically, the suffering which has been so problematic for the person can be transformed into a more emotionally mature way of living, which is characterised by a resolve to leave a valuable stamp on the world and in the lives of others.

NOTE

1 The additive and independent effect of exclusion and rejection was demonstrated experimentally (MacDonald, Borsook, and Spielmann, 2011).

Part I

Theoretical conceptualisation

2 Emotional pain

To distil the core feelings at the centre of a client's painful experience, the therapist and client have to go/work through both the undifferentiated pain with which the client presents (typically depression, hopelessness, and helplessness), and the fear of that pain (apprehensive anxiety), which leads the client to engage in avoiding behaviour. As the client is typically engaged in avoidance of anything that could evoke core painful feelings, the client's underlying pain may often be masked or not readily visible. A warm, caring, security-providing, and validating relationship has, on its own, been demonstrated to have an emotional pain-healing propensity (Panskepp, 2011), and the patient, gentle unfolding of painful experiences in the context of such a relationship can help the therapist and client access the core of a client's emotional pain.

As mentioned in the introduction, in-depth phenomenological analyses (e.g., Crowley et al., 2013; Dillon et al., 2014; Keogh et al., 2013; Keogh et al., 2011; McNally et al., 2014; O'Brien et al., 2012; Timulak et al., 2012; but for similarity, see also wishes reported in psychodynamic studies: Luborsky and Luborsky, 2006) of the presentations in therapy of a sample of clients with depression, anxiety, and traumatic experiences, suggest that emotional suffering concentrates around three main clusters of unmet needs: (1) needs for safety and security (e.g., a sense of calming, reassuring presence, a sense of being protected); (2) needs for love and connection (e.g., care, understanding); and (3) needs for recognition of one's own value and agency (e.g., the space for own pursuits, autonomy, and their respect, acknowledgment, appreciation, validation). It is the learning from our research and clinical experience that the unmet needs embedded in these three domains are typically articulated when clients touch on their most painful feelings. These three domains of unmet needs also have corresponding core painful feelings that signal that the needs are not met. For clients presenting with depression, anxiety, and trauma, these could be clustered into three domains (1) traumatic fear/terror-related feelings (*I am insecure, invaded, I am experiencing terror*); (2) sadness/loneliness-related feelings (*I am on my own, I do not feel loved*); and (3) shame-related feelings (*I am worthless, I feel rejected*) (e.g., O'Brien et al., 2012). Whilst each client's core painful experience is idiosyncratic to that individual, core painful feelings are typically a variation of these three clusters of emotions. Let us have a look at these three clusters of emotional experiences.

SAFETY VS. INSECURITY

We all want to be safe and avoid harm, both in the immediate present, and in the longer term. We want to avoid feeling physical or emotional pain. Safety-seeking guarantees our survival. If we were careless, we may not *be* at all. Anxiety informs us about danger that could be fatal or harmful. That is why apprehensive anxiety of future trauma can be so ingrained as an aftermath of a traumatic experience. Traumatic experience brings a pain that we remember and, therefore, want to avoid. We fear any potential pain that would resemble the trauma and become fearful of any situation that matches the original traumatic situation in some way. This avoidance can be so thorough that it may take place outside of our awareness. We may apprehend without conscious awareness. Furthermore, we also find it very difficult to 'reason' with our anxiety as the location of the fear network in the brain, most of which is subcortical, makes it quite impenetrable to slow rational cognitions (Ohman and Ruck, 2007).

Thus, with every terror/fear experience, we may develop fear of that type of experience. We may become increasingly apprehensive of the traumatic, debilitating bodily reaction that will ensue from such experiences, and of the pain and disorganisation that such trauma and debilitation give rise to. Therefore, in addition to the primary terror/fear itself, we are likely to develop secondary apprehensive anxiety that fears the primary terror/fear bringing experiences. Such apprehensive anxiety not only informs us of potential danger and pain but is, in its own right, incredibly uncomfortable, unpleasant, and painful.

Primary terror and fear are typically experienced in response to traumatic damage to our physiological or psychological self. It is worth noting that the word 'trauma' is often used to describe both the stressor—in other words, the triggering event giving rise to the reaction—as well as the strong, outside-of-regular-experiencing reactions to that stressor (Ford and Courtois, 2009). Stressors giving rise to a traumatic experience may be human or non-human (e.g., an accident), and may be either a one-off, isolated event or repetitive/accumulative in nature. The response to a traumatic stressor is a significantly upsetting, uncontrollable experience that has an immediate, as well as post-traumatic, effect. The immediate effect may take the form of dissociation, profound panic, strong undifferentiated emotional and bodily upset, a sense of uncontrollability, self-disintegration, and an inability to self-regulate. The post-traumatic effect is most evident in the manner by which triggers resembling the original traumatic situation can re-evoke traumatic reaction and experiencing, further traumatising and upsetting the sufferer. Whilst the resemblance between such triggers and the original traumatic event may be clear or unclear, a defining feature of post-traumatic reaction is the avoidance of potential threats or triggers that might re-evoke the traumatic state.

It is interesting to note that we respond to threats to our safety much quicker than to any other stimuli. As a consequence of genetic predisposition, we are also more likely to be conditioned to such stimuli (Ohman and Ruck, 2007). We may fall from a height once and potentially die. Therefore, if we unexpectedly fall from a height in some situation, we will not only be very terrified while we are falling, but we will also become extremely apprehensive of similar situations that may lead to a fall in the future. As noted already, our apprehension may, to a great extent, exist/occur outside of our awareness. For instance, there is strong research evidence documenting autonomic anxious responses to masked dangerous stimuli (visible also as brain activation in the amygdala), meaning that while we may not know what we are seeing, we may already be reacting to it (Ohman and Ruck, 2007). Research also shows that there is variability in biological predisposition to fear, with some subjects responding to potentially dangerous masked stimuli more than others (see studies on masked stimuli such as Ohman and Soares, 1994). Such studies indicate that we differ in our fear proneness. Most likely, this is an inheritance of our evolution. Some of us are perhaps more evolutionary conservative, whilst some are perhaps more modern. Whilst some of us fear flying, as it is not very natural for our bodies—and therefore dangerous—some do not, as it is becoming more natural.

Once traumatic experiencing starts, the resulting terror and fear guide our attention, increasing our engagement with what is possibly dangerous in a manner which is difficult to disengage from (Ohman and Ruck, 2007; Petersen and Posner, 2012). The more of such engagement we have, the more problematic our experiencing can become. Fear circuits are not only easily activated, but once activated, their survival-oriented functioning means that they can become very entrenched. As Quirk (2007) points out, the experiencing of chronic anxiety enhances the ability of the amygdala to learn fear associations, whilst simultaneously reducing the ability of the prefrontal cortex to control fear. This is further problematic as changes to amygdala- and hippocampus-based circuits may be irreversible (Quirk, 2007). So, while on a prefrontal level (where most of our rational thinking takes place) we can reason with our perceptions, such rational efforts may be overpowered by more automatic and powerful impulses deeply ingrained in lower parts of the brain. Whilst we can explain to somebody that flying is not that dangerous, he or she may still have anxious reactions to any sign of turbulence on the plane during the flight.

Experienced traumatic events are encoded in memory and serve as a basis for the creation of emotion schemes, which may be activated when an individual encounters stimuli or triggers that resemble the remembered events. Within emotion-focused therapy (EFT), emotion schemes are conceptualized as "emotion memory structures that synthesize affective, motivational, cognitive, and behavioral elements into internal organizations that are activated rapidly, out of awareness, by relevant cues" (Greenberg, 2011, p. 38). With any problematic emotion schemes that lead to maladaptive experiences and actions, it is important that we are able to rework (or rewire on the neural level) the emotion scheme in such a way that the client's emotional processing once again serves an adaptive function, namely the rapid assessment of situations with regard the client's needs in those situations. Transformation of emotion schemes formed as results of traumatic events is quite complex, as the memory of the danger has an important survival-oriented function. Thus, trauma-based emotion schemes are quite rigid and lasting.

It appears that traumatic memory can be 'undone' through an extinction process (inhibitory learning). In such a process the individual learns to associate memories of safety with benign situations that hitherto, due to their resemblance to the traumatic situation, had triggered terror/trauma (Quirk, 2007). Such 'safety memories' are most effective at undoing trauma when formed early after the traumatic link is developed (Myers, Ressler, and Davis, 2006). On the other hand, inhibitory learning of this type is hindered by the fact that the conditioned fear is very much environment dependent (Bouton, 2004). This means that it is very difficult to 'unlearn' fear experience linked to a particular fearful trigger in an environment that is not exactly the same (e.g., the therapist's office) as the original situation where the traumatic experience occurred.

Overall, it appears that the lack of balance between the traumatic experiences and feelings of safety as well as chronicity of stressor memories can contribute to chronic anxiety (Quirk, 2007). Chronic anxiety is furthermore known to contribute to depression and resignation (Barlow, 2004). From a developmental perspective, traumas encountered in early life may impact neural development and may result in functional changes within the developing brain (Ford, 2009). Most obviously, traumatic experiences may prompt a change from 'learning brain' to 'surviving brain' functioning, the latter being characterised by harm avoidance and a lack of openness to experience. Indeed, the developing brain impacted by trauma may be affected by both biochemical and structural changes (Bateman and Fonagy, 2004; De Bellis et al., 1999; Cohen et al., 2006). Particularly problematic are continuous traumas caused by abusive or neglecting significant others who are supposed to be providing a safe and emotion-regulating presence (Bateman and Fonagy, 2004). Such traumas can lead to the development of both problematic working models of interpersonal interaction and problematic pathways of processing emotional experience. From an EFT perspective, such problematic emotional processing is conceptualised in terms of maladaptive emotion schemes centred on activating trauma/terror/fear evoked in response to triggers resembling the original traumatisation.

LOVE AND CONNECTION VS. LONELINESS

Experiences of love and connection are not only pleasurable (on a biological level, for instance, such experiences stimulate excretion of the 'love' hormone oxytocin), but they also provide us with security. Put simply, we survive in communities. Experiences of closeness and caring are thus antidotes to scary aspects of life. The experience of being cared for has a calming effect on many levels. It reduces physical pain through the release of endogenous opioids (Panksepp, 2011). In addition to alleviating the effect of physical pain, experiences of caring have also been shown to developmentally shape tolerance of emotional pain and the capacity for emotion regulation (Ford, 2009). Indeed, a social loss in childhood (e.g., the death of a parent) increases proneness to depression and brings neurobiological changes to brain functioning (e.g., hyper-reactivity of some neural systems as well as alterations in some neurotransmitter systems, Heim and Nemeroff, 1999). A caring and loving presence expressed in the form of empathy has an affect-regulating impact on children as was powerfully demonstrated by Edward Tronick (Tronick, Als, Adamson, Wise, and Brazelton, 1979; Tronick, 2005) in his still face experiments. In these studies Tronick showed how emotionally dysregulated a baby could become when encountering an unresponsive mother. Conversely, the same studies showed how soothed a baby could be when experiencing a responsive mother.

Similarly, studies on adult love and caring have shown how the presence of a caring spouse can have an immediate, calming effect. James Coan and his colleagues (Coan et al., 2006) showed how a female participant, when anticipating a mild electric shock in a fMRI study, could be calmed by holding her husband's hand. This calming effect was evident in lower levels of neural activation in those parts of the brain related to threat processing. Furthermore, the calming effects of the husband's hand holding on neural activation levels was a function of the quality of the couple's marital relationship, with more satisfied participants being more calmed by the hand holding. A similar study conducted by Master et al. (2009) showed that holding a partner's hand, even if that partner was behind a curtain, led to attenuation of experienced pain (heat). The same study reported that merely showing the subject a picture of the partner had a similar effect. Indeed, some studies suggest (e.g., Holt-Lunstad, Birmingham, and Jones, 2008; Kiekolt-Glaser and Newton, 2001) that marital satisfaction corresponds with health and potentially longevity of married couples.

The opposite of love, care, and connection is loneliness; a lack of experienced closeness, connection, and love corresponds with an experience of loneliness. When lonely, one is organised by unmet needs such as longing for connection, love, and closeness. To have these needs not met leads to emotionally painful experiences of sadness and loss. It can also eventually lead to a secondary psychological withdrawal, but also to physiological resignation (DeWall, Pond, and Deckam, 2011). Loneliness can also be experienced by people who seemingly do not lack social contact, as experiencing social contact without the intimacy of belongingness can also lead to experiences of emotional isolation (Cacioppo and Patrick, 2008).

As physical pain and emotional pain share neural regions, they also share some attributes (Eisenberger, 2011). Interestingly, whilst mild emotional pain (e.g., exclusion by strangers) increases physical pain sensitivity (Eisenberger, 2011), intense emotional pain (e.g., experimental manipulation suggesting that you end up alone later in life) has been shown to result in social and physical analgesia (Eisenberger, 2011; Chen and Williams, 2011; DeWall and Baumeister, 2006). Furthermore, Baumeister et al. (2002) showed that when people were manipulated and told that they would end up alone later in life, not only did they experience physical and social resignation, but their immediate complex cognitive performance also deteriorated. Research studies suggest that experienced social exclusion decreases self-regulation, increases aggression, and decreases prosocial behaviour such as empathic concern for others (DeWall, Pond, and Deckam,

2011). This suggests that lonely people become more irritable and hostile, which perhaps contributes to their further ostracisation.

The negative impact of loneliness is well-documented. People with high levels of self-reported loneliness consume more alcohol, exercise less, sleep worse, and perceive their psychological and social connection in a much worse light (Cacioppo and Patrick, 2008). Experiences of loneliness, indeed, lead to a more resigned style of behaving in which people may not appreciate dangers to their health, for instance, when consuming comforting but unhealthy foods (Cacioppo and Patrick, 2008). Experiences of loneliness may also prompt maladaptive self-soothing behaviour in the form of addiction to narcotics (Panksepp, 2011). Such self-soothing is both short-lived and counterproductive, as withdrawal symptoms, when the narcotics leave the body, typically result in an increase in feelings of sadness. Loneliness can also have other consequences for the person's health. It has been shown to impact adversely on cardiovascular- (Hawkley, Burleson, Berntson, and Cacioppo, 2003), and immune-system functioning (Pressman et al., 2005). Lonely subjects have been found to have higher levels of stress hormones in their blood (Cacioppo and Patrick, 2008), and there are suggestions that loneliness affects gene expression ability to shut off inflammatory response (Cacioppo and Patrick, 2008). Experimental studies inducing a sense of loneliness in subjects (e.g., through hypnosis) have also shown the adverse impact of loneliness on subjects' self-esteem, shyness, perceived social support, and fear of negative evaluation (Cacioppo and Patrick, 2008).

To make the issue even more complicated, it would appear that people who experience loneliness may also be less skilful at eliciting cooperation from others (Cacioppo and Patrick, 2008). This may be partially due to the fact that lonely people are more likely to withdraw from interaction (DeWall, Pond, and Deckam, 2011), as they may be less trusting and may expect abandonment (Jones, Freemon, and Goswick, 1981). Indeed, research studies suggest that the greater the experienced loneliness, the less likely lonely people are to solicit support (Cacioppo and Patrick, 2008). Furthermore, people who do not have high expectations with regards closeness and intimacy may miss signs of the potential for intimacy (MacDonald, Borsook, and Spielmann, 2011).

Although loneliness prompts a desire to affiliate, failure to fulfil this desire can lead to depression, resignation, and apathy (Cacioppo et al., 2006). Thus, experienced loneliness can lead to more loneliness and eventually to withdrawal, shutting down, isolation, hopelessness, helplessness, and depression. The vicious circle is thus complete and is very difficult to break. The unmet needs for closeness and connection are shut down (although the oxytocin levels during the experienced isolation are also elevated, suggesting that they signal the need for being connected to, cuddled; Way and Taylor, 2011). For these reasons perhaps, it is very difficult to bring a client's experiences of loneliness to the fore and identify what is being missed. It is also difficult to mobilise the client to reach out to others, and to open up to the possibility of seeing and letting in any caring and loving behaviour that may be expressed toward him or her. This latter is especially challenging, as in many cases, the unfortunate reality may be that there is very little of such care and love available to the client.

Research studies (often animal studies; see review in Way and Taylor, 2011) also suggest that genetic predispositions to benefit or not benefit from the caring behaviour of caregivers may be quite important in the developmental history of individuals with experiences of loneliness. Genetic predisposition may be responsible for a low tolerance of early adversity, but it might also influence how well we can benefit from the social support that is available to us. For instance, it is possible that the same genetic predisposition that makes us vulnerable to adversity might make us particularly well-attuned to good and caring behaviour. This phenomenon is visible in animal studies (reviewed by Way and Taylor, 2011), which have shown that highly reactive monkeys who are fostered by nurturing mothers develop good social skills, while monkeys of the same type, fostered in a non-caring environment, are more likely to develop as unlikeable.

As with trauma/terror/fear, loneliness (and the sense of being abandoned or overlooked) is often experienced very early in one's life. The internal working models (of interpersonal interaction) and emotion scheme-based self-organisations that develop as a consequence of the experience of loneliness can therefore become heavily ingrained, stable, and self-perpetuating. Animal studies suggest that levels of the hormone oxytocin (the presence of which is stimulated by cuddling behaviour) during early development may have consequences for later social behaviour. So for example, low levels of oxytocin during early development may lead to higher levels of irritability and less interest in social interaction when older (Way and Taylor, 2011).

The activation of historically formed emotion schemes centred around the sense of loneliness by current triggers evokes a whole system of feeling profoundly abandoned. Protection against this painful feeling often takes the form of shutting down or avoiding emotional experience. Such avoidance can include avoidance of social situations, which could potentially result in exclusion. Thus, the most longed-for experience, to experience connection, closeness, and social contact, is not even sought; rather, it is dreaded and avoided.

VALIDATION VS. SHAME

The third cluster of core painful emotional experiences relates to a lack of acknowledgment, validation, and appreciation. Experiences of validation, as with experiences of love, bring a sense of belonging, but they also bring an identity-giving sense of the unique contribution the person is making to the community. Ultimately, experiences of validation are linked to experiences of safety; when we are seen and recognised by those close to us, by our peers, we know that we are important to them. We feel we are part of the community that provides us with relationships and safety.

The opposite of acknowledgment and validation is social or interpersonal rejection. Whereas an experience of rejection is similar to experiences of exclusion, the additive and independent effect of rejection has been demonstrated experimentally (MacDonald, Borsook, and Spielmann, 2001). Exclusion and abandonment evoke feelings of sadness, loss, and ultimately, loneliness. Experiences of rejection and judgment however evoke shame-based emotions (e.g., shame, guilt). In a series of experiments, MacDonald et al. (2011) poignantly showed that social threat (negative, rejecting judgment) led to a more painful impact than just pure non-inclusion. In reality, though, non-inclusion (exclusion) often goes hand-in-hand with rejection. Thus it is not surprising that we often find both closely connected in clients' experiences of the most hurting events in their life. Nor is it surprising that these events, and the memory of these events, evoke in the clients a painful mixture of shame- and loneliness-based feelings (Greenberg and Watson, 2006; O'Brien et al., 2012).

Experienced rejection hurts physically as the neural circuitry of emotional and physical pain is shared and activated in the face of social rejection (Eisenberger, 2011). Experiences of shame are not only excruciating (increasing felt pain and rejection sensitivity; Eisenberger, 2011), but they also come with an action tendency to shrink and disappear. Thus experiences of shame naturally lead to avoidance of contact and to physical, physiological, and social withdrawal (MacDonald et al., 2011). In some cases they may also lead to increased irritability and potentially antisocial aggression (aggressive behaviour as a response to rejection and humiliation seems to be genetically moderated; Caspi et al., 2002; Eisenberger, 2011; Leary, Twenge, and Quinlivan, 2006; Way and Taylor, 2011). Furthermore, rejected individuals, can expect further rejection and thus appear hypervigilant. Such behaviour may be seen as socially awkward by interacting peers and thus, unfortunately, increases the likelihood of rejection (MacDonald et al., 2011). This then leads to a vicious circle. Rejection brings painful experiences of shame and isolation. This painful experience creates an apprehensive fear of rejection, which manifests itself as awkwardness and tension, which then bring on further rejection and humiliation.

The developmental experiences of bullying that often happen in psychologically decisive periods of life so prevalent among the clients of psychological services are good examples of vicious circles of rejection and humiliation (e.g., Arseneault, Bowes, and Shakoor, 2010). Other sources of such shame-based painful experiences are the criticisms and judgments given by harsh, critical, unhappy, or disappointed caregivers (e.g., parents who feel disappointed at the sight of their children's behaviour, performance, etc.). These sometimes subtle, other times explicit, rejections and evaluative judgments often lead to an internalised sense of shame, manifesting as self-doubt, self-rejection, and self-criticism (cf. McCranie and Bass, 1984). Such people then come across as lacking in confidence, as vulnerable, and as socially apprehensive (anxious, fearing rejection), all of which can make them vulnerable to further criticism and judgment.

The toll of experienced rejection and consequent shame, embarrassment, and humiliation is significant, particularly if it is a chronic experience (Dickerson, 2011). Dickerson (2011) summarises research studies showing the negative impact of chronic negative evaluation and rejection on the cardiovascular, neuroendocrine, and immune systems. For instance, chronic rejection leads to the increased presence of cortisol, which has many negative health effects (cf. Dickerson & Zoccola, 2013). The presence of high cortisol levels may be particularly specific for the situation of negative evaluation as opposed to other stressful situations. Gunnar, Sebanc, Tout, Donzella, and van Dulmen (2003) showed that this applies even in pre-school children, whose saliva indicated higher cortisol levels if the sociometric measures indicated rejection by peers.

Shame is a complex emotion that starts to develop in the latter part of the second and particularly in the third year of life (Lewis, 2008). As a self-conscious emotion, its development corresponds with the development of a sense of the self. As with the other core painful emotions of fear and loneliness/sadness, genetic predisposition may make certain people more sensitive to rejection by others. On a biological level, for instance, this can be seen in between subject variability in the functioning of cortisol release, in the moderating function of serotonin levels, or in the production of monoamine oxidase (a neurotransmitter degrading enzyme) during the rejection event (Way and Taylor, 2011). Similarly, there may be variability in the biological/genetic predisposition to solicit and/or to benefit from existing social support (a factor which has clearly been shown to have a blunting effect on the experienced pain in social rejection; Way and Taylor, 2011), with some people benefitting more and some less from this blunting effect. Genetic and biological predisposition may also modulate the response to social rejection with irritability and subsequent aggression being used as a defence to intolerable shaming and shame (Way and Taylor, 2011; Leary, Twenge, and Quinlivan, 2006).

Biological proneness and early experiences of rejection provide a powerful interplay that can lead to long-lasting biochemical and structural changes to the developing brain (Bateman and Fonagy, 2004; De Bellis et al., 1999; Cohen et al., 2006). Long-term traumatic experiences of abuse and neglect, as well as rejecting abandonments, also bring experiences of intolerable shame that may come both from the shaming other, but also from the self-critical processes, by which the child attributes the reasons for significant others' behaviour to the self, in an effort to have some control over it. For instance, a child with an unpredictable, abusive, and neglecting parent may start to look at him- or herself and reason that he or she has some flaws that are responsible for how the parent treats him or her. This self-attribution of the problem can have a temporary adaptive function as it may allow the child some small sense of control over an otherwise unpredictable environment, and may engender hope that finding and changing flaws in the self might potentially lead to a different response from the parent. Of course, with a problematic parent this does not happen (the parent stays the same), which then leads to further self-inspection on the child's part and the vicious circle of self-doubt and self-criticism begins—a vicious circle which may have a lasting effect and which may be carried on further in life.

CHARACTERISTICS OF EMOTIONAL PAIN

Although our studies suggest that at the bottom of individuals' unresolved emotional pain are emotion schemes centring around terror/fear, loneliness, and shame, it is also the case that these emotions are present in different ways for each individual, and furthermore that each individual experiences these emotions idiosyncratically (e.g., Crowley et al., 2013; Dillon et al., 2014; Keogh et al., 2013; Keogh et al., 2011; McNally et al., 2014; O'Brien et al., 2012). Sometimes, particular emotions are explicitly to the fore, while others may be more implicit and inferred. For instance, a client may primarily experience a sense of loneliness and abandonment. Although implicit within these feelings of loneliness is a sense of insecurity (e.g., the sense that *I have no protection*) and this may be inferred from aspects of the client's narrative, feelings of fear or insecurity may not be the fore of the client's experiencing. This does not cause any problem for the therapeutic work as the therapist is primarily led by the client's experience and not the theoretical construction.

The mixture of feelings of fear/terror, sadness/loneliness, shame/humiliation is not the only characteristic of core painful emotion schemes. There are a number of other characteristics which our studies (see above) showed to be helpful when seeking to conceptualise a client's core pain. Core painful feelings always signal unmet needs (e.g., *I feel abandoned—my need for connection and love is not fulfilled; I feel ashamed—my need for validation and self-acceptance is not fulfilled; I feel terrorised—my need for security is compromised.*). There always exist triggers and potential triggers which activate the emotion schemes incorporating painful experience. There is always the person's way of interacting with the triggers through managing the self in the context of those triggers (e.g., self-criticism, self-protection). There is typically fear of the triggers that bring the emotional pain. This fear then leads to emotional avoidance of the pain or behavioural avoidance of the triggers that would bring the pain. And finally, there will almost inevitably be a chain of secondary emotional responses directly and indirectly related to the core pain. Core painful emotions are not only so difficult to bear that the person tries to avoid them, but they also do not lead to adaptive action. Furthermore, the needs implicit in core painful feelings are unfulfilled and the core painful emotions are too painful to be processed; therefore, clients typically present with a chain of secondary emotions, such as hopelessness, helplessness, rejecting (defensive) anger, depression, depletion, tension, frustration, and other forms of (often poorly differentiated) distress.

We will now have a more detailed look at the aspects of painful emotion scheme organisations.

TRIGGERS OF EMOTIONAL PAIN

Emotion schemes containing painful, unbearable feelings are activated or triggered by interactions with the environment (most often social), which in adult life often resemble the historical circumstances that led to unbearable past emotional experiences. Emotional pain is typically activated by historical or current experiences of (1) intrusion, danger, attack, (2) abandonment, betrayal, exclusion, and (3) humiliation, rejection, condemnation. These triggers correspondingly bring experiences of unbearable (1) terror/fear, (2) loneliness, and (3) shame that may be too painful for the individual to tolerate and that lead to profound avoidance or collapse and, therefore, do not inform any adaptive action (Greenberg, 2011). Experiences like these are particularly difficult and impactful if they occur during developmentally sensitive periods of life. This is especially the case during childhood when the person is most vulnerable and is dependent upon the support of adults for protection, love, and validation. Traumatic experiences which happen early in life and continue for a long period of time, or which are particularly devastating (even if they occur much later in life), can lead to the development of maladaptive emotion schemes. Although these emotion schemes could have been as functional as possible in adverse circumstances at the time of the original traumatising experience, over the longer term, they may result in a maladaptive functioning.

For instance, consider an individual who as a small boy experienced aggressive attacks from an alcoholic father. Not only did the father beat the boy, but in times of need, the father was never there for the boy, instead berating or criticising him at every opportunity. Given such experiences, the boy would most likely be terrified, lonely, and ashamed. As the boy grows older, it is likely that similar emotional experiences would be triggered by interpersonal situations where the behaviour of others resembles the behaviour of the father. This would even be the case as the boy enters his adult years. Furthermore, an individual with such history would most likely come to dread such treatment and thus would try to prevent the occurrence of similar triggers. It is also worth noting that these triggers may not even be ones that concern the individual directly, as the individual may begin to worry that the trauma which happened to them could happen to others to whom they are close. As Chen and Williams (2011) powerfully showed using fMRI-based research, emotional pain arising as a consequence of either remembering painful events from the past, or anticipating painful events in the future, activated the same part of neural circuitry as was activated during the actual experience of emotional pain in the present. I will talk about characteristics of the triggers of emotional pain in Chapter 5 (which focuses on case conceptualisation in psychotherapy).

SELF-TREATMENT

The person is not a passive recipient of the triggers of emotional pain. He or she tries to actively respond to these triggers, often doing so by first addressing their own emotional processes triggered by the difficult interactions. Thus, in the context of a difficult trigger, the person can respond actively toward the self in an adaptive way, by supporting the self, improving the self, or by being compassionate toward the self. Alternatively, the person can respond to the self in a maladaptive way, by criticising the self, worrying the self, or by the outright blocking of emotional experience. I will now focus only on the maladaptive forms of self-treatment, as it is maladaptive self-treatment that contributes to the experienced emotional pain.

Maladaptive self-treatment strategies develop gradually, coterminous with the development of the self, and are shaped by interaction between the self and the environment. Initially, they may serve an adaptive function in an otherwise traumatic situation. For instance, I have already mentioned the example of an aggressive and neglecting father who leaves his child feeling insecure, unloved, and ashamed. In such a context, the child may attempt to control the unpredictable behaviour of the father by attributing the reasons for the father's problematic behaviour to the self. Such thinking may leave the child with the hope that if he can in some way be different, the father may behave better. Of course, as outlined above, such efforts on the child's behalf will not change the behaviour of the parent, and whilst the child gets into to a vicious circle of self-criticism resulting in deepening, negative feelings of shame, the parent does not change.

Listening to clients' stories, it appears that self-criticism is indeed one of the main maladaptive strategies that people employ in order to control the impact of social rejection or other types of social adversity (e.g., abuse, neglect, exclusion). Mild forms of self-criticism that are focused on self-improvement can naturally be healthy, as people can improve and thereby win social recognition, both from individuals they are close to but also on a broader social level. However, self-criticism, where the tone is one of self-contempt, is almost never healthy. Such forms of self-criticism are often also introjections resulting from treatment by emotionally salient others, and they can be particularly debilitating, often ending up in profound self-loathing and a concordant sense of shame and worthlessness. Indeed, the level of self-contempt, or self-disgust, appears to be an important predictor of the client's resignation and eventually depression (Greenberg and Watson, 2006).

Sometimes self-criticism may have an explicitly self-protective function. In such instances, the child (and later on, the adult) may brace him- or herself for negative treatment by others. The person may enact self-criticism in order to toughen him- or herself, so that he or she might cope with negative treatment by others. For instance, the person may criticise him- or herself after delivering a performance, so when then the anticipated criticism comes from the other person, it is neither a surprise nor a disappointment. The function of the internal criticism is then reinforced, as the person can see its positive function in preparing the self for potential criticism and thus pre-empting disappointment. At other times, self-criticism may take the form of self-punishment, or even self-harm. It may be an expression of hopelessness, anger, or resignation. Once disappointment comes, the person may need to 'deal' with it somehow, and self-punishment may serve as a channel for anger. It may even indirectly reinforce a hope that if I beat myself now, I might avoid similar disappointments in the future.

Another common self-treatment strategy engaged in by individuals in an attempt to control the core pain elicited by painful triggers is self-interruption (Greenberg et al., 1993). This self-treatment strategy essentially involves attempting to block emotional experiencing and thus stop emotional pain. People can avoid feelings outright by avoiding awareness of those feelings and the emotional pain that they give rise to. They can try to stop or limit feelings by almost physically shutting themselves down or by physically tensing the self. In this way, distinct painful emotions can be hidden in inchoate physical experiences of tension and tiredness, or in specific somatic complaints such as headaches, neck tension, or chest pain. On a behavioural level, this sort of self-interruption can lead to incongruity. The person may not be fully aware of what he or she feels, so might, for instance, offer incongruous nervous smiles, when in actual fact, he or she is terrified. O'Brien et al. (2012) observed that clients with generalised anxiety disorder frequently resorted to a wide range of self-interruption strategies. These included diminishing the extent of their emotional experience, changing the subject of discussion when something painful was being touched on, laughing off painful content, or engaging in behaviour that prevented the therapist from focusing on something more personally or emotionally salient. Clients were also observed as downplaying the emotional significance of important relationships. Early on in therapy, a client may say something like: 'I do not want to talk about my parents. They are insignificant. I did not speak with them for eighteen years. I have no issues with them'. Clearly, this signals that the issue is being avoided at almost any cost.

O'Brien et al. (2012), as well as others before them (see Greenberg et al., 1993) also noted that some clients interrupt primary painful emotions by enacting secondary reactive emotions. A typical example is when an individual becomes angry when humiliated and feeling shame, thus interrupting the experience of shame by substituting it with reactive anger. Take the example of a male client who has an argument with his boss. The client feels put down by his boss, who is also dismissive of him in front of other co-workers. The client is humiliated, but instead of being in touch with and aware of his own humiliation, he jumps straight to rage, expressing a wish to 'strangle' the boss. In this example, the experience and expression of anger serves as an avoidance strategy by which the client avoids unbearable feelings of humiliation.

At others times, self-interruption may take the form of suppressing anger when feeling justifiable anger at mistreatment. So for example, a girl may feel angry toward her neglecting mother. However, she may interrupt awareness or expression of such anger, as to allow such feelings might give rise to intolerable feelings that she is indeed a bad, angry girl, deserving of her mother's rejection.

Self-worrying is another self-treatment strategy that, whilst perhaps once functional, has the potential to become very debilitating. A person engaging in self-worrying anticipates certain triggers that might happen (e.g., *I might be criticised and rejected, as I used to be; I might be attacked as I was before; or Somebody close to me, my children, might get abusive treatment of the kind that I was not able to cope with.*). The person then tries to avoid such triggers, out of the fear that the triggers will bring unbearable pain. The person may play out potentially horrifying scenarios in their mind, and may try to prevent them from happening in reality, by means of their own behaviours. Such behaviours might include over-checking for potential dangers, avoiding activities that could lead to potential dangers, or over-engaging in preparation for what to do in the event that the anticipated dangerous scenarios actually take place.

Individuals can become strongly attached to their self-worrying processes, and worry can be seen as an important asset by many clients. They can view worry as having a protective character. Worry can also prompt people to be very diligent and responsible, which in turn can win them social recognition (O'Brien et al., 2012). On the other hand, the toll of worry can be an overwhelming sense of exhaustion (Murphy et al., 2014), leading eventually to physiological tension, chronic anxiety, and in some cases to psychological and physical collapse. Excessive worry can make all bad scenarios real in a person's experience and thus, can scare the person to an extent that limits the person's capacity to respond to their environment in a manner that is effective or healthy.

Worry can lead to behavioural avoidance, so that the person is not confronted by the feared triggers (e.g., *If I do everything to perfection, I will not be criticised and rejected.*). It can also induce the worrying person to engage in attempts to control others (e.g., *If my partner stays at home and does not go out this evening, nothing bad will happen to her, plus it means I will not have to spend the night worrying about what might happen to her if she does go out.*). Worry can also be closely linked to self-criticism. The person may worry about what might happen, whilst simultaneously blaming the self for what might happen. Thus the seemingly protective function of the self-worry process, to be cautious in order to avoid disaster, may overlap with the seemingly protective function of the self-critical process, to be perfect in order to avoid disaster.

ANTICIPATORY (SECONDARY) ANXIETY

Worry, and in some cases also self-criticism, are often fuelled by *a fear of core emotional pain.* A person with such fear scans his or her environment for signs of triggers that could potentially bring the feared pain. As elaborated on above, the worry process is an exemplary case of avoidance engaged in as a result of this anticipatory fear of pain; the person first worries about potential triggers and their impact, and then acts on this worry by avoiding identified potential triggers. It is important to note that anticipatory anxiety is a fear of pain, but it is not itself the core pain. It is a more surface-level fear (in EFT terms, a secondary emotional response), which needs to be distinguished from the primary fear of terror/trauma, that fear and terror which we feel while we are being violated. Primary fear is sheer distress experienced in response to currently experienced trauma. As such, it has a more specific and more painful quality than the anticipatory fear of pain that we are talking about here.

Nonetheless, despite the fact that apprehensive fear is secondary to the core pain, it still has a very debilitating quality. A good example is social anxiety. Although the anticipatory anxiety with which socially anxious clients present is typically secondary to a more primary unbearable sense of shame and humiliation (*I will be criticised, ridiculed, fooled, or rejected, and left with embarrassment, shame, and humiliation.*), it is this anticipatory anxiety which most sufferers, and often also, most therapists, will focus on. Uncomfortable feelings of panic, tension, worry-induced apprehension, and stiffness will be what will preoccupy the suffering person. However, these symptoms are the result of a process, the function of which is to keep more fundamental and intolerable feelings of shame out of awareness. The suffering person is likely to be very aware of his or her own anxiety and is likely to be knowingly engaged in various strategies to avoid the anxiety (e.g., using tablets, having rituals, using various props and crutches) or avoid situations which might trigger it. Many psychological therapies (particularly cognitive-behavioural therapies) indeed focus on this more secondary and superficial, although very debilitating, anxiety. In fact, intervention at this level may indeed be required, as panic and anxiety can overwhelm a client's capacity to function at the most basic level. A client's level of anxiety or panic can also sometimes increase to a point where it seems unrelated to any discernible triggers in the environment. This is the case in the diagnosis of panic disorder, in which panic attacks appear to occur spontaneously without any obvious triggers. Even in these cases, however, it has been demonstrated (cf. Barlow, 2004) that people are reacting to potential triggers; it is simply that they are not fully aware of what it is that is triggering their responses.

Again, as with other aspects of painful emotion scheme self-organisations, there are likely to be a variety of factors which contribute to the development of anticipatory fear of pain. Much of the discussion outlined earlier in this chapter in relation to the fear/trauma cluster of core painful emotions is relevant here. It is worth noting that it has been empirically demonstrated that highly anxious people are especially sensitive to social and physical pain (DeWall et al., 2011). The obvious suggestion here is that there may be variability between people with regards to how well individuals can tolerate emotional pain and the uncomfortable physical feelings that go with it (see also Barlow, 2004, for his exposition of the view that intolerance of anxiety actually contributes to the development of anxiety disorders). Such individual differences may have both biological/genetic as well as psychogenetic roots. Again, I refer readers to the discussion on safety vs. insecurity earlier in this chapter.

AVOIDANCE

Fear of emotional pain and of the triggers that activate it leads to emotional and behavioural avoidance. For some clients (e.g., clients presenting with GAD), the key process of emotional avoidance is worry (see also the discussion above under self-treatment). However, and as already briefly discussed, although worry fulfils these protective functions, it is rarely fully successful. First of all, the worry process maintains apprehensive anxiety, the consequence of which is that the individual sees potential danger everywhere. Furthermore, the worry process fails to provide complete relief from emotional distress as aspects of feared painful emotional experience (such as shame, terror, loneliness) inevitably filter through and are felt as part of the individual's lived experience. This experience of painful feelings, however limited, leads to further fear and reinforces/fuels the need to avoid.

As already discussed, fear of pain and fear of the triggers that can bring pain lead to behaviour whose purpose is to prevent those triggers from happening. Worry about triggers further reinforces this process of behavioural avoidance. For instance, the person may withdraw from situations that could lead to experiences of insecurity, humiliation, or abandonment. The person may try to be a perfectionist in order to avoid experiences of criticism or rejection. The person may overprotect others, for example their own children, so that those others do not experience pain which resonates with or touches on the person's own pain or fear of pain. The person might also overprotect others from experiences which might result in the person feeling at risk of criticism of responsibility or neglect. Emotional and behavioural avoidance can also be present in the form of rituals performed in order to prevent the dreaded trigger from occurring. It can also be evident in the manner in which individuals use medication (e.g., anxiolytic), or simply keep medication at hand 'just in case it's needed'.

A more subtle form of emotional avoidance is the interruption of already felt emotions (see also the discussion above in relation to self-treatment). This process is well-described as self-interruption in the EFT literature (Greenberg et al., 1993; Elliott et al., 2004). Self-interruption within therapy can be evident in the manner in which clients dismiss the significance of their emotional processes or in the tendency to laugh off painful issues (O'Brien et al., 2012). Clients may also access and express secondary emotion as a way to avoid or suppress primary emotional experiences. For instance, as mentioned above, unbearable shame can be masked by rage at being humiliated, while rightful, assertive anger can be suppressed by guilt at being angry (e.g., *I cannot be angry at my parent.*).

In the self-interrupting process, the client avoids pain by cutting it off. This can occur consciously or without full awareness. With this interruption, however, the person also cuts him- or herself off from his or her emotional needs. By cutting oneself off from painful feelings of abandonment, a person can also bury awareness of the need for closeness and connection. When a person cuts him- or herself off from the experience of shame, the person risks burying his or her need for affirmation. Similarly, in avoiding feelings of fear, the person may not experience the full extent of his or her terror, but the person also loses awareness of his or her need and wish to live freely and to truly feel secure. Thus, out of a fear of pain, the person can choose less pain, but may do so at the expense of not living fully: *I can hide in my shell, but I will miss contact, freedom, and self-realisation.*

GLOBAL (SECONDARY) DISTRESS

Although feelings of sadness/loneliness, shame, or terror/fear are likely to be at the core of clients' emotional pain, when clients present to mental health services, they typically present with more 'superficial' feelings of depression, hopelessness, helplessness, irritation, rejecting anger, or apprehensive anxiety. It is important to state that in describing these feelings as 'superficial' I am not dismissing the possibility that the distress with which clients present is any less painful than the core pain at the centre of their distress. Rather I am highlighting the fact that these feelings (albeit distressing) are secondary to more primary, core emotional pains.

The concept of secondary emotional responses and the usefulness of the concept to psychotherapy have been elaborated on in detail by Les Greenberg and his colleagues (Greenberg and Paivio, 1997; Greenberg, Rice, and Elliott, 1993; Greenberg and Safran, 1987; 1989; Greenberg, 2002; Greenberg, 2011). Secondary emotional experiences are most often emotional reactions to primary emotions (but they can sometimes be also triggered by the cognitive processes linked to those primary emotions). A person might first feel abandoned, but then feel hopeless and helpless that this feeling of abandonment will never change. In focusing on the secondary emotions, a person's unmet need to be connected or to be loved—implicit in the primary painful feeling of abandonment—can become lost or ignored, with the result that the person falls into a depressing state of hopelessness.

Global distress, a term introduced by Pascual-Leone and Greenberg in 2007, is used to describe the emotionally distressing state in which clients typically present when first attending for psychotherapy. Global distress is characterised by a mixture of poorly differentiated, distressing emotions. It is typically characterised by a high level of emotional arousal. Somatisation, itself a sign of unprocessed emotional experiences, is also a defining feature of global distress. Clients frequently present to therapy, reporting variations on the following: tension in the body, sleeplessness, exhaustion, pressure in the shoulders, grinding teeth, jaw clenching, a knot in the stomach, nausea, palpitations, chest pains, breathlessness, a loss of appetite, feelings of suffocation, feelings of paralysis, headaches, dizziness, and so on.

Often it is this secondary distress that mental health professionals focus on. However, this is often an unsuccessful strategy because the meaning of the hopelessness, depletion, or resignation experienced by clients is often unclear to them. A related factor is that such secondary emotion does not inform adaptive action. As Les Greenberg (2002; 2011) puts it, secondary emotions are by definition maladaptive as they do not directly contain the same quality of information about the client's interaction with the environment as is contained within primary emotions. Secondary emotions do not inform us about primary unmet needs, nor do they inform us about potential adaptive actions that could lead to the fulfilment of those needs. Instead, and as already discussed, global distress is characterised by a sense of being unclear. In this state, the client often feels stuck, overwhelmed, and engulfed by their distress. When an individual feels depressed (a presentation typical of the state of global distress), it is often the case that they do not know why they feel that way. It is difficult for them to discern specific wounds and hurts that led to their feelings of resignation and shutting down. Therapeutically, focusing on these secondary, undifferentiated experiences is unlikely to be a productive endeavour.

CORE PAIN

As mentioned above, it appears that at the centre of core painful emotion schemes are primary feelings of fear/terror, sadness/loneliness, and shame/humiliation (e.g., Crowley et al., 2013; Dillon et al., 2014; Keogh et al., 2013; Keogh et al., 2011; McNally et al., 2014; O'Brien et al., 2012; Timulak et al., 2012). Core pain in a particular person is constituted by a unique mixture of these emotions. Typically these emotions are intertwined. So, one can feel that one has never been loved (sad/lonely); one can feel that this experience of not being loved is connected to an essential inner flaw (shame); and as a consequence, one can feel profoundly insecure (fear). Traditional EFT literature refers to core painful emotions as primary maladaptive emotions (e.g., Greenberg et al., 1993). Primary maladaptive emotions are chronic emotions that the person is familiar with and dreads. The person may try to avoid these emotions as they are unbearable, or because touching on these emotions results in a collapse to secondary emotions (global distress) such as hopelessness and helplessness (e.g., *I will never be loved, I will never be accepted, I will never be safe.*). The therapist's first goal, therefore, is to help the client access painful primary emotions and then help the client stay with these painful emotions without trying to avoid them or without collapsing into a state of global distress.

UNMET NEEDS

Core painful emotions signal that a person's needs are not being met. Each emotional experience is a result of an interaction between the person's needs and the person's environment (Greenberg, 2011). For instance, when we need to be loved by the other and we perceive/experience the other as loving us, we feel loved. When we want love or closeness and the other withdraws, we feel sad and abandoned. When we want to be accepted and we are rejected and put down, we feel abandoned and ashamed. The pain contained in core primary emotion signals, therefore, that critical needs (Pascual-Leone [2009] refers to these as existential needs) for security (e.g., being safe, protected), connection (e.g., being loved, cared for) and/or acceptance (e.g., being acknowledged, respected) are not being met. Unmet needs are often not fully articulated in a client's awareness. As the client may be unable to stay with core painful feelings, he or she may not have the opportunity to clarify what it is deep down that he or she wants, what he or she strives for, what he or she longs for. Usually during therapy, awareness of these needs becomes felt and crystallised when the client becomes capable of staying with his or her core painful feelings. So for example, when a client has become capable of accessing and tolerating his or her core painful feelings of loneliness, it becomes possible to prompt him or her to identify what need is being unmet, perhaps by asking 'What are you missing most as you feel that all-encompassing loneliness?' While the primary therapeutic task concerning core pain is to help the client access and bear it, the primary therapeutic task with regards to unmet needs is to facilitate the client's articulation of those needs. In doing so, the possibility of generating the longed-for response to those needs becomes real.

THE ROOTS OF EMOTIONAL PAIN

As already mentioned, phenomenological research (cited above) studying the core emotional pain of clients presenting with depression, anxiety, and trauma, suggests that the experienced *emotional pain* is a response to a—typically interpersonal—injury, which *prevented or violated the fulfilment of the individual's basic human needs*. This same research also suggests that remembered salient interpersonal injuries typically come in the form of (1) exclusion and loss, (2) rejection and negative judgment, or (3) psychological and/or physical trauma and/or intrusive attack. It is possible that the earlier in a person's development the violation comes, the worse its impact is on that individual. Until adulthood, we are all quite vulnerable beings, with relatively limited physical and psychological means to protect ourselves. Even in adulthood this protection may often be dependent upon belonging to a bigger community that can protect us. Thus, unprotected, we can be hurt, and the more developmentally vulnerable we are, the less are our means of coping with that hurt.

The violation and neglect of important psychological needs is typically a process, not just a once-off incident. It usually takes the form of a series of incidents and interactions. This often long-term process shapes the developing person's emotional experiencing, behaving, and thinking. Its impact thus influences the ways in which we process our interactions with the environment in which we find ourselves. EFT posits (Greenberg, 2011) that emotion schemes and the self-organisations based on them are being formed through 'emotion memory structures that synthesize' experience. Emotion schemes set out the ways in which we emotionally process our interaction with the environment. Problematic emotion schemes, formed as a consequence of our interaction with pervasive problematic triggers, hinder our capacity to adaptively process current interactions with the environment. Thus, emotional processing shaped in the interaction with problematic triggers develops limitations and vulnerabilities. These limitations and vulnerabilities then function as attractors for problematic processes (and problematic self-organisations), which in turn further limit our capacity for healthy, resilient, emotional processing. Our emotional schemes and the self-organisations they give rise to are, therefore, not always adaptive.

The emotional injuries which we encounter in life can sometimes be quite subtle. For instance, despite their best intentions, the people around us may directly or indirectly invalidate our efforts to contribute, thereby undermining our sense of feeling loved for who we are. Such interactions may lead us to experience subtle but unpleasant feelings of shame (*I have no worth*) and loneliness (*I feel on my own, not really loved*). Sometimes we may be actively attacked or put down, and if this happens on a continuous basis, we may feel not only humiliated, worthless, and ashamed, but also invaded, intruded upon and ultimately, insecure and unsafe.

This type of experience may bring painful emotions which we cannot control or usefully engage with. We may start to avoid situations which might lead to such experiences out of fear of the pain that such experiences bring. We might give up our efforts to have our needs for love, validation, or security responded to. Our avoidance of different situations or scenarios might mean that we do not acquire experiences of mastery in difficult situations.

Where such hurtful experiences are particularly painful and persistent, and where the individual, perhaps as a child, feels stuck and helpless as to his or her capacity to change the situation, the individual may begin to experience a sense of chronic or traumatic emotional pain. Any future situations which give rise to these types of experiences are likely to become particularly scary and painful. In such instances, efforts to deal with the pain may become frantic and desperate, and introspection as to the root cause of the pain may seem irrelevant or unimportant. What bubbles to the surface is most likely a mixture of poorly differentiated emotions, often dominated by feelings of hopelessness and helplessness. At other times, the pain may take the form of irritability, defensive hostility, or rage. The sense of what needs have been unmet, however, is lost, and any sense of the connection between the unfulfilment of those needs and the painful feelings that those unmet needs gives rise to, lies buried in a global, undifferentiated sense of distress.

The experiences of being impacted by an interpersonal injury may be very painful even when the injuries themselves may not be that visible or apparent to others. For example, parents consumed by their own busy, stressful lives might easily fail to notice the disappointment of an overlooked child. The outward signs of such disappointment may be quite subtle, so that even when parents do notice such disappointment, they might easily underestimate the strength of feeling behind it. The inner psychological pain of the child might be further disguised by the child's own efforts not to appear demanding. Whilst such efforts may stem from an attempt to present as more lovable, the end result may be that the child remains unnoticed. An inner sense of loneliness may set in, without anybody noticing. Furthermore, as children do not have full control over their own lives, they often try to increase their sense of control by attributing the cause of others' behaviour (e.g., overlooking behaviour by the parents) to themselves (*I must be doing something wrong, which explains why my parents are overlooking me.*). This gives children a rationale for what otherwise appears to be uninterpretable and, therefore, uncontrollable behaviour in others (Johnston and Lee, 2005). Whilst such thinking may increase the child's sense of control, it also may lead to negative self-judgment and self-scrutiny.

In many cases psychological injury can be so major and traumatic that its presence is clearly visible and its origins easily understood by all. Compassion will be triggered in most of us, when we consider the plight of an eight-year-old child who hides under the bed in order to avoid the angry outburst of her father. It is clear to us that she most likely feels insecure (*What will happen to me?*), ashamed (*There must be something wrong with me, if my father is angry at me like this.*), and alone (*I do not have anybody in the world who would reach out to me and soothe me now.*). We would not be overly surprised if we learned that this girl often feels anxious and apprehensive as to what might happen to her. Nor would we feel overly surprised if we learned that she feels helpless as to her capacity to protect herself, or hopeless that there is nothing good waiting for her in her future life. To understand her emotional pain in terms of a real fear of traumatic physiological pain—in terms of a real fear of painful experiences of all-consuming shame and profound loneliness stemming from her lived experience of not having her fundamental needs for security, love, and appreciation fulfilled—is empowering and compassionate. Such a child deserves compassion and soothing, as well as protection and being stood up for. She wants to feel loved and to give love. She wants to strive and create and be acknowledged for her efforts. She wants to be secure and safe, so she can live, grow, explore, and develop.

The above example is not untypical of the kind of painful experiences some people and children go through in their life. The western world is relatively free from wars and political instability. Thus, we can hardly imagine what it must be like when one's life is threatened on an everyday basis; when one can be invaded and have no control over his or her own security. It would appear that the long-term implications of such experiences depend upon when in the individual's development such traumatic experiences happen. The impact may be profound and may hinder the future development of the child. Summarising the research evidence, Ford (2009) talks about how in certain situations, the 'survival brain' can replace the 'learning brain'. The survival brain is characterised by rigid neural pathways centring around protection and harm avoidance, susceptibility to pain, and narrowing of openness to experience (Ford, 2009). A lack of emotional maturity when exposed to stressors can lead to experiences of helplessness and hopelessness, prompting fear of overwhelming, dysregulating emotions. The absence of a soothing environment can also limit the development of emotion-regulation capacities, further leaving the child vulnerable and unable to bear new situations, which trigger difficult emotions. Impacted children are thus more susceptible to experiences of painful emotion dysregulation (Ford, 2009). The impact of traumatic experiences during the important developmental phases can also be visible in relational behaviour that may be increasingly disorganised, avoidant, and/or dismissive (Ford, 2009).

Major traumas which threaten our own life or which threaten the lives of those close to us, but which occur later in the life cycle, may also have a debilitating impact (Ford and Courtois, 2009). Stressful events resulting from occupational or family life often trigger prolonged psychological distress, and developmental vulnerabilities may exacerbate the person's reaction to such stresses. A person's problematic emotional schematic patterns are often triggered by current difficulties, with the end result that emotional pain, stemming from current painful events, becomes fused with the old, familiar pain of remembered experience.

As already discussed, emotional pain can also be triggered through identification with the emotional pain of close ones, especially one's own children or one's own parents. For instance, it may be particularly difficult and debilitating for me as a parent to see my ten-year-old son being bullied, humiliated, and shamed. I will most likely feel his pain, his sense of exclusion, his sense of feeling alone and ostracised. I might feel powerless as my attempts to improve the situation for him have been ineffective. Thus, like him, I can start to feel hopeless and helpless. Fortunately, however, I can do something about it, as I can provide him with compassion and love, and I can validate him and his rights by expressing healthy anger, clearly stating that he does not deserve this type of treatment.

This type of identification with the pain of those whom we are close to is potentially complicated. We are empathic and sense the distress of others, but we can also project onto them our own vulnerabilities and our own pain. If our own past experiences have been too painful, and if those experiences have left us with a sense of hopelessness, helplessness, and dread at the possibility of encountering such experience again, then our reaction to the pain of individuals close to us, will be stronger. Our pain will become fused with the pain which we see our close ones experiencing. Our past pain will be reactivated and re-enacted.

In this chapter, I talked about emotional pain based on what we know about it from reviewing therapy sessions and from basic psychological research. In the next chapter, I will look at a particular theory outlining how the underlying emotional pain at the core of psychological suffering can be transformed in therapy, thereby increasing the person's maturity, resilience, and adaptive sensitivity to the complexities and difficulties of life.

3 Transforming emotional pain

How should the therapist approach emotional pain? First of all, we have plenty of evidence that even in the face of adversity, many people fulfil their strivings to belong, develop, and create (Rutter, 1985). The support of another human being would seem to play an important part in overcoming adversity. Such support may have a healing physiological impact as it can produce a lowering of the physiological aspects of pain (cf. Panksepp, 2011; Hyde, Gorka, Manuck, and Hariri, 2011), but it also provides psychological support, breaking isolation and helping the individual in his or her concerted effort to overcome the situation causing emotional pain.

Each of us has a different capacity to tolerate emotional pain. We are each shaped by genetic predispositions that influence not only our sensitivity to emotional pain (Way and Taylor, 2011), but also our physiological capacity to bear distress. Furthermore, we each have had a different developmental history of being supported or not being supported by important caregivers. Whilst one person may have had a history of nurturing experiences that led to the building of emotional resilience (Feder, Nestler, & Charney, 2009), another person may have had a history of neglect, invalidation, or abuse (Keyes et al., 2012) leading to quite the opposite. One path resources the person, better equipping him or her to meet adversity; the other path leaves the person vulnerable to such encounters. People also vary as to their degree of exposure to traumatic experiences, the emotional pain of which may have left them emotionally bruised, apprehensive, hopeless, or helpless. Thus, the capacity to process and transform experiences triggered by adverse situations such as rejection, abandonment, or attack, differs widely from one person to another, and is to a significant extent the result of each individual's unique constellation of lived experiences.

This unique constellation of past experiences impacts then on the manner in which each person processes stressful, difficult emotion-triggering situations in the here and now. The unique mix of biological predisposition and a particular developmental pathway explains the unique individualised responses people have to adverse situations. This also means that any form of social support (such as psychotherapy) has to be fine-tuned to the individual's manner of dealing with pain and pain-bringing situations.

So how does emotional pain transform into resilience, maturity, and increased sensitive attunement to others? The model presented here is based on work examining and refining a model of emotion transformation in therapy first proposed by Pascual-Leone and Greenberg (2007). Pascual-Leone and Greenberg (2007; Pascual-Leone, 2009) studied good sessions of emotion-focused and client-centred therapy and observed that the sequence of emotions within these sessions followed a particular pattern. They observed that in good outcome events, clients first showed *global distress* (characterised by an undifferentiated emotional pain, hopelessness, helplessness, etc.). This was then followed by a stage whereby the client displayed chronic primary painful feelings such as *fear and/or shame.* These chronic painful feelings were typically accompanied by *negative self-evaluation* (e.g., self-criticism, *I do not like myself*) juxtaposed with a statement of existential *need* (e.g., *I need to be accepted*). Chronic painful feelings were then transformed by the experience and expression of *assertive anger* (*I deserve to be accepted*) and/or *self-soothing* (*I feel accepted*). These transformatory experiences were followed by a stage of *grief/hurt* in which clients grieved missing experiences (e.g., of acceptance). The emotional processing pathway culminated in a sense of *acceptance and agency*. Pascual-Leone and Greenberg also observed an alternative pathway by which emotional processing occurred in 'good outcome' sessions. In this pathway, *global distress* was followed by a *rejecting anger* stage (typically targeting the hurtful other). This *rejecting anger* was then transformed into *assertive anger* before continuing on the above-outlined pathway through *self-soothing* and *grieving* stages, before culminating in *acceptance and agency*.

Pascual-Leone (2009) further showed that clients' emotional processing progressed along the outlined stages in a 'two steps forward, one step back' manner. So for example, clients might reach a higher level of emotional processing but might then fall back to a lower level. However, over time the duration or degree of regression shortened. Thus, successful in-session emotional events showed signs of clients building both *emotional resilience* and *emotional flexibility,* with clients becoming increasingly capable of generating more adaptive and healthy emotional experiences.

Pascual-Leone's studies led the Trinity Emotion-Focused Therapy Research Group (a collaborative group of my students) to a series of studies (Crowley et al., 2013; Dillon et al., 2014; Keogh et al., 2011; Keogh et al., 2013; McNally et al., 2014; Timulak et al., 2012) that used the model of within-session emotional processing developed by Pascual-Leone and Greenberg (2007) as a basis for observing emotional processing in psychotherapy, across sessions. In these studies, we observed similar phenomena as were described in Pascual-Leone's papers. However, we also observed some discrepancies and variations that led us to reconceptualise some aspects of Pascual-Leone and Greeneberg's original work (see also Timulak and Pascual-Leone, 2014). What follows is a summary of the processes we observed through the lens of the client and therapist's interaction. First, we will look at how client suffering showed in therapy sessions; second, we will look at the process by which suffering was transformed across therapy.

THE INITIAL DISTRESS PRESENT IN THERAPY

As already mentioned, clients present to therapy often in a form of undifferentiated emotional pain—or global distress that I described in the previous chapter (here I offer a very brief recap of the description of the initial distress). Global distress usually shows in the form of a variety of psychopathological symptoms such as hopelessness, helplessness, low mood, irritation, anxiety, and so on. Global distress is typically characterised by high emotional arousal (cf. Warwar and Greenberg, 1999), but in controlled and emotionally avoidant clients, it may show more subtly, for instance, in the form of somatic complaints.

Often in the context of pain-provoking interpersonal triggers, clients displayed a tendency to treat themselves negatively, holding themselves somehow responsible for the pain that was triggered. It would seem that clients often did this out of an attempt to control the pain (*If I am responsible, than it is in my hands*), which often appeared to be a strategy that they learnt in childhood (e.g., *The only way I can understand why I am being attacked by my alcoholic father, and therefore the only way I can become capable of doing something about it is to have a sense that somehow I provoke his responses by simply being who I am.*). In other instances clients simply appeared to have internalised how they perceived the salient other as viewing them (e.g., flawed, not deserving [full] love; *You are just not smart enough, you are just not good enough, you are just not strong enough.*). In these instances, it appeared that the salient other was so important for the client that the client took the other's reality and allowed it to define him or her.

While negative self-treatment can be seen as a way of coping with the triggered emotional pain, it can also in itself become a source of additional pain. Furthermore, it contributes to the confusion often experienced in global distress. In other words a client may be in pain whilst also beating him- or herself up for being in pain (*Why am I so weak?*). With distress initially triggered by the experiences or perceptions of others' actions, but then further prolonged by negative self-treatment in the context of those triggering situations, clients can feel overwhelmed by inner turmoil. They can also collapse into hopelessness and helplessness, feeling that the pain is simply too much, and that any effort to shift the pain is failing. Whilst this is happening, the actual core of the painful experiences (*What is it in fact that hurts so much?*) is often obscured, lost under layers of avoidance, fear of pain, hopelessness, and helplessness.

Classic EFT (e.g., Greenberg et al., 1993) literature refers to the emotional experiences present in global distress as secondary emotions, because they are usually secondary responses to more primary, underlying emotions. For instance, the client may feel desperate and hopeless (secondary emotions) because of feeling abandoned and lonely/sad (primary emotions). As proposed in the previous chapter, the underlying pain is typically constituted by feelings of loneliness/sadness (*I am on my own*), shame (*I am flawed*), or traumatic terror (*I am falling apart*). These feelings signal that important needs for love, validation, and safety are not being met.

As mentioned above, one of the reasons why underlying primary painful emotions are obscured is that they are unbearable, and thus feared. Fear of feeling pain, and fear of encountering triggers that might provoke pain, motivates the clients' efforts to avoid both the pain and the triggers that might give rise to it or provoke it. Both within therapy and in their lives outside of therapy, clients engage in a variety of emotional and behavioural strategies to avoid primary painful emotions. By numbing themselves, distracting themselves, or tensing their muscles, clients can emotionally avoid otherwise overpowering, all-consuming feelings of shame, loneliness, or terror/fear. By avoiding situations in which they might encounter rejection, exclusion, humiliation; by not standing up for themselves; or by managing situations in such a way that the likelihood of conflict or judgement is reduced, clients seek through their behaviour to avoid the triggers of painful experience. Such behaviours can even be engaged in so as to avoid pain triggered by one's own self-critical processes.

The consequences of such avoidance are that the client's feared, painful, unresolved, emotional experiences are not processed, and therefore are not transformed. A chance to see underlying pain as a natural reaction to adversities encountered in life is thus missed. The unmet needs embedded in painful emotions are not recognised or owned. Without access to what it is that would allow him or her to feel better, the client becomes stuck in a mixture of painful, upsetting, and undifferentiated experiences. The client may seek to fight against these feelings, or may seek to avoid them, but more often than not, the sense of stuckness and helplessness does not shift. The core emotional pain, the discrete painful emotions of sadness/loneliness, shame and/or fear/terror, are not attended to and in that absence, needs for love, validation, and safety are not responded to. The client falls into helplessness, resigned to the unlikelihood of present suffering ever lessening, and apprehensive of any further pain which might make things worse.

THE PROCESS OF TRANSFORMING EMOTIONAL PAIN IN PSYCHOTHERAPY

Successful therapy interrupts the above-described pattern of distress and avoidance. It helps the client first to become capable of overcoming avoidance; then to bear emotional pain; and thereafter to differentiate the core aspects of that emotional pain. Such a process leads naturally to the articulation of unmet needs, and once articulated, these needs can be responded to within sessions, through the generation of healing emotional experiences of compassion and protective anger. Healing experiences are typically followed by a spontaneous grieving process, whereby the individual grieves the hurts that gave rise to the emotional pain and which left fundamental needs unmet. Healing experiences also typically lead to spontaneous feelings of relief and give rise to a sense of empowerment and personal agency. This process has been described and documented across a range of successful experiential therapy cases (e.g., Pascual-Leone and Greenberg, 2007; McNally et al., 2014). Let us have a look how it actually happens.

ACCESSING THE CORE EMOTIONAL PAIN AND ARTICULATING UNMET NEEDS

Theories of psychotherapy variously assume that change has to come through an understanding of the causes of psychopathological problems and their maintaining factors; through the learning of a variety of powerful coping strategies; through a corrective (interpersonal) experience; through altering one's thinking about the experience; or through altering one's behaviour. Many of these theoretical models seek to deal with the client's presenting, secondary distress (see above; typically undifferentiated painful emotions, hopelessness and helplessness, depression and anxiety, etc.). In contrast with the above processes, the model of change proposed here posits that long-lasting psychotherapeutic change is the result of accessing, processing, and transforming idiosyncratically formed core emotion schemes and self-organisation. Indeed from our own position, some of the approaches briefly alluded to above may be viewed as inadvertently supporting the avoidance of underlying pain rather than its processing and transformation. For instance, when we intellectualise around the causes of suffering, we may in turn be trying to avoid actual felt pain.

The model of transformation, based on the studies of successful emotional processes in therapy, assumes that transformation is a sequential process, and proposes that it consists of several steps. The very first step is to acknowledge the client's global sense of suffering; the individual's idiosyncratically experienced sense of unhappiness, hopelessness, despair, helplessness, fused sadness and anger, and/or reactive anger at being wronged. In psychotherapy, the therapist provides acknowledgement through empathic and compassionate communication, actively trying to understand the person's emotional suffering but also actively sharing this understanding with the person. It is important that this understanding is provided by a therapist who is not overwhelmed by the client's emotional distress, and who can therefore hold on to his or her own sense of being as a solid, firm, helping presence. The therapist has to have confidence that the emotional pain and suffering experienced by the client can be borne by the client; that the client can be helped to regulate their level of distress where necessary; and that this emotional pain, in itself, contains important information.

The therapist has to understand the desire of the client to avoid his or her distress and that that emotional and behavioural avoidance of pain is driven by fear of further pain. The therapist has to acknowledge both the avoidance, and the fear which drives it, and communicate through his or her presence and understanding, compassion for the client's position. At the same time, however, the therapist has to focus on the client's underlying pain, on that which is at the core of the client's pain; ultimately, on that which is unbearable for the client.

As mentioned in the previous chapter and above, the psychotherapy process research studies indicate that with clients presenting with depression or anxiety, core emotional pain is constituted by idiosyncratic variations of a triad of clusters of painful primary emotions. The first cluster of emotions contains experiences of sadness, loneliness, abandonment, loss, and other such similar emotions.

The second cluster of core underlying primary emotions contains experiences of shame, humiliation, embarrassment, failure, and worthlessness. Finally, the third cluster of core primary painful emotional experiences includes experiences of basic insecurity, terror, physiological upset, physical injury, and trauma. These experiences are typically the consequence of violation of our attachment- and identity-related needs (Greenberg and Goldman, 2007), such as to be safe, loved, and acknowledged. Developmentally, crucial interpersonal injuries can contribute to the development of emotion schemes centred around unbearable and feared core pain. Current situations containing aspects similar to the original injuries can then trigger these emotion schemes and self-organisations. Although shame-based, sadness/loneliness-based, and fear/terror-based painful emotions can be understood as discrete clusters, they may often be associatively linked (see Greenberg and Watson, 2006).

Core emotional pain is also linked to the unique personal narrative by which the individual summarises the developmentally significant cornerstones which shaped how he or she experiences current pain-provoking situations. Each individual has their own unique patterns of underlying emotional experience and their own idiosyncratic needs embedded in that experience. The pain they experience has a flavour and quality that is unique to them. The manner in which unfulfilment of needs triggers secondary distress, resignation, or fear of pain is idiosyncratic to each client, as are the particular ways each client seeks to avoid pain, or responds to it with a problematic self-treatment.

In therapy, core pain is first accessed in its unproductive form (Greenberg, Auszra, and Hermann, 2007). Core painful emotions are chronic (classical EFT literature refers to them as primary maladaptive emotions; Greenberg et al., 1993) and are experienced as too overwhelming. In addition, (or alternatively), core painful feelings may be truncated as a consequence of the client's attempts to avoid or interrupt them. It is the therapist's role to support the client's emotion-regulation capacity. The therapist does this by helping the client stay with painful emotions rather than avoid them; by facilitating the client's differentiation and articulation of these painful experiences in language and narrative (putting experience to words helps to regulate arousal; Lieberman, Eisenberger, Crockett et al., 2004); and eventually by helping the client articulate the unmet needs those painful emotions point to. Expression of the unmet needs embedded in core emotional pain mobilises the suffering person to have those needs met.

THE RESPONSE TO THE UNMET NEEDS: COMPASSION AND PROTECTIVE ANGER

The above-mentioned studies of transformative processes in therapy (e.g., Crowley et al., 2013; Dillon et al., 2014; Keogh et al., 2011; Keogh et al., 2013; McNally et al., 2014; Timulak et al., 2012) suggest that once unmet needs have been articulated, it is important that they are responded to with compassion and protective anger. Experiences of compassion provide a sense of being loved, acknowledged, and soothed, while experiences of protective (as opposed to reactive) anger provide a sense of entitlement to be loved, acknowledged, and secure.

For the healing and curative potential of compassion and protective anger to be truly felt and appreciated, it is important that the clients experience these emotions and their impact whilst they are in touch with their core pain, and whilst they are aware of the unmet needs at the root of that pain. The therapist plays a crucial role in generating these emotions. First, the therapist can directly express compassion toward the client, and can express rightful anger on behalf of the client. The therapist's compassionate presence and understanding reaches out to the client, breaking the client's existential isolation. Furthermore, the therapist's interpersonal affirmation can strengthen the client's sense of entitlement and worth.

The aforementioned studies also indicate that healing experiences of compassion and protective anger can be facilitated by a skilful therapist in a more technical manner by the use of specific therapeutic interventions. For instance, after first facilitating the client's accessing of core pain, and then facilitating the articulation of unmet needs, the therapist may ask the client to remember and enact the compassionate presence of a caring person from the client's own life. Thus, for instance, a male client might be encouraged to enact his caring father who, when the client was a child, woke him up every morning, made breakfast for him every morning, and went with him to the doctor when he felt sick. In an imaginary dialogue, the client can enact the father's presence, and, as his imagined father, respond to his son's unmet need for closeness and connection. The therapist facilitates this dialogue, encouraging 'the father' to speak from how he feels in the moment when he sees his son (i.e., the client himself) feeling so profoundly alone. Alternatively, the therapist may facilitate the expression of compassion from the client to his or her younger self imagined in the empty chair. Take for example the case of a female client who, after entering into an episodic memory of what it was like to be her ten-year-old self, expresses the profound sense of loneliness felt as a result of her alcohol-dependent mother's unavailability. In such an instance, the therapist might ask the client to imagine her child self sitting in another chair, feeling lonely, lost, and desperately in need of a caring presence. The therapist might encourage the client to respond as her adult self to the needs of that small child, thereby facilitating the expression of compassion from the adult client to her younger, hurting self.

The experience of compassion in response to need has a healing quality. Hearing, saying, and feeling that I am loved, that I do matter, and that somebody wants to protect me, fulfils unmet needs. It is a soothing, calming experience, and it is important that such exchanges are savoured experientially. Experiences of compassion also contribute to the re-scripting of problematic emotion schemes as emotional processing does not end up in a global sense of distress, but rather at the mixture of distress and subsequent pain and need articulation that is responded to by balancing adaptive emotions. This process is thus increasing the person's emotional flexibility and consolidating access to compassionate self-organisations.

Of course, it may not be that straightforward to access, experience, express, and accept experiences of compassion in therapy. In some instances the degree of injury and hurt experienced by clients throughout their life can have an irreparable, or difficult to repair, impact. Therefore, the therapist has to be patient. He or she needs to have a profound understanding of how the client's pain feels; how the loneliness, shame, or terror feels; what can make these feelings more bearable; when it is important to attend inward and feel, but equally so, when it is important to have a break from paying attention inwards; when it is important to put things to words and make sense of them; when it is important to focus on the need; how to help the client access, articulate, and express that need; and how to generate compassionate responses, and so on. While negative self-treatment can interfere with client's accessing and acceptance of compassion, it also appears to be the case that self-compassion is best generated by the witnessing of one's own pain. In EFT such experiences are facilitated by the use of imaginary dialogues. We will look at these complex processes in the following chapters.

Experiences of healthy, protective anger also validate and support the client and thus are effective responses to unmet needs. Although it is likely that experiences of both compassion and protective anger are necessary in order to feel secure, belonging, and purposeful, our studies suggest that for some clients, the experience of protective anger may be even more fundamental than the experience of receiving compassion. Protective anger allows the suffering client to recover his or her agency and control. This is because experiences of felt entitlement energise the client and encourage him or her to look after unmet needs. The felt entitlement is affirming and provides a sense of personal power, thus essentially counterbalancing the fear, withdrawal, hopelessness, and helplessness present in the suffering and pain. Take the example of a male client who was terrified in childhood, in part as a consequence of his parents often leaving him alone at home for extended periods of time. Experiencing protective anger in therapy helps such a client develop the sense that as a seven-year-old boy, he did not deserve to be unsupported and left alone; that instead, he deserved to be better looked after. He can gain a sense that as a seven-year-old boy he was entitled to a feel a sense of security. Thus empowered, he can, as an adult, access a sense of entitlement to have people around him now, people who are more responsive at times when he feels isolated and unsupported. The experience of such entitlement is likely to fill him with a sense of power and strength that, experientially, balances the overwhelming vulnerability he used to feel as a child, and sometimes feels now as an adult.

The experience of feeling protective anger is enlivening for the person. It brings a felt sense of energy, personal resilience, personal power, and agency. It differentiates the person from others. It mobilises the person to stand up for what he or she is entitled to. All of this implies a tendency to thrust forward, a tendency which is very different to the withdrawal which characterises the collapse into hopelessness and helplessness. Protective anger thus, not only lifts the person's mood, but also counterbalances the sense of pain experienced by the person. The person is less consumed by feelings of loneliness, shame, and fear, and thus does not need to be so avoidant of these feelings. The more a client accesses protective anger in therapy, the more likely he or she is capable of accessing appropriate protective anger when necessary in real-world situations. Thus the client's emotional flexibility develops.

In our studies, we observed that for some clients it was difficult to feel an entitlement to have their needs met, or to express this entitlement in the form of healthy anger. In some instances, this difficulty appeared to stem from a fear that such anger would carry them to situations where they would lose control over themselves and act in a way that might be hurtful to others. In other instances, the difficulty appeared to originate in a fear that assertions of anger would not be accepted by people around them. Such fears appeared to be rooted in developmentally significant events where efforts to stand up for the self were suppressed and turned against the person trying to assert him- or herself. In these encounters, efforts by the individual to assert him- or herself were also often labelled by the significant others as unacceptable. For instance, a female client who felt suffocated by her mother's over-controlling anxious behaviour had difficulty standing up to the controlling mother in an imaginary dialogue, out of fear that mother would get hurt and imply that the client is an ungrateful daughter.

Fear of anger and the negative evaluation of anger are also natural phenomena. From an evolutionary perspective, it makes sense that cooperation and harmony, and not conflict, are what allow a community to grow and to look after all its members. Thus, caution around anger is understandable and reasonable. On the other hand, a point can be reached whereby expression of anger is the only way to ensure justice is served. In such instances, the expression of appropriate anger can be viewed as promoting growth and security. Striking that balance and facilitating access to, ownership of, and expression of adaptive anger is at the core of the transformation of core emotional pain. Thus in therapy, the therapist *validates* the client when he or she recognises and acknowledges a sense of entitlement to have the client's needs met. The therapist does so especially when this recognition on behalf of the client arises *naturally* in response to a sense of being wronged (e.g., excluded, rejected, intruded upon, etc.). The therapist acknowledges such an entitlement, validates it, affirms it, and encourages the client to both feel it and express it in enactments during therapy sessions. The therapist's support thus aims to give the client permission both to generate anger and to accept it once it occurs.

The above-mentioned studies observed that the experiencing and expression of protective anger is best facilitated when the client is confronted with a live, heartbreaking, non-responsiveness in the other. For instance, in the example above the female client who cannot stand up to her mother may access the anger after the therapist asks her to sit in the opposite chair and be her controlling mother in her most controlling and suffocating way. Once this behaviour is escalated, the client may be asked to go back to her chair and observe the controlling behaviour and its impact, and see whether she wants her mother to control her in this way. Often when a client experiences the imagined other responding to the client's own vulnerable, hurting self with harsh non-responsiveness, hurtful behaviour, and/or rejection, client anger spontaneously emerges. The client's capability to stand up for him- or herself, and fight for his or her own needs, is naturally mobilised. For instance, if the client expresses vulnerability and a need to be loved and accepted, and the other person (e.g., the imagined mother) responds with ridicule, the client is likely to either collapse into despair and hopelessness, or stand up for him- or herself with empowering anger (*I do deserve love and acceptance and not to be ridiculed.*). It is the therapist's role in these instances to help the client be assertive rather than collapse into despair (see Chapters 7 and 8).

There are several other ways by which the therapist might do this. One option available to the therapist is to coach the client to express protective anger. For instance, a male client who was bullied may be instructed to look at an imagined/remembered bully, adopt a firm posture, and firmly express to the bully what was not right about the bullying behaviour. Additionally, he might be encouraged to express to the bully what the client as a child was entitled to (e.g., safety and respect). Another option for the therapist might be to emphasise the client's collapsed, non-assertive state through a paradoxical intervention, for example, by instructing the client to look at the bully and state: 'I will be scared of you for the rest of my life'. Such an intervention typically provokes rebellion in the client, leading him or her to state something like 'I will not be scared of you anymore'. A number of other intervention strategies useful for helping clients access and express healthy anger will be looked at in Chapter 7.

Emotion-focused therapy typically gives a central role to enactments of interactions with hurtful, significant others, with such enactments typically taking the form of imaginary dialogues. Such dialogues evoke intense emotions in clients, and thus have been found to be powerful strategies by which existing problematic schemes and self-organisations can be activated within the therapy session and eventually transformed (cf. Greenberg and Foerster, 1996; Greenberg and Malcolm, 2002). Where the client has memories of times when the significant other was more responsive to their needs, these memories typically feed into enacted dialogues in the form of a remembered compassionate presence of the other, that can also be responsive to the client's unmet needs in the here and now of the session (cf. Greenberg and Foerster, 1996; Greenberg et al., 1993). If such memories do not exist, and the imagined significant other is remembered only as non-responsive, abusive, or neglectful, then enactments of that significant other usually trigger a collapse into hopelessness and helplessness (i.e., that the unmet needs will never be responded to: *I am not loved and accepted and it will stay like that*) or they provoke the emergence of protective anger. Which of these two options prevail is dependent upon a variety of factors, including the nurturing and affirming presence of caregivers or important people in the client's developmental history; the presence of assertive role models; biological predispositions; and perhaps also the level of adversity. Taken together, the client's experiencing of a compassionate response to core pain and assertive affirmation of his or her right to stand up for the self result in the creation of a facilitative environment within which it becomes possible for despair to be transformed. In turn, the client can be transformed into a vulnerable yet powerful and engaged person, following his or her natural and healthy needs.

Genuine pain signals that the natural needs of a person are being violated or overlooked. The natural consequence of witnessing such pain is to feel genuine compassion and to endeavour to respond affirmatively. This is why we get such a boost from watching films or listening to stories in which injustice is overcome by the bravery of heroes. We like such victories, especially in cases which initially looked hopeless or impossible to change. We are happy when once-wronged people win, and until their moment of victory, we are moved to the core of our heart by their suffering and pain. Paradoxically, we are moved even more so when the turning point is reached and they start to win (see crying at happy ending phenomenon; Weiss, 1993).

THE IMPACT OF EMOTIONAL TRANSFORMATION EXPERIENCES

Primary maladaptive emotions, such as maladaptive shame, loneliness, or fear, are transformed in therapy by primary adaptive emotions such as compassion and adaptive anger (Greenberg, 2011). The client's experiencing is thus no longer solely organised around hopelessness, helplessness, fear, despair, rage, or avoidance. These latter experiences are balanced by a sense of being understood, cared for, looked after, supported, affirmed, and entitled. These new experiences not only balance the pain, but increase the likelihood that the client will be able to generate such adaptive emotional responses when feeling painful maladaptive emotions. Problematic emotion schemes are thus changed and re-scripted (one can hypothesise that this includes changes in neural connections), and new emotional processing patterns start to develop. Emotional processing is no longer stuck in painful primary maladaptive emotions and in the avoidance of such experiences. Rather it now also contains adaptive emotions such as self-compassion and protective anger, as well as experiences and behaviours which elicit compassion and supportive anger from others.

The studies mentioned throughout this chapter suggest that as a consequence of accessing and differentiating emotional pain, and eventually transforming it, clients also learn to be more tolerant of, and more capable of bearing, difficult feelings. Clients can also become aware of important emotions, reflect on them, and put them into personally meaningful narratives. Clients may also become more aware of the needs embedded in salient emotions and can generate the emotional responses and actions required to respond to these needs. Thus the person can be more adept at pursuing the meeting of their own needs. The in-session experiences of being able to bounce back from despair also leads to personal maturity and a developing sense of one's own agency in life. These experiences also bring about learning to face adversity and the pain which such adversity can bring. Taken together, these experiences ultimately contribute to a broadening of emotional flexibility and a greater accessibility to a variety of self-organisations (Paivio and Pascual-Leone, 2010; Pascual-Leone and Greenberg, 2007).

The experiences of bouncing back from adversity, combined with the experiences of transforming painful feelings into a richer palette of emotional responses, ultimately makes the clients more resilient in the face of future adversity. Clients learn a subtle but powerful skill—a way of being—that helps them face future difficulties and adversities in their lives. This way of being can be supported through other nurturing and supportive relationships, such as responsive parenting (in case of children), transformative education, or community and/or peer support.

The experiences of an empowered sense of self, supported by experiences of compassion, and bolstered by experiences of protective anger, do not, in and of itself, mean that past hurts are healed and overcome. In a sense, the client remains sad and pained by the memory of these experiences. However, once the debilitating power of these memories has been overcome, the client can properly grieve, a process which has been clearly seen in the studied cases (e.g., Pascual-Leone and Greenberg, 2007; Crowley et al., 2013; Keogh et al., 2013; McNally et al., 2014; Dillon et al., 2014). Clients become capable of experiencing and expressing sadness and grief at those adversities, difficulties, and hurts which met them in the distant or more recent past. Clients become capable of grieving these hurts in a less upsetting manner and with more of a letting-go flavour. Whereas once these memories of hurt brought only unbearable pain and hopelessness, now novel experiences of compassion and protective anger allow for the hurts to be grieved without the client becoming overwhelmed. They can be grieved in a way that allows the client to be fully aware of what happened to him or her without being immobilised and tortured by that awareness. Thus, clients' emotional maturity may increase, and they may become more sensitive to the pain of others. The transformation of emotional pain not only makes the clients more resilient, but it also makes them more sensitive and more human, more capable of connecting with others, and more willing to stick out their neck and offer others a compassionate presence or firm affirmation and determined support if needed.

Part II

Practical applications

4 Therapeutic relationship promoting emotional transformation

People are social beings, and we live our lives in supportive social networks. Relationships help us to overcome adversity; they have the potential to calm emotional pain (Panksepp, 2011), regulate affect (particularly in childhood; Schore, 2001), help to bear physical pain (Coan et al., 2006), break existential isolation, provide protection, and offer affirmation. From the perspective of Damasio (2012), functional social networks provide opportunities for people (including at an organic and cellular level) to fully live to their potential. Therefore, it is not surprising that psychotherapy researchers, developers, and practitioners noticed early on the powerful potential of a caring and supportive relationship (Rogers, 1942). Indeed, it is now widely accepted that the fundamental bedrock for any psychological therapy is a good therapeutic relationship (Horvath, Del Re, Fluckinger, and Symonds, 2011).

The EFT therapist attempts to create a therapeutic relationship with his or her clients that has a healing quality and can serve as a base for emotion transformation work. The main feature of the therapist's contribution to the development of a healing relationship is his or her offer of a transparently authentic relationship in which the therapist openly shows his or her caring intentions and warmth (cf. Rogers, 1957). The therapist is not hiding behind any facades and may be quite tentative and somewhat vulnerable in the presence of the client (cf. Timulak, 2014).

PERSONAL ACCOUNT

Recently, I described my own experiences of providing emotion-focused therapy (Timulak, 2014). Early on in therapy I am quite anxious, as I am a naturally shy person as to meet a new person on an intimate basis requires a level of engagement that is challenging. I am also anxious because even though I will use all my expertise when working with the new client, I cannot guarantee that the therapy will work as the transformation of emotional pain and suffering is always a very complex process. I am, however, using my experience and confidence based on that experience to instil hope in the client that I will do my best to successfully help the client to meaningfully change his or her life. From early on in therapy, despite my position as an expert who is visited by the vulnerable client, I am trying to form a relationship that will promote equality. I am attempting to build trust in the relationship with the client by being open about how I work and what is happening inside of me during the therapeutic work (obviously without burdening the client, but with an openness to reveal what is happening in me if asked by the client). I am open with my commitment to the client in terms of using all my skills and knowledge. Additionally, I am very open about my understandings of the client's difficulties throughout the therapy, and I share and collaboratively develop conceptualisation of the client's difficulties with the client (see Chapter 5).

From the first moments of therapy I am seeking to generate warmth inside of me and show caring in my posture, my voice quality, and in my concentrated focus on the client's experience, in particular its painful aspects. My focus is on the client and his or her presenting issues, bracketing off those things which are not relevant to the client and consciously attempting to be of help to the client (cf. Geller and Greenberg, 2012).

In the session, particularly in those moments when we are touching on the raw painful feelings in the client, I often feel a very strong connection. As we touch on the client's pain I am always genuinely moved when witnessing the client's struggles and vulnerabilities. I believe it brings out the best in me, the most caring and facilitative qualities I possess. I am deeply touched by the client's pain and I am not trying to hide it, but on the contrary I share with the client that I am being moved, touched, angry at what he or she went through and so on. I am trying to be relational and state my support and validation openly. Together with Les Greenberg (Welling and Greenberg, 2011), I can say that witnessing the client's pain evokes a lot of compassion in me (indeed I say to my students that the signal for them that they have accessed their client's core pain is that they are being moved by their clients and feel very gentle, protective, and compassionate toward them). In those moments, I am identifying with aspects of the client's pain and feel particularly tender and caring toward the client's raw primary emotional pain (cf. Geller and Greenberg, 2012). In such moments, I am aware that I need to proactively show my warmth and presence in the language I use and in the interventions I employ, so the client can sense my presence and connection. On a technical level, as the client's core pain is accessed in therapy, my aim is to bring clarity, to name the different aspects of the pain, and to shed light on the unmet needs that are present in that pain. Additionally, I am working to facilitate an emotional experience that brings a response to those unmet needs and as a result transforms the pain.

I am supporting the client in the moments of fundamental vulnerability and its transformation. Witnessing the client's suffering in its rawness, as well as seeing the client battle the pain through caring self-compassion and protective assertion, inspire and change me. This is what is most rewarding in my profession. The moments of transformation, those moments when the client shows the resolve to protect the self and to recognize the importance and validity of his or her own needs and responds to them through caring or validation, inspire me in dealing with my own aches and fears. These experiences with the client are changing me. In such moments, I have a sense that I can connect with my own hurts and vulnerabilities better and connect to people around me who can offer support. I am also determined to be braver and address injustice.

As therapy ends, it is often experienced as a loss for clients; this can often be my experience too. It may be filled with sadness, but also with celebration and recognition of important achievements. If therapy was not particularly successful or if it is finished prematurely, it may fill me with disappointment and I may find myself asking questions of what I could have done differently. However, those difficult moments can be balanced by memories of successes with other clients (for more about my experience of providing emotion-focused therapy, see Timulak, 2014).

THEORETICAL PERSPECTIVE

Apart from being a very human and impactful experience, the relational provision of emotion-focused therapy requires it to be an intentional, theoretically and empirically informed, professional activity. The entire work of transforming emotional suffering is taking place within the context of a therapeutic relationship. This relationship is the central vehicle for conditions conducive to transformative work as well a central agent of transformation itself. The therapeutic relationship in emotion-focused therapy has several functions. Here I will focus on three of the major functions: the provision of safety, emotion regulation, and corrective emotional experience.

Safety

The first function of the therapeutic relationship in emotion-focused therapy that I will discuss is its provision of safety. The clients come to therapy vulnerable and apprehensive of what will happen in therapy. They are in pain, but they are also anxious about the possibility of experiencing further pain in therapy. They also have concerns regarding whether the therapist will be knowledgeable and skilful enough to help them. Occasionally, they may have their own experiences with psychologists or other health professionals that may sometimes make them doubtful of the professional's ability to help them. Furthermore, they may also have concerns regarding judgement by the professional and whether they will be liked or not. Particularly, they may fear that the professional may concur with people in their life who did not like them or criticised them or were not sympathetic toward them. This may be specifically the case for those clients who are filled with self-doubt and who do not have a very positive sense of the self. They may fear that the therapist will see through them and will view them as weak, unintelligent, responsible for their own problems, not having nice personal qualities, and so on. Therefore, it comes as no surprise that the clients in therapy are very vigilant and scrutinise the therapist (see Rennie, 1990; 1994; Timulak & Lietaer, 2001) and his or her actions from early on until they feel more comfortable and safe with the therapist.

How can the therapist respond to the client's understandable vigilance and vulnerability? First of all, the therapist should be aware of the possibility of these feelings and also be aware of the fact that the client may not communicate what he or she finds difficult (see the studies on clients' deference by Rennie, 1990; 1994). Furthermore, the therapist should be forthcoming and explain how he or she operates (cf. Timulak & Lietaer, 2001), so the client does not have phantasies about what is happening in the therapist's mind. The therapist may decide early on to provide a rationale for the therapy that fits idiosyncratically with the client's presenting issues as they are unfolding (e.g., *I see that those issues with your mom bring up a lot of things for you emotionally. We will be trying to look at it so it would perhaps be somewhat less upsetting.*). Concurrently, the therapist also works with the client to agree on the goals of therapy (e.g., which issues need to be worked on) and the tasks of therapy (e.g., by providing the rationale that the emotionally painful issues will have to be accessed and experienced in the sessions in order to be transformed), and provides a warm presence that can hopefully contribute to a firm bond between the therapist and the client (cf. Bordin, 1979; Horvath, Del Re, Fluckiger, and Symonds, 2012).

The process of agreeing on the goals and tasks of therapy is typical of the first therapy sessions, in which the client is still discovering what the therapy is about. When the client has had a prior therapy (a phenomenon that is becoming increasingly common as people are attending therapy at an increasing level), it is prudent for the therapist to inquire about the client's prior experiences of therapy. These experiences are likely to inform the client's current perspective and expectations from therapy. In some cases, these experiences may not have been positive or may have been very different to what the client can expect in emotion-focused therapy.

The main focus then in early sessions, as well as in the overall therapy, is encouragement given to the client to bring the issues that are most painful, troublesome, and upsetting to the session. As the client shares what troubles him or her, the therapist 's empathic stance allows the client to unfold the story (cf. Angus and Greenberg, 2011) and feel the emotional tone of it. The therapist 's empathic responding is aimed at communicating understanding and also to facilitate the client 's exploration of his or her experience. The therapist 's empathy is embedded in the attitudinal qualities that convey acceptance of the client 's emotional experience and the therapist 's authentic presence (Rogers, 1957). It is important that the therapist 's empathic presence, which focuses on the exploration of the client 's difficulties, is embedded in the therapist 's non-defensive presence that allows the therapist to stay relational (open and transparent about own experience) with the client even in situations when the therapeutic relationship may be rocky or very tentative (see Timulak, 2011). As I expressed previously (Timulak, 2011, p. 30): 'a non-defensive therapist is not withdrawing or hiding things from the client. He or she is open to share his or her experience if it is important for the therapeutic relationship or therapy. This openness and transparency may be a model for the client 's engagement in therapy '.

The therapist 's non-judgmental stance is another defining feature of the EFT therapist. The non-judgmental stance refers to valuing the client and welcoming every aspect of their experience (Barrett-Lennard, 1998). Importantly, the therapist should not only have an open attitude toward the client's feelings, thoughts, and actions, but also he or she should not be afraid of the client's emotional world. As clients are generally fearful of their painful emotions, it is imperative for building the clients' emotional safety that they have a sense that no matter what they experience, the therapist is not scared of that experience, but rather welcomes it and is confident in working with it. Indeed, this is often a problem with junior therapists in training, who can be ambivalent about the EFT focus on pursuing emotional pain throughout the therapy sessions. Some therapists in training are afraid of these painful emotions and may feel that they are arousing pain in the client that they do not feel confident to deal with (e.g., soothe or transform into an empowering experience). They may also fear their own emotional vulnerabilities, which may leave them feeling hopeless to address the pain in the other, particularly if the client's painful feelings and experiences are similar to their own. Therefore, it is an important aspect of training that therapist's emotional tolerance, emotion recognition, and understanding—alongside developing their emotional work skills—are focused on in order that they become confident to guide their clients through the pain.

For some clients emotional expression can be difficult as they may see it as socially embarrassing to get emotional or upset in front of the therapist. This may particularly be the case for clients who received subtle or direct messages throughout their development, suggesting that emotional experiences should not be expressed openly, because they are difficult to bear by others, or are signs of vulnerability that may attract abuse, and so on. In this situation, the EFT therapist is accepting of the client's hesitation, but also directly encourages the client to access and experience emotions as this is the only way they can be worked with and eventually transformed.

Regardless of the therapist's efforts to be warm, present, caring, and skillful in working with the client, the possibility of strain in the therapeutic relationship remains high due to clients' natural vulnerabilities and sensitivities. When clients engage in therapy, they are likely to come in a state of vulnerability and may be particularly sensitive to a less-than-optimal response to their emotional needs within the session. It is, therefore, important for the therapist to detect any reservations on the client's part and then focus on them in the session. The therapist should try to encourage the client to share what is difficult while remaining mindful that client may avoid expressing these feelings directly out of the fear that they may cause tension in the relationship with the therapist (Safran and Muran, 2000). The therapist should be tentative and facilitative in order to help the client express what he or she has experienced and to encourage the client, through empathic exploration, to give voice to the difficulties perceived in the relationship (see the work of Safran and Muran, 2000, on the ruptures in the therapeutic relationship).

The therapist's humility and courage to explore the client's reservations about the therapy or therapist, as well as an openness to admit their own part in any constraints that can appear in the therapeutic relationship, seem to be important components in successfully overcoming ruptures in the therapeutic relationship

(Rhodes, Hill, Thompson, and Elliott, 1994; Safran and Muran, 2000; Safran, Muran, and Eubanks-Carter, 2012; Timulak, 1999). Overcoming such ruptures may be crucial for forging a solid relationship that is experienced as safe by the client.

Emotional regulation

The therapeutic relationship in which the therapist conveys a non-defensive, open, non-judgmental, and accepting interest in the client's emotional world and in which the therapist conveys these attitudes through empathic understanding and exploration, has the potential to calm the client's upset and the pain. Similar results were found in terms of a calming impact in the presence of a caring person (Panksepp, 2011), the effect of a good quality romantic relationship, and the presence of a caring other to alleviate physical pain (Coan et al., 2006). The EFT therapist aims to develop such a relationship which provides that potent emotion-calming presence. In this calming presence the therapist conveys empathy and genuine caring (Timulak, 2011). Research provides solid evidence that the therapist's empathy contributes to therapeutic outcomes (Elliott, Bohart, Watson, and Greenberg, 2011).

Of course, the regulating presence of the therapist is a complex issue. The therapist's activity does not only focus on the delivery of compassionate empathic soothing responses. An EFT therapist is promoting access to the most painful emotional experiences so that they can be transformed. The therapist typically achieves this through focusing on the pain and actively evoking it in the session through the use of evocative responses. Additionally, active experiential interventions such as imaginary dialogues (see Chapters 6, 7, and 8) are used to elicit the particular emotional pain. It is important to be mindful that all evocative work takes place within the context of the caring empathic relationship in which the therapist actively conveys his or her caring presence.

The therapist contributes to emotion regulation and soothing by helping the client to have an experience whereby they can stay with the core painful emotions. The therapist models this by welcoming (rather than fearing) all emotional experiences, even those that are scary and painful at the core of the client's emotional pain. The therapist's consistent approach in accessing such emotions encourages the client to stay with them and thus to build the capacity to be able to tolerate them. Furthermore, the therapist is actively helping the client to articulate the experience by finding a language to name the various aspects of the emotional experience (e.g., *And it brings this profound sense of loneliness inside.*). The most poignant aspects of the client's emotional experiences are focused on by the therapist inviting the client to stay with the experience. The therapist is aiming to facilitate the client to not only savour and feel the experience, but also to articulate it in appropriate language. Another important part of this articulation is exploring which needs are not being met in the painful experience (e.g., the need for connection, acceptance, and or safety). The therapist also encourages the client through tentative empathic responses as well as through active inviting questions to articulate the emotional experience in the client's own words (e.g., *See what is happening inside. How does it feel inside when you get that?*). The research evidence suggests that naming the feelings can have a regulating effect (Lieberman et al., 2007). Indeed, some experiential therapeutic approaches (and some of the EFT interventions presented in Chapters 6 and 8) are built around that concept (Gendlin, 1996). It is further hypothesised that as the client and the therapist are forging their relationship, the regulating function of the relationship is strengthened and internalised by the client who can then mirror the therapist's attentive, caring, and understanding presence in the treatment of self. The client thus internalises the therapist's function and fulfils it even without the presence of the therapist. The regulating function of the therapist is thus gradually replaced with self-regulation.

Corrective interpersonal emotional experience

Apart from the regulating function of the therapist's caring presence and empathic responding, the therapist often enacts the type of relating that provides an antidote to the treatment provided by hurtful others whom have contributed to the client's interpersonal injury and consequent emotional pain. Thus, the therapist's compassionate attentive responses, such as empathic understanding, affirmation of unmet needs, or acknowledgment of being moved by the client's painful story, are providing the client with direct experiences that contradict prior abusive or neglectful actions of the hurtful others. The client's loneliness can thus be broken by the therapist's reaching out and being with the client. The client's shame is being undone by the therapist's validation and affirmation. The client's fear and insecurity is met with the therapist's protecting presence. Such interpersonal experiences in therapy are not planned, but rather authentic spontaneous responses of the relationally oriented EFT therapist. The therapist is non-defensively present and prepared to share his or her humanity (e.g., that he or she is moved by the client's suffering or perhaps angry at maltreatment on behalf of the client). The therapist's spontaneous compassionate responses are typically elicited by the client's raw pain; the client's vulnerability thus calls for a caring presence that is actively expressed by the EFT therapist. In such circumstances the EFT therapist does not hide behind the professional mask, but shows compassion toward the client's pain and unmet needs entailed in it. The therapist also affirms the protective and self-affirming, assertive stance that is an antidote to feelings of abandonment, invalidation or abuse, and similar types of hurtful experiences in the client's past and present. The impact of such a therapist's actions is then seen as one of the important transformative mechanisms of change in EFT. In such instances, new corrective emotional experiences are transforming the existing self-organisation centred around the core problematic emotion schemes (Greenberg and Elliott, 2012). These corrective, interpersonal, emotional experiences are supplemented by corrective emotional experiences generated from within the client (see Chapters 6 and 7; see also Greenberg, 2011; Greenberg and Elliott, 2012).

Existential meeting

The experience of conducting EFT also leaves the therapist somewhat vulnerable as he or she is always very transparent and takes the risk of revealing his or her caring presence to the client. This is particularly so at moments of intense vulnerability for the client, in which the therapist stays active and genuinely reaches out to the client through empathic responses, but also through genuine relational disclosures that are attempting to show the therapist's compassion and/or justified anger on behalf of the client. For some clients their vulnerability may increase their sensitivity to any misattunements they may experience emanating from the therapist. Thus the therapist's caring presence also leaves him or her more open to the client's rejection. The EFT therapist purposefully differs from some people clients may encounter who, out of the fear of not knowing how to respond to them when they are in pain, consequently hesitate to provide comfort when it is needed.

I mentioned in the beginning of this chapter that I am often directly affected by emotion-focused work. I am moved, inspired, challenged, saddened, wanting to fight for the client, and impacted in many ways when working with clients who are in pain. I believe that this is the case for many therapists in a variety of therapeutic approaches. In EFT, with its focus on the most vulnerable areas of the clients' experiences, it is very likely that work will be impactful on the therapist. The impact often comes in an unexpected way and may change how the therapist experiences his or her own vulnerability and how he or she addresses it (for more, see Timulak, 2014).

Case vignette

Throughout the rest of the chapters, I will be presenting various vignettes. The transcripts and vignettes in the book are based on actual clients and therapy sessions of individuals who underwent therapy as part of my research group. All material used was provided by clients who gave consent to take part in various studies. They allowed their material to be analysed and published while preserving their privacy and personal details. Therefore, the vignettes and transcripts are altered to protect the clients' confidentiality and identity. They have also been edited for communication purposes in order that they would depict the main points that are to be illustrated.

Here, I would like to present a brief segment from a therapy session which aims to illustrate moments in which the client touches on the core painful emotions which are also very moving for the therapist. They require the therapist to be very active and convey a compassionate presence and verbal empathic responses aimed at the core of the pain and unmet needs in that pain. This segment illustrates a poignant moment in which the client Ann (who will be described in more detail in the next chapter) expresses her experiences of loneliness and her unmet need for a caring and present mother in her childhood. Ann's core painful emotional issues covered several areas, one of the main ones being an experience of neglect by her mother (who also died quite early in her life) that left Ann with a profound sense of loneliness and feeling unsupported. The excerpt comes from one of the early therapy sessions where, in an empty-chair dialogue with her mother, she touches for the first time in therapy in a very emotionally aroused way on this core pain of loneliness and abandonment. The therapist provides a caring presence that hopefully breaks Ann's existential isolation. The therapist, attempting to help Ann to access the pain, puts it to a narrative that potentially helps to regulate the pain.

In the beginning of the segment, Ann compares her childhood to that of her own children:

Ann: *But I know, from my kids growing up that we should have had that childhood. And we didn't (choking quality).*

Therapist: *I gave it to my children.*

Ann: *I gave it to my kids (voice strained with emotion, words are almost inaudible).*

Therapist: *Yeah.*

Ann: *You should have given it to me (almost a whisper, crying).* [This is directed to her imagined mother sitting in the empty chair. Ann is engaged in an empty-chair dialogue, an EFT task described more fully in Chapter 6; see also Greenberg et al., 1993; Elliott et al., 2004].

Therapist: *There's pain in it, and anger, yes? It's painful what's missing yes when it was like this.* [The therapist is naming the experience and also points to the unmet need through highlighting that there is something missing.]

Ann: *My kids would never see what you put us through (crying). We'd tell them sometimes (sniff) but they can laugh about it, because they never had to live with it, and they never will.*

Therapist: *Yes, but it's not laugh, laughing for me yes.*

Ann: *It was never laughing for me.*

Therapist: *Yea, yea ... It's like full of pain. The pain that I can feel now, I can stay with it.* [The therapist speaking on behalf the client.] *Yea ... So I need you, what would you need from her?* [The therapist is trying to help to articulate the unmet need.]

Ann: *(sniff) Not an apology, but an explanation (voice collapses with emotion). And back then when we were kids, I needed a mother (tearful).*

Therapist: *Ok.*

Ann: *I didn't know it at the time. Cos I thought life would be better without you.*

Therapist: *Yeah.*

Ann: *And it was. God forbid me for saying it but it was.*

Therapist: *Yea yea... this is how it felt. I just wanted you not to be there, so I have, I can achieve some peace or something yea?*

Ann: *Yeah (crying) but I was still not getting the peace from her.*

Therapist:	*But I know that I needed real mother, yea? For you to be there as a mother.*
Ann:	*Yeah, and I'd nobody to turn to (very tearful).*
Therapist:	*So there was nobody for me there, yea?*
Ann:	*No (crying).*
Therapist:	*It just aches.*
Ann:	*With things like that, when me kids are sick. I know I have [a husband] and I know he's there and he does everything he needs to do for me. But then I would have liked my own mother to be there (choking with tearfulness). Just to go and say Mum 'I need a cup of tea, sit and talk to me.' Try and help me deal with it. Instead of having to let me deal with it myself. Which I'm gonna have to keep on doing.*
Therapist:	*Yeah.*
Ann:	*But it would have been nice just to have her there.*
Therapist:	*Yea 'I needed you there'.*
Ann:	*Yea (crying).*
Therapist:	*I was so on my own just to deal with all of it.*
Ann:	*It's not even that. It's every now and then a girl needs her Mum.*
Therapist:	*Yea. Just to have you there.*
Ann:	*The boys mightn't need them. But every now and again a girl does need her Mum (crying heavily).*
Therapist:	*Yea. Every girl needs it and I needed it as well. I needed you so much yes in my life.* [The therapist actively speaks on behalf of the client.]
Ann:	*I did (crying) and it's only now that my own kids are growing up. I realise that because I'm there for them, and they know I am, and they know I always will be ... It's very annoying, and it is very hurtful that she wasn't there for us, or for me. She could have been there for the others I don't know.*
Therapist:	*Yea, you were not there for me.*
Ann:	*She wasn't there for me.*
Therapist:	*You weren't there for me. Yea and this is just so painful. And it's just such a loss yea? And such a sense of being on my own in my life.*
Ann:	*(nodding) Yea. Even though I have [a husband] and I have the kids, you still do feel lonely. You'd love to just go up to them and say I'm going to me Mum (crying).*
Therapist:	*Every girl needs it, and I need it and I needed it.*
Ann:	*Yeah (sniff).* (A portion of the dialogue taken from Witnessing client's emotional change in psychotherapy: An emotion-focused therapists experience of providing therapy. Timulak, L. *Journal of Clinical Psychology*, *70,* 741–752. © 2014 John Wiley and Sons doi: 10.1002/jclp.22109)

This excerpt poignantly shows how the EFT therapist empathically follows but also guides Ann to the core of her painful experience and how he stays with the Ann's pain and articulates it in an appropriate language. He also focuses on the unmet need in the painful experience (the client missing a caring mother). The therapist is caring, compassionate, and actively communicating empathic understanding, but is also evoking various aspects of Ann's experience. The therapist is moved in the segment, his voice quality conveys how fragile the client's process is and how the therapist sensitively tries to attune to it. The therapist also offers a calming and regulating presence as he does not shy away from the experiences that are at times overwhelming for the client. Ann (in one of the later sessions) spontaneously comments that she has a sense that the therapist 'gets her' like nobody else in her life. This just points to the strength and unique quality of the bond that is being developed through the work demonstrated in the above segment.

5 Conceptualising core emotional pain

Case conceptualisation is a defining feature of any psychological therapy. Each therapist attempts to understand the presenting issues of his or her clients using a particular theoretical framework, in order that he or she can apply a therapeutic strategy aimed at overcoming the client's difficulties. Humanistic and experiential approaches to psychotherapy (amongst which EFT belongs) traditionally did not pay much attention to the therapist's conceptualisation of client difficulties. Conceptualisation was seen as impeding the therapist from having an authentic relational encounter with the client (e.g., Rogers, 1951). In line with this tradition, the developers of emotion-focused therapy were initially reluctant to formulate a firm conceptual framework that would guide therapeutic strategy. Rather, in its earliest incarnations (Greenberg et al., 1993), in-session markers were used within EFT to identify specific tasks that the client was engaged in within the session, and which the therapist could respond to, or collaborate on, with the use of specific experiential techniques. As the development of EFT progressed, a more complex and multi-layered approach to case conceptualisation evolved (Greenberg and Goldman, 2007; Greenberg and Watson, 2006; Watson, 2010). The conceptualisation approach proposed by Greenberg and colleagues contained *eight steps* that were to be understood as following fluidly across therapy sessions (at the time of the writing of this book, Goldman and Greenberg [forthcoming] have further refined those eight steps, however, their new book on EFT case conceptualisation was not available at time of writing so below I describe the original eight steps). They focused on (Greenberg and Goldman, 2007; Greenberg and Watson, 2006):

1 *Identification of the presenting problem.* Here the EFT therapist not only focuses on what brought the client to therapy, but also, as initial sessions progress, reframes the presenting problem in terms of problematic emotion schemes and problematic self-organisations centred around those schemes.
2 *Exploration of the client's narrative about the presenting problem.* As the EFT therapist empathically explores the client's presenting issues, he or she pays attention to certain characteristics of the client's narrative (Angus and Greenberg, 2011). The therapist tries to facilitate optimal interplay between the client's emotional experience and personal narrative in the session. Optimal interplay is understood as being one in which there is a balance between

access to emotional experiencing, the expression of that emotional experiencing in narrative, and subsequent reflection on it.

3 *Gathering of information about past and current identity and attachment experiences.* The EFT therapist expects that the problematic emotion schemes, on which therapy needs to focus, will be centred around current, and developmentally significant, relational and personal identity experiences. It is assumed that specific significant experiences are responsible for the development and maintenance of problematic emotion schemes (Greenberg and Goldman, 2008). The therapist collaboratively gathers relevant information from the client in order to understand the origin and maintenance of the core painful emotion schemes.

4 *Identifying the core pain.* Greenberg (2002) describes the EFT therapist as following a 'pain compass'. According to Greenberg and colleagues, by focusing on the most painful and poignant experiences that the client presents with, the therapist is led almost inevitably toward the client's chronic enduring emotional pain. This pain represents maladaptive emotional experiences, and identification of the 'core pain' thus helps to develop the main focus of therapy.

5 *Observation and attention to the client's style of processing emotions.* Apart from following poignant narrative, the EFT therapist also observes, from the initial moments of therapy, whether the client is over-regulating or under-regulating his or her emotions. The therapist, for instance, assesses the client's voice quality (Rice and Kerr, 1986) and level of experiencing (Klein, Mathieu, Gendlin, and Kiesler, 1969). Narrative style is also taken into consideration (Angus and Greenberg, 2011). Furthermore, according to Greenberg and colleagues, the therapist distinguishes whether the experienced and expressed emotions are primary, secondary, or instrumental (cf. Greenberg and Safran, 1989). Emotions are assessed as to their adaptive or maladaptive potential, and also, as to their productivity in terms of whether they serve productive emotional processing (Greenberg, Auszra, and Herrmann, 2007). By being attentive to the client's core pain, the therapist essentially focuses on primary emotions, typically primary maladaptive emotion. The therapist tries to increase the productivity of primary emotions, and tries to generate adaptive primary emotions in order to counteract and transform the presenting primary maladaptive emotions.

6 *Identification of thematic interpersonal and intrapersonal processes.* The client's presentation in therapy centres around particular interpersonal and/or intrapersonal themes (see also step 3) that the therapist and the client explore and work with experientially.

7 *Identification of markers informing the choice of therapeutic tasks.* EFT, in its attention to moment-to-moment process, utilises a number of therapeutic tasks that address the thematic and emotional aspects of the client's presentation (see Elliott et al., 2004; Greenberg et al., 1993). The therapist initiates such tasks on the basis of an appropriate marker, in other words, an in-session indicator of a particular emotional processing problem. Tasks in

EFT are research-informed experiential techniques that promote activation of the problematic emotion schemes and their subsequent transformation. In other words, problematic emotion schemes are worked with by the use of experiential enactments (e.g., two-chair dialogue for identity-related self-critical process, empty-chair dialogue for an unresolved interpersonal injury, etc.; for details, see Elliott et al., 2004, and Greenberg et al., 1993); first to activate maladaptive emotions; and second to transform those maladaptive emotions via the generation of adaptive emotional responses.

8 *Attending to moment-to-moment process within the session and tasks.* The EFT therapist does not set an agenda early in therapy. Rather the therapist responds to the ever-changing in-session experiencing of the client. For instance, when a client is involved in a specific experiential task, the therapist uses micro-markers (e.g., emotional arousal, voice quality, self-interruptions) to inform the adjustment of a given task and its direction.

This traditional form of EFT case conceptualisation (Greenberg and Watson, 2006; Greenberg and Goldman, 2007) presents a clear framework that informs the therapist as to what he or she should pay attention to in therapy. It is important to emphasise that while this model of case conceptualisation guides the therapist to pay attention to particular aspects of the client's experience and presentation in the therapy session, conceptual understanding of the client's difficulties does not take precedence over the constant moment-by-moment tracking of the client's in-session experiencing. The same is true for the case conceptualisation approach presented below.

This book presents a somewhat different approach to case conceptualisation. While it is informed by the work of the above-mentioned authors, it is particularly influenced by the recent research on sequential steps in emotional processing and emotion transformation in EFT already presented in Chapters 2 and 3 (i.e., the initial work of Pascual-Leone and Greenberg, 2007 and Pascual-Leone, 2009; and further work building on that initial research; Keogh et al., 2011; Timulak et al., 2012; O'Brien et al., 2012).

As we (in the Trinity College Dublin emotion-focused therapy lab) started to examine videotapes of therapy cases and track the process of emotion transformation, we also noticed that the emotion transformation model helped us to understand clients and their progress. We (myself and my students), therefore, started to develop a case conceptualisation framework that could be used in our thinking about clients and our strategies for therapy. My thinking was then further influenced by a collaboration with Antonio Pascual-Leone where we tried to come up with a shared view on case conceptualisation that might be useful for EFT therapists (see Timulak and Pascual-Leone, 14). Also very influential were my discussions about clients, and about the nature of client change, with Les Greenberg on his many trips to Ireland. What follows is a conceptualisation framework that has already been presented in a recent paper by Timulak and Pascual-Leone (2014). Here I offer a somewhat elaborated version of our thinking.

EMOTION-FOCUSED CASE CONCEPTUALISATION BASED ON EMOTIONAL TRANSFORMATION MODEL

The research studies inspired by the original work of Pascual-Leone and Greenberg (2007) carried out at the Trinity EFT lab led to the development of a conceptual framework that can be used as a guide by the therapist in his or her understanding of the client (Timulak and Pascual-Leone, 2014). Such an understanding can inform the therapist's overall strategy for therapy. It can also increase therapist sensitivity to the client's moment-to-moment therapeutic process. The framework assumes that through the observation of regularities in the client's narrative and emotional processing, the therapist can tentatively determine the core painful emotion scheme self-organisations that are central to the presenting issues that the therapist and the client have agreed to work on in therapy. The tentative conceptualising framework pays attention to the underlying core pain (primary maladaptive emotions in the traditional EFT language; cf. Greenberg et al., 1993); the unmet needs embedded in core painful feelings; the interpersonal and situational triggers that bring about the pain; the client's self-treatment in the context of triggers, and the manner in which that self-treatment contributes to pain. The framework further captures the global distress into which the client collapses out of an inability to process underlying pain; and the fear (of emotional pain) that drives avoidance and emotional interruption strategies (see the first part of Figure 1—until the need [out of interest I include also Figure 2 (page 74) that is a variation of Figure 1 conceptually clearly outlining its similarity with the original work of Pascual-Leone and Greenberg, 2007; however, throughout the rest of the text I will be referring to Figure 1 only]). This conceptual framework then guides the therapist to facilitate emerging self-organisations (e.g., compassion and protective anger), the presence of which transforms core pain and responds to unmet needs (cf. the second part of Figure 1, from need to the transformed feelings of relief and empowerment).

As already emphasised, any case conceptualisation framework has to be seen as hypothetical and tentative. It should not override the therapist's continuous observation of, and empathic responding to, the client's ever-unfolding presentation in therapy. However, observing clients in clinical practice and in detailed case studies (using video tapes of the sessions), we observed some shared features that clients with mood and anxiety disorders (and interpersonal or personality difficulties) frequently presented with. We found the model presented in Figure 1 helpful as a means to visually represent the dynamic present in the client's core painful emotion scheme self-organisations. It helped us to think about the cases when we wanted to conceptualise them, but also helped us to orient ourselves toward what needed to happen in therapy.

It has been our observation that when initially presenting to therapy, clients typically present in a state of distress, and furthermore that this distress (which using Pascual-Leone and Greenberg's terminology I refer to as *global distress*; see Chapters 2 and 3) often shows in the form of undifferentiated painful emotions.

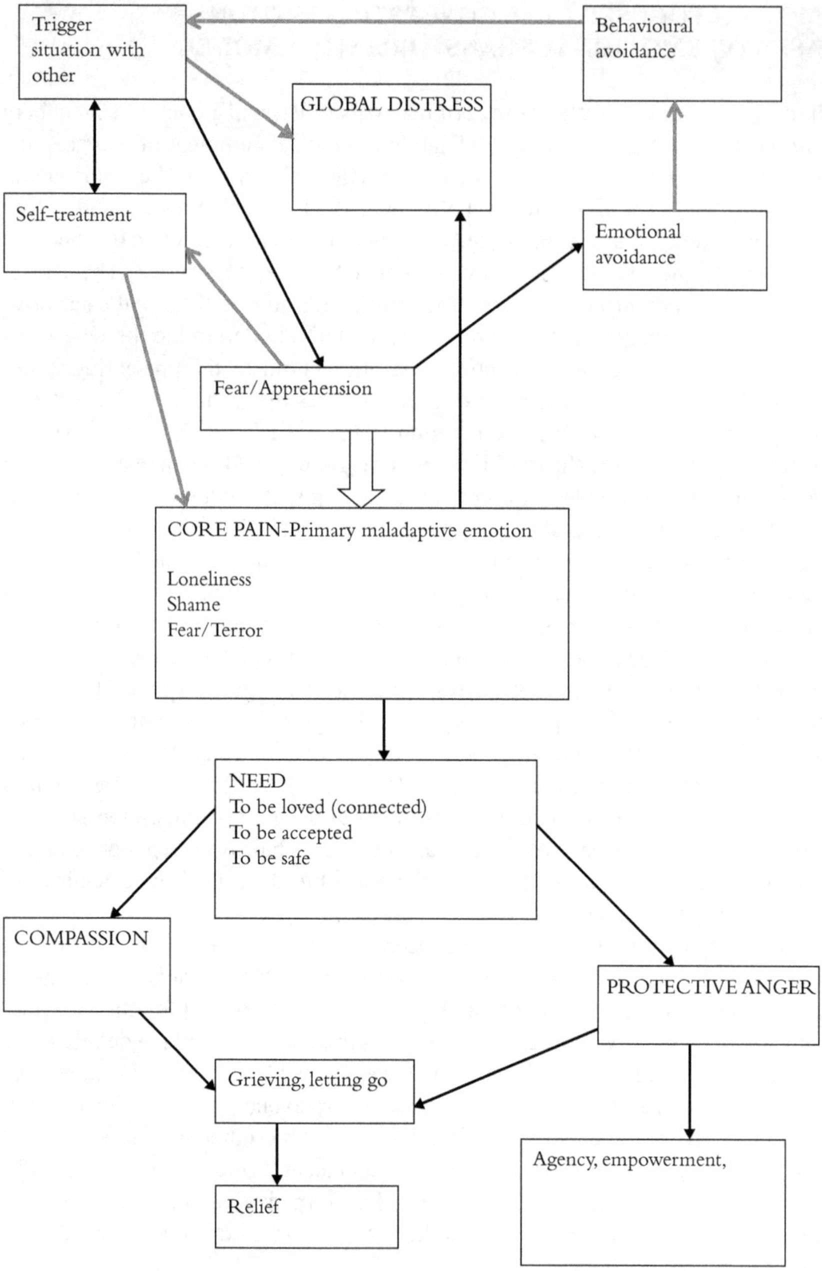

Figure 1 Case Conceptualisation Framework Based on Emotion Transformation Model (adapted from Transforming emotion schemes in emotion focused therapy: a case study investigation. McNally, S., Timulak, L., & Greenberg, L. S. *Person-Centered & Experiential Psychotherapies, 13*, 128–149. © 2014 reprinted by permission of the publisher Taylor & Francis doi:10.1080/14779757.2013.871573)

Global distress is often characterised by hopelessness and helplessness (but sometimes also rage and reactive anger) and is a response to current and past (typically interpersonal) triggers. These triggers represent (interpersonal) situations, in which the client's needs were, or continue to be, violated or not responded to. This leaves the client with painful emotions (*core pain*) which signal that these needs are not being met. The aforementioned studies of the presentation of depressed and anxious clients (e.g., Crowley et al., 2013; Dillon et al., in press; Keogh et al., 2011; Keogh et al., 2013; McNally et al., in press; Pascual-Leone, 2009; Pascual-Leone and Greenberg, 2007; Timulak et al., 2012) suggest that the core painful emotions are shame-based, loneliness/sadness-based and/or terror/fear-based (see Chapters 2 and 3), and that these core painful emotions correspond with unmet needs for approval, closeness, and safety.

Core painful emotions are difficult for the client to bear, a difficulty further compounded by the fact that clients often find it unimaginable that the needs embedded in that pain will ever be fulfilled. Core painful emotions are therefore also scary for clients, and clients often engage in emotional avoidance strategies in order to mitigate those painful feelings. Clients may also avoid situations or interactions that might trigger that pain (Behavioural Avoidance in Figure 1); for instance, they may be trying to avoid situations where they experience rejection. Core pain can also be reflected in the manner in which clients, aware of their difficulties, and seeking some way to make sense of and manage those difficulties, assume responsibility for their own pain and/or blame themselves for their own pain.

We will now look in more detail at the individual aspects of this case conceptualisation framework. Whilst a variation of the framework has already been presented in Chapters 2 and 3, here the focus will be on how the framework informs the therapist's treatment strategy.

Triggers/Perceptions

The triggers of emotional pain (see also Figure 1) are typically evident from a client's narrative about what is most painful and difficult for him or her. The therapist listens for triggers such as current and/or past interpersonal situations which evoke in the client difficult-to-tolerate feelings. These triggers are often actions or perceived actions of important others that leave the client with feelings of rejection, exclusion, invalidation, humiliation, intrusion, terror, and so forth. Important others are seen and experienced as invading, rejecting, blaming, neglecting, invalidating, humiliating, or harsh. Interestingly, in some instances the perceived other may trigger distress, not because he or she is abusive in some way, but rather because he or she is too vulnerable or fragile, thereby evoking in the client guilt that the client is in some way responsible for the other's fragility or for any pain that the other might feel.

Often the triggers of emotional pain are current events or situations that are happening in the client's life (e.g., the hurtful behaviour of a spouse). The client may report several of these current triggers in early sessions, corresponding to a variety of difficult interactions in the client's day-to-day life. However, as therapy progresses, the therapist is likely to observe that some of these current interpersonal difficulties (and their attendant triggers) contain features that resemble developmentally salient interpersonal events during which the client experienced emotional injuries. These original hurtful interactions typically occurred at times when the client was particularly vulnerable, for instance not yet fully matured (e.g., in childhood, adolescence). Thus these hurtful interactions typically occurred at times when the client did not have the internal resources to process the pain caused, stand up for him- or herself and/or seek appropriate external support. Take for instance, a hypothetical client who is socially anxious, and is fearful of criticism, and the subsequently felt humiliation, in situations where as a part of his job, he has to speak in front of an audience. Such a client may have had regular experiences of being undermined and 'put down' by 'friends' during adolescence. Furthermore, such experiences in adolescence may have been preceded by experiences of being undermined, humiliated and/or doubted by his father during childhood. Situations where the client, as an adult, anticipates or fears criticism, therefore evoke anxiety, and this anxiety, propels the client into avoidance of such situations. The client fears humiliation and shame, and thus seeks to avoid situations which will trigger such humiliation and shame. However, these efforts to avoid being shamed stem from an intrinsic sense of being someone who should be (self-criticism; see below) shamed. Despite efforts to avoid these situations, the client often intrinsically experiences a sense of *shame* that is self-defining; that is felt as a central trait of the self (*I am flawed.*).

The therapist's strategy with regards to the triggers of the client's emotional pain is to observe these triggers and bring them into the client's awareness. The therapist observes and highlights nuances of the triggers that are often non-verbal (e.g., being looked down upon). The therapist brings the triggers to the client's awareness often by facilitating the client's enactment of the triggers in imaginary dialogues (typical EFT tasks; see Elliott et al., 2004, and next chapters) in which the client is asked to enact the hurtful behaviour of others toward the imagined self. The implicit messages contained in the other's behaviour are unfolded and the idiosyncratic impact on the client experienced and further worked with (see more in Chapter 6). In other cases, triggers are accessed through the use of the systematic evocative unfolding task (Greenberg et al., 1993; Elliott et al., 2004), in which the client reconstructs perceptual aspects of situations in which he or she experienced puzzling emotional reactions. In some instances, problematic self-treatment (e.g., self-critical or self-worrying processes) triggers emotional pain. The nature and function of these triggers can be explored using self-imaginary dialogue tasks (see the following chapters). Since EFT is an experiential therapy, the therapist is not focused on discovering the triggers through theoretically based speculations, but rather seeks to identify triggers by exploring and unfolding the client's perceptual field (the remembered triggers) and aspects of those triggers that evoke painful feelings.

Global distress/secondary emotions

As already mentioned, global distress (see Figure 1) is a label used to describe an aroused emotional state in which the client expresses an undifferentiated form of emotional pain (see Pascual-Leone and Greenberg, 2007; see Chapters 2 and 3). Global distress is what is typically seen when a client attempts to talk about what brought him or her to therapy, and it is a type of distress characterised by what EFT literature terms 'secondary emotions' (Greenberg and Safran, 1989; Greenberg et al., 1993). Since the EFT therapist is trying to facilitate the client's access to emotion in the session, global distress often shows in an aroused form. Another feature of this emotional state is its low differentiation with regard to the felt emotions, but also with regard to the personal meaning of these emotions. The client simply feels the pain and is overwhelmed by it, fears it, and wants to avoid it. He or she is rarely able to say why they feel this way.

While the feelings in global distress are not well differentiated, there are some emotions (and some distinct combinations of emotions) which occur with enough frequency as to be almost characteristic of global-distress–type presentations. These are often feelings of hopelessness and helplessness at the impossibility of ever having unmet needs met (*This will never change. I am just unhappy*). Hopelessness and helplessness are typically secondary to more primary feelings of loneliness/sadness, shame, or terror. Apart from hopelessness and helplessness, clients often present with irritability, anger, and frustration at not having needs met (*How could you do it? I hate you [directed at the person causing hurt and distress]*). Global distress often takes the form of a mixture of anger and sadness (*Why did you hurt me?*). Whilst the anger points at the violation of need, the sadness is a response to what is actually being missed. Clients with anxiety disorders also often show a lot of secondary (apprehensive) anxiety, which is an anticipatory response to potentially painful triggers. Anxiety and a constant expectation of further pain or attack, leads almost inevitably to exhaustion. Thus, global distress can show also in the form of physical exhaustion.

Whilst the above presentations are common, the distress each client presents with has its own unique, idiosyncratic form. This presentation, this mixture of secondary and poorly differentiated emotion, obscures more primary, core emotional response to triggers. The therapist tries to acknowledge and empathise with the experienced distress. He or she responds to and communicates an understanding of it. This in and of itself can have a soothing, regulating impact on the client. However, the therapist's primary goal is to try to access the core of the client's painful emotional experience, those underlying primary feelings which point to the unmet needs. The therapist, therefore, focuses on what is the most painful in the client's experience; on what is the most hurtful in the triggering situation. The therapist also encourages the client to pay attention to painful emotional experience, to allow emotional experience to come to the surface, and to speak from that emotional experience. As already mentioned, the therapist attempts to follow a 'pain compass' (Greenberg and Goldman, 2007; Greenberg and Watson,

2006), following what is most painful, in order that both the client and therapist can arrive at the underlying painful emotions at the core of the painful emotion scheme self-organisation.

Problematic self-treatment

The therapist not only observes the client's perceptions of triggers and the pain that those triggers bring; he or she also notices how the client treats him- or herself in the context of those hurtful triggers. People respond to such triggers in a wide variety of ways. Some may, for instance, calm themselves, offer themselves support, or fight for themselves. For a majority of emotionally suffering clients, however, such supportive self-treatments are often limited or missing. What comes instead is a problematic self-treatment. It has been our observation and of other EFT authors (see, for instance, the original work of Greenberg et al., 1993) that problematic self-treatment typically takes one of two forms. The first of these are a variety of self-treatments the function of which appears to be to try to avoid painful feelings (e.g., emotional avoidance, self-worrying, self-scarring, etc.). I will address this form of self-treatment separately below. The second are a variety of negative self-treatments which are essentially self-attacking in nature; for example, self-judgment, self-contempt, self-dissatisfaction, and especially self-criticism (see also Chapters 2 and 3). Whilst this latter self-critical/attacking treatment appears to be central for clients presenting with depression (Greenberg and Watson, 2006), socially anxious clients also typically present with the former, either in the form of an anxiety split (e.g., scaring themselves with regard to upcoming social interaction; Elliott, 2013) or in the form of worry (Timulak and McElvaney, 2012).

The therapist may notice that problematic self-treatment can show in many forms. Some are more superficial than others. For instance, the client may be critical of him- or herself for being depressed (*I should not be depressed*). However, this superficial criticism is typically an expression of a more core negative self-attitude (*I am flawed*). Case observations reveal processes indicating that to some extent problematic self-treatments may be rooted in the introjection of criticisms coming from significant others. However, there are also indications that it might be a coping process, a functional response to neglectful and/or abusive treatment by others during childhood and adolescence. For instance, a child experiencing abuse or neglect may attribute the reason for this treatment to aspects of their own intrapersonal character that might merit others treating them in this way (*I deserve rejection, humiliation, exclusion, judgment—something in me is flawed, unlovable, etc.*). Although this self-attribution of negative characteristics is painful, it may offer the child some rationale for what is happening, and therefore a perceived (and perhaps felt) control over the otherwise unpredictable and hurtful behaviour of the other. It also offers hope in so far as it holds out the possibility that *if I improve, I can become more lovable*. The fallacy in this self-treatment is that the other does not change, and thus the child continues to blame him- or herself.

It is not surprising therefore that a client's attempts to deal with problematic triggers ultimately contribute to the client's pain. Indeed, a lot of shame and loneliness related painful emotions are also representations of negative self-attitudes (e.g., *I am unlovable, I am worthless, I am weak.*). The problem of negative self-treatment is further compounded by the fact that clients may have experiences of problematic self-treatment actually serving them well. For instance, if the client constantly criticises him- or herself and wants to do everything perfectly, such a client can actually be praised by others for being perfect and reliable. Such examples further confirm the idea that the function of self-attacking behaviour is often to help the client, in this instance, giving the client the longed-for approval.

The therapist observes the client's problematic self-treatment and seeks to bring it into the client's awareness. In bringing this process to the client's awareness, the therapist proposes the possibility of working on this process. Subsequently, when appropriate markers of self-critical processes present themselves in session, the therapist proposes the use of an experiential task, a two-chair dialogue for a conflict split (Greenberg et al., 1993; Elliott et al., 2004); first to explore the self-critical process; then to transform it. In a two-chair dialogue, the client is guided first to enact the criticism toward the self; then to see the impact or toll of this criticism on the self; and then to see what needs are not being met, or are being neglected or violated by such self-treatments. The work then focuses on how the client can access a more self-compassionate and more self-protective stance in order to counterbalance the negative self-treatment. In other words the therapist is trying to help the client have experiences of love and protective anger that will counterbalance experiences of shame and exclusion (see Chapter 6 and particularly Chapter 7).

Emotional and behavioural avoidance

Another form of problematic self-treatment (arising in the context of triggers which evoke painful emotions) is *self-interruption* (cf. Greenberg et al., 1993), which can be understood as a process of *emotional avoidance* of evoked painful feelings (see Figure 1). This process of avoiding uncomfortable emotions is driven by both the felt emotional pain, and apprehensive fear of further pain. It can also prompt *behavioural avoidance* of the triggering situations that could bring further pain (see Figure 1).

Emotional avoidance can take many forms, all of which can be seen in session; deliberate numbing of feelings; intellectualising; dissociation; changing the topic of conversation; diverting attention by using humour, and so on (O'Brien et al., 2012). It can also show in the form of physical symptoms, such as a tightening of the muscles, as if the client is bracing for emotional pain by controlling bodily responses. In the case of clients presenting with generalised anxiety disorder and similar anxiety problems, emotional avoidance may take the form of worry. Anxious clients worry about triggering situations that might elicit emotional pain (e.g., being blamed, criticised, rejected, attacked, etc.). Worry is typically also intertwined with behavioural avoidance, in other words, behaviours in which the client engages (or not) with the hope that doing so will reduce the likelihood of being confronted with the feared triggers. For instance, a client may be over-compliant in order to prevent criticism. Alternatively, a client may be avoidant, refusing to take responsibility, in order to prevent evaluation by others. A very good example of emotional avoidance is the agoraphobic behaviour so prevalent in panic disorder. Clients with panic disorder avoid any situations in which they previously experienced feelings of panic, but they also avoid situations in which, were the panic to come on, they would not have any access to a safe, private space where they could calm down without being observed. Emotional and behavioural avoidance, and the underlying fear which drives such avoidance, all play an important role in the individual clients' problematic emotion schemes. Although the ultimate motivation in these processes is to avoid felt emotional pain, these processes ultimately fail to achieve their goal. In the short term, pain is rarely kept fully away, and in the longer term, avoidance is counterproductive as engaging in such avoidance actually lowers the client's pain tolerance threshold. Furthermore, avoidance does not allow the client to process painful emotions in a way that would facilitate the generation of adaptive emotional responses to counterbalance the felt pain (e.g., soothing or protection). Avoidance thus paradoxically contributes to global distress, leading to tiredness and fearfulness, and contributing to a sense of limited control focused solely on unsuccessful self-protection.

The therapist observes the client's avoidant processes and brings them into the client's awareness. The therapist may help the client to see the role the avoidant processes have in the overall dynamic of his or her problematic schemes and self-organisations. As with any other part of the conceptualisation framework presented here, the therapist's observation are collaboratively shared with the client and discussed at points in therapy when the conversation has a direct relevance for what is being explored and experienced by the client at that point in time. Avoidance and self-interruption processes can also serve as markers for specific experiential tasks, most notably the two-chair dialogue for self-interruption (Greenberg et al., 1993; Elliott, 2004). In this experiential task the client is instructed to enact the interruptive processes in one chair, i.e., to do what the interrupter is doing to the imagined self in the other chair (*How do you make sure that he (or she) does not feel? Please do it.*). This is done in order to help bring this self-interrupting/avoiding process more fully into the client's awareness, and thereby help the client take ownership of what he or she is doing to him- or herself. It is also done, however, to elicit the impact this self-treatment has on the client. After enacting the interruption, the client is asked to sit in the other chair, and describe what it is like to be the object of the interruptive process (e.g., *What happens inside when you get this?*). The therapist helps the client feel the toll of the self-interruption, and guides his or her focus to what is being missed (e.g., which needs are not fulfilled), in order that a more compassionate or self-protective stance be evoked. Similar dialogues are focused also on the worry process (Murphy et al., 2014). We will look at the details of work on overcoming avoidance in Chapter 6.

Anticipatory anxiety

Anticipatory fear (see Figure 1) of situations that might evoke painful emotions, combined with fear of those actual painful emotions, drives emotional and behavioural avoidance. It is important for the therapist to remember that this fear needs to be distinguished from a more basal, core fear felt as a primary response to some triggering situation, e.g., the fear that a client might experience when attacked. While apprehensive fear is characterised by an apprehensive anxiety, primary fear is characterised by a quality of terror. A good example is fear of flying. If I am scared to fly, my fear can be understood as an apprehensive anxiety of what could happen. On the other hand, were the plane to actually start falling from the sky, and were I to feel physical upset in response to the free fall, this primary fear has a quality of terror. The actual fall is scary, intrusive, and upsetting to my body as a whole.

Another distinction that can be helpful for the therapist is the understanding that apprehensive fear (anxiety) is actually the fear of triggers and the corresponding underlying core, painful emotions that, as I have already elaborated on, appear to be predominantly shame-based (e.g., *I am worthless*), loneliness/sadness-based (e.g., *I am not loved*) and terror/fear-based (e.g., *I am weak to face intrusion.*). Again, the terror/fear-based emotions here need to be distinguished from apprehensive fear. In this case it is a fear (apprehensive anxiety) of the fear (the core primary response to intrusion).

Anticipatory fear is a defining feature of clients with anxiety disorders difficulties. For instance, this type of fear (anxiety) is the main presenting feature of social anxiety. While what is most visible is the client's fear of social situations, the core underlying emotion is the feeling of shame that would be triggered in those situations. It is this shame that the person wants to avoid and cannot bear. Thus the client fears the triggers (e.g., criticism) and own uncomfortable feelings of shame. The anticipation of shame (of being ridiculed, negatively evaluated, and humiliated) shows on the surface in the form of apprehensive anxiety. This anxiety is then at the fore, while shame may not be at the centre of attention, and may in fact be missed. This anxiety then also leads to behavioural avoidance of social situations.

The distinction of primary vs. secondary (anticipatory) fear is crucial for the subsequent treatment strategy. For instance, EFT, in contrast to cognitive-behavioural therapy, does not focus primarily on anticipatory anxiety but rather focuses on the underlying shame. The therapeutic work focuses on helping the client to be able to access and regulate this shame, to be able to articulate the need embedded in shame (e.g., to be valued, appreciated) and eventually to access self-organisations of self-compassion and protective anger that would validate and respond to the natural need for appreciation. It is then assumed that the fear of social judgement will not be that strong as the client will have a sense of inner confidence in him- or herself, as well as the sense that he or she will be able to bear potential criticism.

In therapy sessions, the therapist pays attention to anticipatory fear as it can help the therapist in sharing his or her understanding of the dynamic at the core of the client's problematic emotion scheme-based self-organisations. Again, the therapist shares this understanding at appropriate times in the session when the apprehensive anxiety is activated. There is one important feature of apprehensive anxiety that we observed in our studies (O'Brien et al., 2012, Murphy et al., 2013). We noticed that anticipatory anxiety is seen by clients as having a *protective* function, in that they can be aware that it prevents them from encountering triggers and triggered painful feelings. However, as already argued, this protective function is outweighed by the cost of the ensuing avoidance, in other words, avoidance prevents healthy, flexible emotional processing that would successfully help transform the feared underlying emotions. Clients are thus crippled by apprehensive fear and do not develop a strong sense of their own resilience and personal agency.

Core emotional pain

The core emotional pain (see Figure 1 and Chapter 2) is the underlying painful emotional response to the triggering situations or perceptions. For instance, the client may perceive somebody as humiliating him or her, and he or she can experience painful feelings of humiliation and shame. Compared to undifferentiated global distress, core emotional pain is typically present in the form of discreet emotions that quite clearly provide information about the client's unmet needs in the particular triggering situation. While these core emotions have the potential to be clear and differentiated, in early therapy sessions, core pain is typically obfuscated by client states of global distress. Since core primary emotions are scary and difficult to bear, they essentially become buried in secondary emotions such as hopelessness and helplessness, irritation, pain, hurt, unspecified sadness, anger, anxiety, and so forth. The predominance of secondary emotions represents the client's collapse into a hopelessness that the needs embedded in core painful emotions will never be met. Global distress is further compounded by client avoidance strategies, the function of which is to avoid primary core painful feelings.

The core emotional pain contains primary emotions that are painful and which do not give rise to any adaptive action on the client's part (Greenberg and Safran, 1987; 1989). They are usually familiar, well-known, and dreaded feelings that are in the centre of the problematic emotion schemes self-organisations (Greenberg, 2002; 2011). They are uncomfortable feelings, and the client typically feels overwhelmed by them. The client is not able to stay with the pain they contain, nor is he or she able to process and counterbalance these feelings. Instead, secondary emotions, which are responses to those primary maladaptive emotions or to the cognitive processes accompanying primary emotions, come to the fore. What the therapist initially sees in fact is the consequence of the client's emotional processing collapsing into global distress, secondary hopelessness, helplessness, and other form of distress. The client's effort to avoid feelings may also come to the fore. Various EFTs studies of mood, trauma, and anxiety disorders (e.g., Greenberg and Watson, 2006; O'Brien et al., 2012, Paivio and Pascual-Leone, 2010) suggest that the feelings that I refer to here as core emotional pain, centre around shame, loneliness/sadness, and terror/fear experiences. These are the emotions that the therapist is then most sensitised to hear in the client's presentation.

Shame-related primary maladaptive emotions (shame, guilt, embarrassment, humiliation, etc.) can be simple or complex emotional experiences that prompt an action tendency to hide, shrink, disappear, stop existing, and so on. Verbally (narratively) they are expressed in self-statements alluding to characterological deficiency such as *I am flawed, I am worthless,* or *Something's wrong with me.* They are typically experienced in the context of interpersonal situations (triggers), in which the client sees others as rejecting, judging, humiliating, bullying, putting the client down, or conversely when the client views others as being harmed by the client's own actions. It seems that in the context of these situational triggers, the client treats him- or herself negatively (e.g., *I deserved to be bullied, because I was weak; I am selfish.*) (see the section on negative self-treatment above). The experienced shame and its variations point to embedded unmet needs to be *valued, appreciated, recognised, accepted,* and so on. These unmet needs may relate to either past experience or to the present.

Loneliness-related primary maladaptive emotions are variations of emotional experiences of profound isolation, abandonment, and/or loss. The typical emotional quality these experiences bring is sadness. It may be a sense of missed connection or the missed presence of a caring other. Or, it may be the sense of loss accompanying the loss of a loved one, which can be particularly difficult if the loss is of a defenceless dependant other such as the client's own child. Client verbal expressions (narrative) that point to this type of experience can include expressions that refer to a sense of emptiness, such as, *I feel empty, on my own, alone, lonely* or to what it is that is missed, for example, *I miss my mom, child, partner, friend.* The triggering situations in which the client can experience variations of loneliness may be situations where there are elements of neglect, exclusion, or loss. The experienced sadness may speak to unmet needs, such as the need for *closeness, support, love,* or *connection.* Again these might be needs that are not being met in the client's current life, or the pain may relate primarily to needs that were not met in the past.

Terror/fear-related primary maladaptive emotions are responses to a traumatic trigger that intrudes on either the physical or psychological world of the client (e.g., physical attack, verbal attack, an accident, etc.). These triggers provoke a variety of primary, painful fear-based emotional responses such as intense terror, horror, dissociations, and so on. They evoke physiological and psychological upset over which the client may have limited or no control. The experienced pain causes significant physical upset in the body. The action tendency is typically to stop the upset (either by fleeing or fighting). In therapy sessions, these emotions typically appear when memories of traumatic experiences are activated. The obviously inferred unmet needs in these types of experiences are needs for safety and predictability, in place of the experienced significant discomfort.

The core emotional pain often consists of a unique mixture of shame-based, loneliness/sadness-based, and terror/fear-based emotions. For each client the core emotional pain may contain an idiosyncratic variation of the particularly defining painful primary maladaptive emotions that serve as attractors for a particular problematic self-organisation (or self-organisations). These central painful emotions and the dynamic whereby they are triggered by particular situations and by own self-treatment in those situations, are embedded in emotional schematic structures (and it is hypothesised, represented in neural pathways—structural as well as functional) that are based on emotional memory of developmentally and currently salient difficult experiences. The core emotional pain as it manifests itself in the present is thus typically an activation of, and a representation of, an underlying vulnerability, built through a dynamic interaction between past injuries and unbearable experiences in the client's currently lived life. The roots of emotional pain can often be found early on in the client's life, when the client was limited in his or her resources to process adversity. However, traumatic/adverse experiences later in life can also be responsible for the development of particular emotional vulnerabilities. Furthermore, in many instances biological and genetic predispositions can potentially limit a client's resources to cope with adversity (see Chapter 2 for the discussion of the roots of emotional pain).

The therapist's primary focus in therapy is to access and transform the core emotional pain (see Chapters 6 and 7). The therapist seeks to help the client access core painful feelings, which also means that he or she seeks to help the client refrain from engaging in avoidance of their emotional experience. The therapist aims to help the client to stay with their core painful feelings, to feel them, to reflect on them and articulate the unmet needs in them, and eventually to be able to process them through transforming them by activating balancing emotional experiences (e.g., compassion, care, protective anger). The core emotional pain is typically activated through enactment of the painful situations, either through imaginary dialogues with the pain eliciting others or through the self-self dialogues which activate painful self-treatments. In some cases the core pain is accessed through a vivid entering of the painful situation in imagination. Sometimes the experienced core emotional pain can be accessed through imagining vulnerable others, whose painful experience is in some way similar to that of the client (for details of this type of work see the next chapter and also Greenberg et al., 1993; Elliott et al., 2004).

Through such experiential work, the therapist discovers, together with the client, what it is that is at the centre of the client's difficulty. The development of such a shared understanding, a shared conceptualisation, is important for good client–therapist agreement on the tasks and goals of therapy, and for this reason, the therapist is quite transparent with his or her own observations. He or she seeks to share observations with the client in a bit-by-bit manner that does not distract the client from engagement in the actual, experiential emotion-focused work in therapy. The manner in which the therapist shares his or her evolving case conceptualisation can be thought of as similar to what Greenberg (2002) describes as 'hot (experience close) teaching'; the therapist reflects on and shares those parts of the case conceptualisation that resonate with, and are pertinent to, what it is that the client is feeling at that point in the session.

Unmet needs

It is very important for the therapist's understanding of why some emotional experiences are particularly painful, to be aware that those painful emotional experiences signal that the client's needs in some difficult situations were not or are not being met (see Figure 1 and the discussions in Chapters 2 and 3). The fact that the client's lived experience of interaction with his or her environment did not, or does not, bring an adequate response to these needs, is the root cause of the unbearable pain which the client experiences, and it is this in turn that can lead to feelings of resignation (global distress, secondary hopelessness, helplessness—depression) or apprehension of further pain (emotional avoidance—anxiety). A focus on the unmet needs of the client is the central aspect of both case conceptualisation and the ensuing transformative therapeutic strategy, as it is the unmet needs that have to be emotionally responded to in therapy in order to bring about emotional transformation.

Studying clients' painful emotions as they show in the course of emotion-focused therapy (for instance, studies on depression, anxiety and trauma; Greenberg and Watson, 2006; O'Brien et al., 2012; Paivio and Pascual-Leone, 2010) offers some light on what type of needs are not being met. These unmet needs can be discerned from closely observing the core primary maladaptive emotions at the centre of clients' suffering. Unsurprisingly, each type of need is closely linked to a type of primary painful emotion. Thus the unmet needs embedded in *shame*-based emotions include needs to be *valued, seen, accepted, appreciated, respected, acknowledged, recognised, or validated.* The unmet needs embedded in loneliness-related emotions include needs to be *loved, connected to, reached out to, hugged, cared for, included*, but also the need *to love, to connect to, to reach out to, to care for,* and so forth. Finally, the unmet needs embedded in *primary fear*-related emotions include the need *for protection, for safety,* and *for control.*

The therapist focuses on distilling the unmet needs. Unmet needs cannot be accessed through an intellectual exercise or exploration. They can be accessed only when the client is fully feeling the core primary painful emotions. When the client is feeling rejected, abandoned, or scared and is prompted by the therapist to reveal what is he or she is missing most (or what he or she needs) at the moment of this intense pain, the client is able to access what is missing (or needed) most; the unmet need. The articulation of unmet need by the client happens typically in moments of high emotional arousal and vulnerability. Such articulation is central to the emotional transformation that ensues. In transformation, adaptive experiences provide an emotional response to those unmet needs (both inside and outside of the session). We will focus on this in Chapters 6 and 7.

Case Example

The case presented here is an extended version of the case presented in Timulak and Pascual-Leone's paper (2014). The client, Ann, was a female in her early fifties who struggled with generalised anxiety, self-criticism, and low mood. To protect the anonymity of the client, some facts about her are altered. I also incorporate some facts from other clients with similar experiences, thus the case can be seen as a composite example. Visually, case conceptualisation is presented in Figure 2 (it will be referred to also in Chapters 6 and 7).

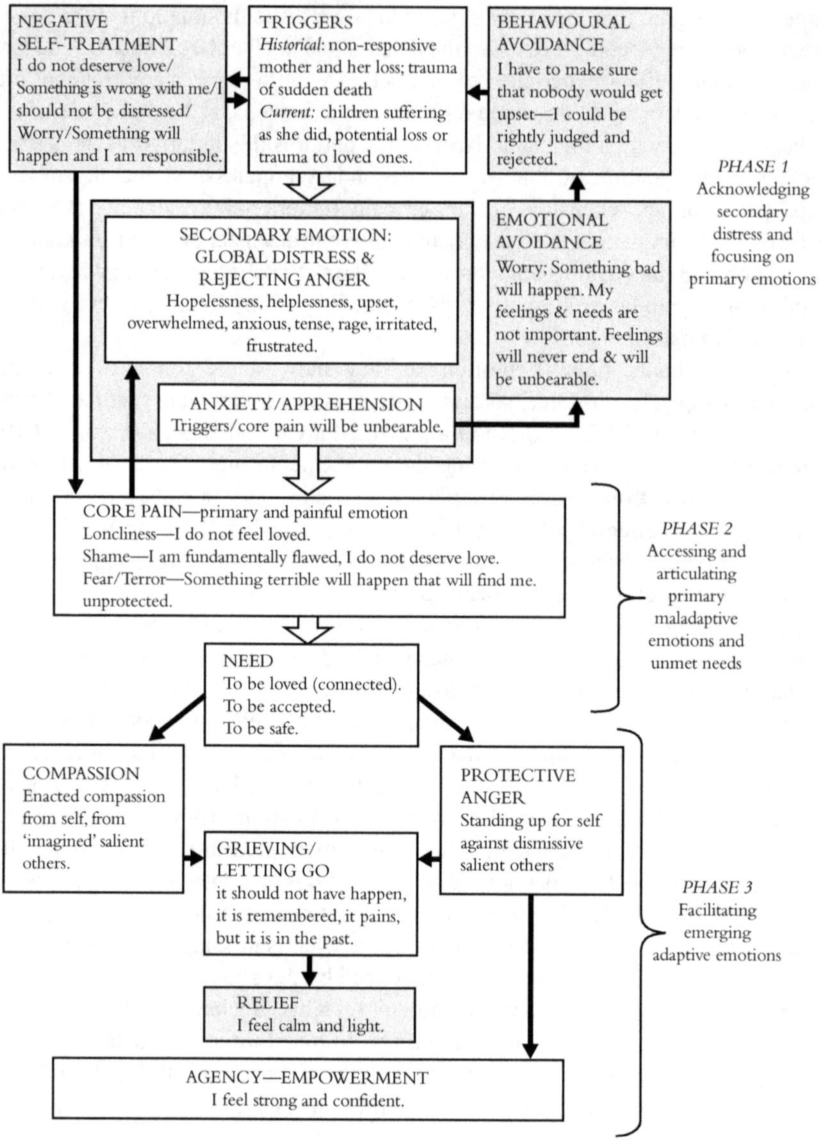

Figure 2 A Variation of case Conceptualisation Framework (adapted from New developments for case conceptualization in emotion-focused therapy. Timulak, L., & Pascual-Leone, A. *Clinical Psychology & Psychotherapy*. Advanced online publication. © 2014 John Wiley and Sons. doi: : 10.1002/cpp.1922)

Global distress

Ann was referred for counselling by her GP as she was highly distressed. She was not interested in using an antidepressant medication; however, she occasionally took valium when she was not capable of calming herself. In the first few sessions, she showed a very significant level of global distress that caused the therapist to wonder whether she should not be referred onwards for a more intensive treatment. She worried constantly. She particularly worried about the well-being of her children, but also other close ones. For instance, she would worry that her adult children would make a mistake if they went to the doctor without her *(I'm afraid they won't say the right thing. They won't ask the right questions. And then they'll make a mistake.).* She also could not sleep well (*It feels like if I go to bed and go to sleep, I'm not being the responsible person that I should be.*). Her worries often led her to protect and check on others, so that she could prevent anything bad from happening to them. She could get easily agitated about things that needed to be done. This over-commitment exhausted her.

Ann was also worried about her own physical health and her own mental health; her mother had a mental illness, depression, and alcohol abuse, and she died suddenly when the client was only nine years old. Ann also experienced a number of physical symptoms such as tension across the back of her shoulders and a tense stomach. She presented as overwhelmed and confused by her current levels of anxiety and distress, and described the significant impact this distress had on the quality of her life: 'Sometimes I just want scream at the top of my lungs and for what I don't know', and 'It's just not being able to cope with things when it's happening to me that's freaking me out more or less'. She presented with high levels of emotional arousal, getting easily upset and often crying. For instance, as one of the early sessions was ending, Ann started to cry and sob, saying that she just wanted to 'Walk and walk and walk and walk and walk …'. She expressed a lot of hopelessness and stated that she could not see how anything could help her. She was also very negative about herself, blaming the self for her own difficulties (see more in the part on the problematic self-treatment below).

Triggers

The current triggering situations were mainly situations relating to health (e.g., potential health issues affecting her son; her own health issues, etc.) and situations in which she witnessed suffering of others who were close to her (e.g., an extended family). An exploration of poignant and salient memories showed that those current triggers were firmly embedded in past hurtful life experiences. As a child Ann experienced a lot of neglect from her mother, and the sense of not being loved was familiar to her (*She didn't love me.*). Therefore, she could easily identify with the abandonment felt by children who were secluded from mum (*It hurts because I know what it's like … I know what it's like to grow up without a mother and it's not very nice.*). Ann relayed anecdotes of times when she had felt very ashamed; for example, she spoke about the time when her mom became drunk on Ann's birthday and fell down on the street: 'All these relatives … and the smell of drink on her … and she fell twice. … So that's my memory. … Other kids' mothers aren't like that'. Ann not only experienced neglect and a sense of abandonment but often spoke about times when her mother had attacked her. In one of the very first sessions she said, 'I was worried when I was a kid going home and seeing what humour my Ma was in … if she's going to be ranting and raving or what.

You just didn't know what was going to happen when you walked in through the hall door ...'. She always hoped that her mother would change; 'Every day there was hope that she would, she wouldn't be drinking', but her pleas to her mother requesting her to change, instead led to her mother blaming Ann for her drinking: 'I asked you to stop and then you made it out that it was all my fault'.

Nevertheless, Ann longed to have a better relationship with her mother. She felt profound loneliness and craved her mother's love (*I never had motherly love.*). In one of the early sessions she admitted, 'not to have the love and affection of your mother ... it's a very big hole'. Her longing for a better relationship showed in her wish for her mother to be around: 'I always had the recurring dream that she was missing ... and that one day she's going to come back'. When she compared what she was missing in her childhood with what she gave to her own children, she shared the realization that 'it's heart-breaking, when I know what it could have been ... what we should have had'. Her sense of loneliness and lack of love was further deepened when her mother died suddenly when Ann was just nine (*You died and left me.*). She was not only traumatised and shocked by this, but was also scared that something similar could happen to others in her family; that they might die suddenly and leave her even more alone. Ann used to check at night whether her close ones were still breathing. This fear continued right into the present, and she reported worrying that she would not survive death of anybody in her family (*I would die with them.*).

The trauma of her mother's sudden death most likely played a significant role in Ann's anticipatory fear of physical illness or of the death of close ones. Interestingly, she reported how although forty years had passed since her mother's death, she continued to have imaginary dialogues with her mother in her head almost every day. Worries around other current potential triggers also appeared to be linked to these historical triggers that were still quite alive. For instance, Ann's current worries and overprotective behaviour focused mainly on her children not having to undergo situations in which they would be alone and unsupported. She also did not want her close ones to be harmed by somebody and unprotected.

A lot of information on the historical and current triggers was shared by the client in an early empathic interview led by the therapist. However, their most poignant aspects were disclosed during imaginary dialogues (e.g., with her mother, and other close people in her life such as father, partner, children, siblings, etc.). The potency of those triggers showed in early dialogues. For instance, in initial empty-chair imaginary dialogues with her mother, Ann would easily fall into undifferentiated upset or she would experience a highly reactive (secondary) anger that masked the experienced hurt. She would criticise herself for still being upset about the past and for getting angry at her mother. She would feel hopeless that her experiencing of past hurts would never change, and that the profound loss of not being loved and looked after, could never be resolved.

Self-treatment

In the midst of difficult triggers and the upset that they evoked, Ann was often quite self-reproachful and self-contemptuous. She blamed herself for difficulties.

She recalled that early on in her life, she had a sense that if her mother treated her as she did, then there must be something wrong with her. As an adult, she accused herself of being moany and weak, the very qualities she did not like in her mother, whom she reported would always present herself as a victim. Ann somehow had a sense that she deserved harsh treatment. In initial imaginary chair dialogues, she clearly indicated that she did not deserve any compassion and indeed had a huge difficulty in expressing anything resembling self-compassion. She hated her own vulnerability (*I just need to cop on.*) and her need for more compassionate and supportive treatment from the self and others (*Stop feeling so flaming sorry for yourself. ... There's no point in feeling like this.*). She also put herself under a lot of pressure, assuming responsibility for any suffering that might befall those close to her (*If I fail to look after others ... I will be responsible.*). It was her job to prevent any harm from coming to those close to her (e.g., children, father, husband). She also displayed a tendency to make herself feel incredibly guilty if anything did go wrong. She always suspected that because she had somehow let go, the bad thing had happened. She then would be unforgiving toward herself. The depth of her harsh self-treatment showed in early, but also later, experiential therapy dialogues (for more on this, see later chapters) when she could not soften even toward her own vulnerability (e.g., when she was enacting how she felt as a small girl). Her harsh self-treatment visibly resembled the treatment she described getting from her mother. For instance, when she drew on memories to enact her mother, she enacted almost solely her mother's punitive, dismissive, rejecting treatment of her. As the following excerpts illustrate, when enacting her own critical self, Ann responded to her own vulnerability and needs with a harsh, dismissive contempt.

Ann (in the critic chair); it is a chair in the two-chair dialogue in which the client enacts the part of the self that is critical and dialogues with the imagined self in the other chair—the experiencer chair; cf. Elliott et al., 2004):	*Right. You've had your whinge. Give it over. Get ... Get yourself together and start getting your head around it.*
...	
Ann (in the critic chair):	*... You're like a big over grown forty-eight-year-old cry bag.*
...	
Ann (in the critic chair):	*... it's just get over it now. Like you know come on. You ... You're almost hitting fifty so start behaving and doing and going like you're fifty and not twelve again and like a scared little kid ...*
...	
Ann (in the critic chair):	*No. You, you haven't got the right to even think about having a day off.*
...	
Ann (in the critic chair):	*You are weak ...*

In addition to the harsh verbal content, Ann's critical self also displayed strong non-verbal contempt and rejection toward her vulnerable self.

Emotional and behavioural avoidance

The main feature of Ann's emotional avoidance was, as would be expected from a client presenting with GAD, her worry process. Ann had reported that worry was one of the main difficulties that brought her to therapy (see previous discussion on global distress). She felt that worries were constantly overcoming her and that she had no control over them. Within sessions, Ann worried about her own physical and psychological health. She worried that something bad would happen to her children (e.g., they would be sick or hurt), or to other close ones (e.g., that they would die). She worried that she would 'not be able to help' them. Furthermore, the worry led Ann to engage in behavioural avoidance, to act in such a way as to prevent any potential disaster. For instance, she reported going to all her children's doctor's appointments, even though they were now adults. This served to prevent scenarios arising whereby she might feel responsible if anything went wrong at an appointment and she had not been present to prevent it. Ann was particularly sensitive to, and worried about the possibility that anyone close to her might feel neglected, unsupported, or on their own, in other words that anyone close to her might experience the type of suffering which she had experienced as a child. She also dreaded any potential traumatic loss (e.g., sudden death of her close one) and worried about such possibilities. The worrying process is depicted in this brief transcript:

Therapist:	*I see. But the thing is also that you almost feel the pain or complications that will happen in future. I mean that you ... almost see what your daughter or partner will have to go through and you so much feel for them in it.*
Ann:	*I know ... I know ... The way I see things then 'If I can do everything possible in my own power' ...*
Therapist:	*Yeah.*
Ann:	*to make things right, well then if it goes wrong ...*
Therapist:	*Then at least ...*
Ann:	*It's, it's not my fault.*

Anticipatory anxiety

Generalised anxiety was a defining feature of Ann's presentation. She feared many potential triggers. She feared triggers that threatened to bring pain to her or to those close to her. She also feared triggers that might evoke painful feelings of traumatic loss; of physical upset; of isolation or shame; of failing others; or of being weak. Anxiety was also present with regard to triggers of an older origin. Ann was scared to engage with the memories of her mother as she found these memories too upsetting. However, she reported fear not only of the upsetting memories themselves but also fear with regards to her own anticipated emotional reaction to those memories. She anticipated feelings of loneliness, shame, and terror, and reported feeling dread in relation to these feelings, a sense that she would not be able to bear them. This primarily manifested as Ann's stated fear that she would end up like her mother (e.g., profoundly unhappy and depressed), but it also showed in her fear of expressing anger toward her imagined mother. To do so would be upsetting, as it would evoke and further confirm the shameful sense that she was somehow 'bad' for being so angry at the mother she had missed throughout her life.

This secondary, anticipatory anxiety (as distinguished from a more primary terror that she could feel when she did not avoid the triggers) visibly drove Ann's emotional and behavioural avoidance. However, despite her efforts to reduce this anxiety by avoiding the potentially dangerous situations and the feelings they evoked, her anxiety was unavoidable. It continued to seep out, and clearly constituted part of the global distress that Ann continually experienced (*I expect turmoil. My head is going ninety to a dozen.*).

Core emotional pain

Loneliness. Ann's underlying, primary, core painful feelings centred around a profound sense of loneliness, shame, and terror. She often felt profoundly on her own. She reported feeling very much alone, particularly with regard to developmentally significant points in her life (such as when she was a small girl, or when her children were born and she missed having the female support of her mother to help with them). For instance, in session 3 when Ann explored her own upset at seeing her neighbour's children without their mother, she would get very emotionally distraught and in an imaginary dialogue broke down crying, stating, 'I know what it's like to grow up without a mother. And it's not very nice. It's not'. Ann further stated how she would have wanted her children to meet her mother. 'I wanted … I always said when my children were born. I would have loved them to meet my mum'. She also said how she was missing the support of her mom 'to help me to look after them [kids] … and guide me to help me guide them'. The following excerpts illustrate the profound extent to which Ann missed her mother (parts of the transcript were used in Chapter 4):

Ann: *With things like that, when me kids are sick. I know I have [a partner] and I know he's there and he does everything he needs to do for me. But then I would have liked my own mother to be there [choking with tearfulness]. Just to go and say Mum 'I need a cup of tea, sit and talk to me.' Try and help me deal with it ...*

…

Ann: *The boys mightn't need them. But every now and again a girl does need her Mum [crying heavily].*

…

Ann: *... [crying] and it's only now that me own kids are growing up. I realise that because I'm there for them, and they know I am, and* *they know I always will be ... it is very hurtful that she wasn't there for us, or for me.*

...

Ann: *[nodding] Yea. Even though I have <husband> and I have the kids, you still do feel lonely ... [crying].*

Ann's vulnerability to feeling overwhelming loneliness also showed in her fear of her elderly father (with whom she was always close) dying. In an imaginary dialogue with her father, she reported how she would profoundly miss him, even when he just went away on holiday.

Ann: *'Nobody goes near the sitting room. The curtains aren't even open'.*
Therapist: *Yeah.*
Ann: *'Nobody turns on the light'.*
Therapist: *Ok.*
Ann: *'So the sitting room is just left now'.*
Therapist: *Yeah.*
Ann: *Because you're not there'.*
Therapist: *Yeah.*
Ann: *'And then I'm waiting for you to get out of the bed and you're not getting out of the bed. Then I have to remind myself that you're on holiday'.*
Therapist: *Yeah.*
Ann: *'It was the same the last time you were away'.*
Therapist: *Yeah. So it's just huge emptiness. Yes? Huge.*
Ann: *Yeah.*
Therapist: *'Kind of loss or hole almost?' Yes? 'In me'. Yeah?*
Ann: *... It's like somebody took him and put him somewhere else. And then half the time I do say 'Where's my dad?' and I do forget where he is.*

...

Therapist: *Yeah. 'You were everything that I was missing in Mam'. Yeah? 'That I didn't have from her but I had it all in you'.*

Ann's loneliness is closely linked to her sense of being overwhelmed, of being intruded upon, and of not being able to manage. Indeed, being unsupported was a pervasive feature of her personal history. She married when she was young and had children when she was young. As is evident from the transcripts above, she felt very unsupported and overwhelmed by the responsibility of looking after her children, and exhausted by her anxious efforts to prevent them being harmed in the manner that she had been.

Shame. Another distinct emotional quality at the centre of Ann's core emotional pain is the sense of shame. She reported how as a small child she somehow had a sense that she was to be blamed for the lack of love showed to her by her mother. This sense that there was something wrong with her persisted into her adult life. 'I feel like I am doing something wrong'. Ann's mother contributed to this sense by blaming Ann not only for both her own, but also for Ann's upset. In an imaginary dialogue Ann told her mother how 'You always made me feel like I wasn't worth it …'. It is possible that Ann attributed the blame for her mother's behavior to herself when she was small, because it provided her with some sense of control in this otherwise hopeless situation (*If I'd just be a bit better, she may love me.*). Unfortunately, if this was the case, it did not help to get the response from her mother that she hoped for.

Shame for Ann was also connected to embarrassment about being neglected (e.g., not having clean clothes for school), but also embarrassment about her mother's drinking and emotional instability. She particularly remembered how her mother caused embarrassment when she fell in a public place witnessed by a lot of people who knew the family: '… and the smell of drink on her … and she fell twice. … So that's my earliest memory. … Other kids' mothers aren't like that'. Ann also talked about how she wished for her mother to be different when she was small: 'every day there was hope that she would, she wouldn't be drinking'. However, Ann was also often criticised by her mother whenever she expressed upset at her mother's drinking and asked her mother to stop drinking. In these instances, Ann's mother blamed Ann for her own drinking, inevitably sowing seeds of self-doubt in the young child (*[you] made it out that it was all my fault.*).

Ann's felt sense of shame also showed in the responsibility she assumed for her children. Her taking responsibility for everything was driven by an expectation that she would be blamed (in others as well as her own eyes) for anything that went wrong. She thus sought to prevent that familiar sense that there was something wrong with her, by ensuring that she did not let others down, and by ensuring that others close to her came to no harm.

Terror/fear. The primary fear (as opposed to a more superficial anticipatory anxiety of the core pain) aspects of Ann's core pain related to experiences when Ann was not able to avoid scary, intruding situations, for example, when her relative died or was suffering. These primary fear experiences mixed with the sense of shame and profound unsupported loneliness. The origins of this fear were most likely in traumatic experiences such as the intrusive and invalidating criticism of her mother. The impact of her mother's attacks were powerfully illustrated in Ann's reported memories of '[being] worried when I was a kid going home and seeing what humour my Ma was in … if she's going to be ranting and raving or what. You just didn't know what was going to happen when you walked in through the hall door … nine times out of ten it would be anger'.

The sense of an unpredictable, terrifying event to happen was further worsened by the sudden death of Ann's mother. This was experienced as an unbearable trauma. Its overwhelming nature continued to impact Ann in her fifties, filling her with the dread of experiencing something similar in relation to her children or others close to her. The experience of death was something so unnatural that it was terrifying, bringing physical pain. This fear of death was coupled with a fear of witnessing the suffering of those close to her, pain she herself (over) identified with and could feel. Furthermore, for Ann the death of a close one could lead to her feeling alone and missing the other. Another aspect of Ann's primary fear was her being scared of losing control, a fear stemming from her experience of seeing her mother being hospitalised. When she experienced upset, Ann experienced it as uncontrollable and scary; as such it was understandable that her fear precluded her from being able stay with painful, upsetting feelings.

As can be seen, the sadness/loneliness-based, shame-based, and terror/fear-based aspects of Ann's core pain were intertwined. Ann was terrorised by her upset at experiencing the death of a close one. Such loss deepened her sense of loneliness and contributed to her fear that she was on her own, she was unsupported and unprotected. In such traumas she also was prone to feelings of shame and guilt, stemming from a sense that she in some way failed the other by not protecting them. The three aspects of Ann's core pain (loneliness, shame, terror/fear), however, could also be felt relatively independently. The profound sense of being on her own was always present. The terror felt when something bad (e.g., death) happened could be felt quite distinctly. And her shameful sense that there was something wrong with her was ever present. On the other hand, the interconnections of those vulnerable emotion-schemes were also evident. For instance, Ann's experience of not feeling loved (abandonment—loneliness), was closely linked to feelings of rejection, shame, and humiliation, and to an attendant feeling that she deserved such treatment.

In summary, a unique mixture of loneliness/sadness-based, shame-based, and terror/fear-based emotions was at the centre of the Ann's painful emotion-scheme self-organisations. These emotion schemes clearly had their origin in Ann's personal history, but they were easily activated by a variety of triggers that somehow (perhaps through sharing similar characteristics with the original painful triggers) evoked senses of loneliness, shame, or fear in Ann's current life.

Unmet needs

As Ann was able to access her core painful emotions, with the help of the therapist, she was also able to articulate unmet needs. This happened later in therapy. Needs are most productively accessed in the context of painful emotions that are not avoided but actually felt in the session, and it took a certain amount of time before Ann developed a capacity to stay with, rather than avoid, her emotions. Furthermore, Ann had great difficulty expressing and owning what her vulnerable experiences suggested she needed. Her initial tendencies were to harshly and contemptuously judge any need as selfish. However, as the therapy progressed, she was eventually able, in heart-breaking dialogues with her imagined mother, children, father, and husband, to articulate and express what she needed most, what was missing, either in the past or in the present, and what it was she continued to long for.

The unmet needs embedded in Ann's experience of loneliness showed in imagined dialogues, where she expressed a craving for closeness, love, and caring from her mother. At the time of therapy, Ann still needed this closeness, love, and caring from her father, husband, and children, as she often felt lonely in their presence. We can see Ann's first expression of need in this transcript from an early session, where with a heart-breaking emotional quality, Ann expressed how she missed and needed her mother (fuller version is in Chapter 4):

Ann: *But it would have been nice just to have her there.*
Therapist: *Yea 'I needed you there'.*
Ann: *Yea [crying].*
Therapist: *I was so on my own just to deal with all of it.*
Ann: *It's not even that. It's every now and then a girl needs her Mum.*

With regard to her experiences of shame, Ann needed to hear that there was nothing wrong with her, and that she deserved validation and acknowledgment. The articulation of this need occurred to a limited extent in imagined dialogues with Ann's mother; predominantly, however, it occurred in imagined dialogues with her own inner critic, where Ann expressed clearly that she needed a break from the criticism, more freedom to be herself, and the right to feel OK about it. The following is an example of such a dialogue:

....
Ann: *(expressing her perspective to the critic from her own experience [experiencer] chair): Yeah. And instead of ... Instead of giving out to me just let me have the whinge [still quite critical of self even in the experiencer chair as she sees herself as not being in pain but rather whinging].*
...
Therapist: *Yeah. It's like, 'I need a space ...'. Yes?*
Ann: *Yeah. I need a space.*
...
Therapist: *... 'And I need you to give me that space'. Yes? 'And then I'll put myself together and I need your support' or something? Yeah?*
Ann: *'Show me another way to do it' ...*

With regard to her primary fear and experiences of terror, Ann was able to articulate her need for safety and protection. She expressed the need to be in the presence of a caring and protective other. She also expressed the need to have the strength to face debilitating and fear provoking situations. She expressed a wish to not always have to be worrying, running away, hiding, or focusing on just getting through. She expressed a strong need to feel free and powerful, and to have the support around her that she needed to make this possible. A poignant expression of the need for safety is given here. The extract is taken from an imaginary dialogue between Ann, as her younger, vulnerable self in one chair, and as her adult self, offering care and comfort in the other chair. The exchange begins with Ann speaking as a small girl, and follows an exchange where her adult self in the other chair communicated a protective, caring presence.

> *Ann [enacting herself as a small girl to her current adult self in the other chair]:* *'I'd still have to go back to the madness' [of her mother's attacks].*
> *Therapist:* *Yeah.*
> *Ann:* *'I'd still have to go back to them'.*
> *Therapist:* *Yeah. 'I can't stay here forever' or something? Yeah?*
> ...
> *Therapist:* *'So I need ...'. What would you need from her? From that adult Ann? Yes? That you see here. 'I need from you ...' what? 'To have understanding how difficult it really is for ...'.*
> *Ann:* *'Probably understanding. Yeah. And to make it go away' [make madness of her situation to go away].*
> *Therapist:* *Ok.*
> *Ann:* *'To make it stop happening. And to ... When I ... When you're talking ... When ... When I was a kid for people to listen'.*

As is perhaps also visible in the sample therapy excerpts the core painful emotions and the needs embedded in them were always close to each other. Similarly close to each other are the different processes that have been highlighted in this case conceptualisation framework. Triggers evoke the core pain, the vulnerability toward which, is based on past injuries and unbearable experiences. Since the triggers bring painful emotions that are not possible to process, the client collapses to global distress. The client, although collapsed into global distress, has to also attempt to deal with the core painful feeling, and these efforts often result in coping strategies (self-treatment) that actually hinder the processing of the core painful feelings (self-criticism, emotional avoidance). The core underlying painful feelings are thus unprocessed and obscure the unmet needs embedded in those feelings. All of these processes while presented separately here happen very quickly and are experienced by the client as a whole. The therapist slows down the process and deconstructs the client emotion schematic process, while still helping the client to feel different aspects of the holistic experience and reflect on it. How this process leads to emotion transformation will be illustrated in the next two chapters, which focus on how emotional pain is processed and transformed.

6 Strategy for therapy—accessing core emotional pain

The case conceptualisation approach presented in the previous chapter informs the therapist's strategy for therapy. The traditional EFT strategy for therapy has been to offer an empathic therapeutic stance, promote the client's exploration of problematic experiences, and wait for particular in-session markers such as unfinished business or harsh self-criticism. The therapist then responds to such markers by initiating particular research-informed therapeutic tasks such as an empty-chair dialogue task for unfinished business or a two-chair dialogue task for conflict splits (cf. Greenberg et al., 1993; Elliott et al., 2004). From this traditional perspective, these experiential tasks are considered to be decisive for resolving (transforming) problematic emotion schemes (see research overview in Elliott et al., 2013, and Greenberg, 2010). The important role of these experiential tasks is recognised in the following pages. However, the following discussion will consider these tasks, not as standalone tasks to be engaged in when appropriate markers present, but rather as key therapeutic interventions that can be utilised within a broader therapeutic process (i.e., the conceptual framework already presented in previous chapters). From the perspective presented in this book, the experiential tasks described in the landmark books on EFT such Greenberg et al.'s (1993) *Facilitating Emotional Change* or Elliott et al.'s (2004) *Learning Emotion-Focused Therapy*, can be viewed as building material that the therapist uses creatively while following a number of key overarching therapeutic goals and principles. These principles and goals will be described in the chapter that follows.

The fact that the therapist is working from his or her conceptualisation, and utilising specific tasks, does not mean that the therapist prescribes what the client should feel. The therapist's strategy is firmly anchored in a collaborative client-centred relationship. It constantly refers to the client's emotional experiencing and to the client's needs in that moment. Therefore, the framework for emotion scheme transformation presented below should be seen as a framework that offers guiding principles but should not be adhered to rigidly. It is conceived as something to be followed flexibly, in such a manner that the therapist never loses sight of the quality of the alliance and the bond, the client's needs at any moment in therapy, or the client's overall goals for therapy.

The therapist's higher-order therapeutic strategy is grounded in an understanding that particular problematic self-organisations are rooted in specific problematic emotion schemes that need to be transformed. Core painful emotions (shame, loneliness, terror/fear) need to be accessed; the unmet needs in these painful emotions must be articulated; and these needs then have to be emotionally responded to from self-organisations characterised by compassion and protective anger. Within this framework, the focus on particular markers and tasks (so well developed in EFT, cf. Elliott et al., 2004) becomes a lower-order strategy that is used flexibly to promote the healthy emotional processing of unprocessed pain and to facilitate the restructuring of emotion schemes centred around that pain. In this conceptualisation, the overall aim of therapy is not the resolution of problematic emotional experiences or tasks (as is traditionally conceptualised in EFT; cf. Elliott et al., 2004), but rather, the transformation of emotional experiencing, emotion schemes, and self-organisations. Emotion transformation is characterised by increased emotional flexibility and by increased emotional resilience (Pascual-Leone, 2009) rather than by a particular state-bound task resolution (Greenberg et al., 1993).

This chapter focuses on steps that a therapist can use as a conceptual map, orienting him or her to what needs to happen in therapy in order to promote the chances of a successful outcome. The steps are presented here sequentially; however, they should not be seen as always occurring in a linear sequence. Whilst in well-proceeding therapies, the sequence presented here can be visible, even within an individual session or across therapy sessions, there can often be slips backward (see Pascual-Leone Greenberg, 2007; two steps forward, one step back nature of progression in successful emotion processing transformation). The steps presented here are typically repeated again and again in therapy. What should be visible in successful cases of therapy, however, is progress with regards the ease in which a client moves through this sequence of steps (e.g., from painful emotions to more healing and expansive experiences), in later sessions as compared to early sessions of therapy. In other words, the client's emotional flexibility and resilience should be growing as therapy progresses (Pascual-Leone, 2009).

ACCESSING CORE PAIN

In general, clients initially present in therapy in a state of global distress characterised by hopelessness, helplessness, general upset, irritability, or rejecting anger (e.g., *I am unhappy, all I feel is a darkness, nothing brings joy*). This presentation of global distress also tends to be accompanied by various avoidance strategies, which can be conceptualised as attempts on the client's behalf to regulate emotional distress. The EFT therapist meets this distress with empathic caring responses that focus on the client's emotional experiencing. If the client is so overwhelmed by global distress that he or she actually cannot engage in self-exploration of emotional experiencing, the therapist responds to the client where he or she is at in that particular moment. For example, the therapist might focus on helping the client regulate his or her emotion, in order that the client can develop an appropriate capacity to stay with, rather than run from, his or her own distress.

An original task was developed in EFT for dealing with the experience of being emotionally overwhelmed. The task is known as 'clearing a space' (Elliott et al., 2004) and is based on Eugene Gendlin's work on focusing (Gendlin, 1996). In this task the therapist first helps the client to identify where distress is felt in the body. The client is then instructed to name the felt experience of the distress and to imagine putting the felt experience aside to a comfortable distance. The client is then instructed to check inside to see how he or she now feels now; if he or she is still too distressed, the process is repeated until there is a sufficient level of relief for the client to take a pause and appreciate relief or to proceed with further therapeutic work. We will return to this task in Chapter 8, where I discuss working with various difficulties that can arise in the therapeutic process.

Once the client has been helped to regulate his or her level of emotional distress sufficiently for him or her to proceed, the therapist's next goal is to access the client's core underlying, painful emotions. The therapist listens attentively and focuses on what is at the core of the client's suffering. The therapist balances focused exploration and evocation of emotional experiencing with the communication of an empathic understanding that he or she is aware of the impact of the felt pain, and the difficulty it brings the client. The therapist also acknowledges that the self-exploration of painful emotions and the sharing of vulnerability with a complete stranger is a challenging and anxiety-provoking activity. With this acknowledgement and with offers to support the client through the process, the therapist maintains an enquiring focus on what is the most painful aspect of the client's self-exploration. The therapist may simply ask questions such as 'What is the most difficult thing? What is the most painful?' or more elaborately, he or she might enquire, 'If you stayed with those tears and if you spoke from them, what would they say? (see Greenberg, 2007). Again, such questions are interspersed with responses communicating empathic understanding, and the process as a whole is supported by the therapist maintaining a warm therapeutic stance.

Despite therapist efforts to help clients clarify the painful aspects of their experience, it is often the case that clients struggle to fully know what it is that is actually at the core of their distress. Often, clients have been chronically suffering for such a long time, and/or have been struggling to such an extent, that the secondary level distress with which they are living is all that they are aware of. In early therapy sessions, therefore, we often see exchanges such as the following:

Therapist:	*Ok. So [you are saying] I feel this tension ... because if I let go of the tension, what would happen? What would be the bad thing that would happen? 'I would just cry forever'. Or 'I don't know what ...'*
Client:	*I don't know really what would happen. I, I just feel so wound up all the time (crying).*
Therapist:	*Ok. Ok. 'Just the sense that I feel so unhappy ...'*

As already stated, the therapist must balance two tasks. On the one hand, the therapist empathically acknowledges and validates the client's distress; on the other hand, he or she seeks to achieve the first step in processing undifferentiated distress by accessing underlying, though not readily accessible, primary painful feelings. The therapist attempts to access these underlying feelings by focusing the client's awareness and exploration on those aspects of the client's internal emotional experiencing that are the most difficult to stay with. To access painful underlying feelings, the therapist may also use evocative language, focusing on the inner emotional experience of the client. The therapist may focus on personalised or specific aspects of the client's narrative in relation to their difficulties. He or she may ask what was happening inside for the client at a given moment in a described, difficult situation. He or she might promote the accessing of core emotional pain by focusing on the client's sense of unmet needs in recent or past situations described by the client. In essence, the therapist gently focuses on that which is most painful for the client; that which aches the most; that which he or she is most missing. The therapist's gentle focus on the client's inner emotional world can be seen in segments such as the following:

Client: *I've nothing, well you would know probably better than me, but I've nothing ... I've a nice enough life and not any worries or anything. I don't know why I'm like this ... I kind of feel like I shouldn't be, I'm ashamed of being like this because there are people a lot worse off than me, I've nothing to be like this.*

....

Client: *I think I'm a great actress, you know.*
Therapist: *But inside ... it's really ...*
Client: *Yeah, fighting with myself all the time.*

Here, the therapist gently focuses the client on her inner experience, with the hope that it will lead her to focus her attention inwards and elaborate on aspects of her felt experience.

Accessing the core pain through evocative unfolding

In some cases, the client's core painful feelings can be accessed by employing aspects of the systematic evocative unfolding task (Elliott et al., 2004; Greenberg et al., 1993; Rice & Saperia, 1984), a task which was originally developed in EFT as a therapeutic response to instances when a client presented in the session with a puzzling, emotional experience. Aspects of this task can, however, also be used for a general exploration of a client's emotional experience. Clients often describe situations in which they felt uncomfortable, scared, or particularly distressed. In order to process and transform these painful emotions, it is necessary that they are brought into the therapy session and felt in the present. The therapist may, therefore, invite the client to re-create vividly the memory of the difficult situation.

For instance, a male client tells the therapist how he came home during the week and found his wife sitting behind the computer. She did not pay any attention to his arrival home, and this led him to feel 'down'. In such an instance, the therapist may ask the client to revisit the event in question. He may ask the client to imagine that he is reliving the event again, to slow it down, to describe what he sees, and to try and notice how it makes him feel. For example, the therapist may say something like 'Take me through that event as if through a slow motion movie. First of all, how do you feel inside as you are going home? What are you noticing around yourself?' (It is worth noting that when giving such directions, the use of the present tense can be especially evocative, helping make the reimagined experience more vivid and real.) The client's response to these instructions might be that he feels exhausted after the long day but also that he feels a bit vulnerable as several people were critical of him during the day. As he imagines walking home, he describes how he is walking along a dark street in a part of the city where he did not grow up, and that this leaves him feeling quite sad and alienated. At this point, the therapist may enquire, 'So what is the expectation inside as you are approaching your house? What is it that you need in your sadness and alienation? What do you see in your house?' The client responds to this by observing that he 'sort of hopes' to come home and be comforted by his wife. He describes how, as he enters the house, everything is silent. He describes how, when he enters the room where his wife is, she does not even raise her head from her engagement on the computer. The therapist asks, 'What do you see?' The client continues: 'Her interest is elsewhere, she does not register me'. The therapist asks, 'What happens inside as you see her non interest? Stay with that picture of her not registering you and looking to the computer and see what is happening inside'. The client describes feeling upset in response to this. He describes feeling profoundly sad and alone, and reports wanting to just withdraw, lie down, and cry. This type of sadness and loneliness is a primary maladaptive, painful, and chronic emotion that the client is familiar with, and knows. This is the type of emotional experience that needs to be accessed in therapy in order for it to be transformed.

Accessing the core pain through imaginary dialogues

Perhaps the best way to access underlying painful emotions is via an enactment of the triggers that bring about those painful emotions. This is typically a hurtful behaviour by another (e.g., rejection, exclusion, or abuse), though in some cases, it can be a negative self-treatment which happens in the context of situational or interpersonal triggers. In order to enact the triggers and problematic self-treatment which evoke a client's underlying pain, EFT utilises a number of specifically developed and intensively researched chair dialogues (Elliott et al., 2004; Greenberg et al., 1993). The two most frequently utilised chair dialogues are an empty-chair dialogue, in which the trigger (e.g., the hurtful other) is enacted by the client in a way that highlights the hurtful aspects of the other's behaviour; and a two-chair dialogue, in which the client re-enacts the self-attacking behaviour that triggers a painful emotion response.

Enacting the core pain in an empty-chair task

The empty-chair dialogue for an interpersonal injury (or unfinished business) is an EFT task initiated when the client in session refers to either lingering (Elliott et al., 2004; Greenberg et al., 1993) or strong adverse feelings toward another person (typically a significant other). As the therapist and the client explore the client's difficulties, they often find that a lot of the client's experienced pain is linked to interpersonal situations or problematic relationships. The therapist and the client can then focus on those interpersonal situations/relationships which provoke the most distress. These interpersonal situations/relationships are therefore seen as triggers (see Figure 1) of the underlying primary core painful emotions that need to be accessed and transformed in therapy.

The therapist seeks to bring a focus onto these underlying feelings by initiating the empty-chair task for interpersonal injuries. The therapist asks the client to imagine the identified person in the other (empty) chair. The therapist asks the client to focus internally and notice what happens inside as he or she imagines the person sitting in the other chair. After checking how the client feels, the therapist empathically responds to the client's experience, and asks the client to express these feelings to the imagined other.

For instance, in the third session of therapy, the aim of which was to treat her anxiety and depression, Mary, a female client in her mid-forties, spoke about her now deceased mother, describing how her mother had always been very contemptuous, rejecting, and dismissive of her as a child. The therapist decided to further Mary's exploration of the pain she felt as a consequence of her mother's treatment of her, by suggesting the use of an empty-chair task. The therapist suggested that Mary picture her mother in the other chair, asking, 'What is the feeling if you stay with the picture of her?' Beginning the process in this manner increases the likelihood that the client can get in touch with his or her internal experiencing, with his or her feelings. The following excerpt shows how the therapist initiated Mary's first experiential dialogue with her mother.

Therapist: *Ok. So if you imagine her here. Yes? See what happens inside? I mean what is the feeling like when you picture her? ... What is the feeling if you stay with the picture of her?*

Mary: *Sadness.*

Therapist: *Ok. And we will actually try to talk to her ... So it is like 'Mam I am sad' and I am sad for what? What is the sadness for? 'For what we didn't have in life'? Tell her.*

Mary: *Em. Why you were always hurtful?. ... She would look at me and just look at me and shrug and ...*

Therapist: *Yeah. Yeah so this is what was painful, yeah? So I would go like 'Mam this is why it was so painful to get those shrugs' and so on, yeah?*

The distress in this edited example is still undifferentiated, but the goal at this point is to orient the client to the task itself and to facilitate her initial engagement with the task. As the dialogue progresses, the client will be encouraged to pay attention to different aspects of her hurt feelings, to name these feelings, and to express them to her imagined mother. This 'dance', whereby the client focuses attention inwards, names the felt experience, and expresses it to the person to whom the feelings refer, makes the empty-chair dialogue a powerful experiential intervention (Greenberg, 2002). Clients quickly start to feel as if the dialogue is happening in reality. As such, the dialogue becomes an emotional reality for the client, and as a consequence, the felt emotions are real. This allows the client to fully feel various aspects of their painful experience, to explore these various aspects, to pay attention to them, to symbolize them (e.g., to name them in narrative), and to express them.

The therapist facilitates this exploration and further deepens access to painful emotional experience by asking the client to enact the particularly hurtful aspect of the other (i.e., those aspects of the other which function as a trigger for the client's pain). The therapist asks the client to come to the other's chair and be that part of the other that they found particularly painful. This is done to highlight the perceived triggers that are painful and bring them thus into awareness, but also to help the client deepen the presence and experience of the painful emotional experience in the original chair from which they engaged the imagined other (in EFT referred to as the experiencer chair). The change of chairs usually happens as the client expresses the perceived aspects of the other's behaviour that were difficult to bear in the experiencer chair. For the dialogue to flow smoothly, the therapist has to ensure that the client is fully in *contact* with the other chair; that he or she is expressing his or her own feelings directly to the imagined other; or after the change of chairs, that he or she is communicating directly from the enacted imagined other to the now imagined self (in the experiencer chair).

The following excerpt illustrates what this looked like in Mary's first empty-chair dialogue with her mother:

Therapist: *Could you come here? [pointing to the empty chair]. And if you could be the rude mother that you remember for a moment, yes, it is just to convey the message what she was doing. Yes? [Mary changes chairs.] ...*

Therapist: *So how would she behave? How would she deliver this rudeness to you and to others?*

Mary: *She would look at you and then she would go 'thththh'.*

Therapist: *Ok. Do it ... And the message of it is almost like as if she is saying what? Like 'I don't care about you'? [Therapist brings to awareness the most painful aspects of the mother's behavior.]*

Mary: *She would say 'come' and you would go over to her, and she ... then she would grab me hand, and she would be pulling at me and everything, but couldn't ...*

Therapist: *Ok so I am really angry. So do it for a moment, convey to it Mary. But is it 'I am really pissed off with you' or?*

Client: *Yeah. Absolutely, all the time. I want to insult you.*

....

Therapist: *Yeah and what would be the insult? What would be an example?*
Mary: *Em. 'You're very fat'. 'You're getting fatter'.*
Therapist: *You are fat. Tell her again. [Therapist emphasises the painful message that should help in accessing the hurt afresh when Mary will be asked to sit in the experiencer chair again.]*

The client is thus encouraged to convey the hurtful behaviour of the other. As the therapist is trying to distil the essence of what it is that the client perceives as hurtful, he or she instructs the client to focus on identifying and enacting the implicit message in the other's behaviour. The therapist may also highlight what is most emotionally salient and hurtful by asking the client to repeat the most hurtful statements or behaviours. This type of intervention highlights and brings to the client's awareness both what they see in the other's behaviour, and how they react to it. After the client has enacted fully the hurtful behaviour of the other (i.e., the trigger), the therapist instructs the client to move back to the experiencer chair, and to notice the impact of such hurtful behaviour on the self. So for example, as the client sits back down in the experiencer chair, the therapist might say, 'See what happens inside when you get that'. In the example already discussed, the dialogue proceeded in the following manner:

Therapist: *Could you come here? Yeah? [Pointing to the experiencer chair; Mary moves chairs.] ... This is what we see [The therapist highlights the perceived hurtful trigger.]. This behavior of her, yes? So what happens inside when you get this? 'You're fat'. 'You are getting fatter'?*
Mary: *Go straight out and stuff me face. Go straight out and eat like there is no tomorrow. [The client highlights the devastation she feels and how she attempts to protect herself by overeating.]*
Therapist: *What happens for you inside? It's like? [The therapist wants to focus client on the felt emotional experience.]*
Mary: *I just think 'You're vicious'. [The client goes to defensive secondary anger, the underlying shame and rejection is not revealed.]*
Therapist: *Could you try to tell it to her? [Although it would be better for the process if the client came with the primary painful feelings, the therapist respects where the client is and promotes emotional expression anyway—this helps to get the client engaged in the task.]*
Mary: *Vicious horrible old cow, I would actually think.*
... *[a bit later]*
Therapist: *Ok. 'And I mean it is so painful and hurtful because I so much would like to have a mother-daughter relationship with you and all I get is this vicious horrible attacking me, targeting me'. [The therapist is probing for underlying painful feelings.]*

....

Therapist:	*'It is just so sad to see that you behaved like this to me and to others'. Yeah? [The therapist conjectures the client's underlying feelings.]*
Mary:	*Absolutely, yeah ... and always a big influence in me life. Even at fifty years of age you are still controlling me in a way'.*

....

Therapist:	*Ok so it is like I am scared of your anger, or what is it? What?*
Mary:	*I did always feel afraid of her, you know? Always.*
Therapist:	*Could you tell her? [The therapist is encouraging the client's expression and the client staying in contact with the imagined other.]*
Mary:	*I always felt afraid of you all my life.*

...

Therapist:	*'Because like this was so scary but what I really needed was'? What was that you really needed? [The therapist facilitates differentiation of the underlying feelings through asking after the unmet needs.]*
Mary:	*Didn't have a childhood at all. It was all work.*
Therapist:	*'I needed you to be there for me'?*
Mary:	*Mmm. I did. I needed you to be there.*
Therapist:	*'I needed you to show me affection'?*
Mary:	*Show me affection. You never even took us out to the park or anything. You never did anything with us as children, any of us.*
Therapist:	*Yeah. Could you tell her what you missed? 'I missed'. [Asking after what is missing helps to get access to the underlying primary sadness.]*
Mary:	*I missed the affection, the love, just what a mother should be doing. You did nothing. The only thing you did do was you always kept us lovely and you did keep your house nice and everything but that was ... there was no love whatsoever from you. [The client expresses the mixture of anger and sadness.]*

The above excerpt demonstrates the therapist's constant focus on unfolding the underlying experiences of fear of being attacked and shamed, and sadness at being rejected and missing the care of a loving mother. The therapist helps the client to unfold the primary painful feelings by focusing on what needs were not met; by focusing on what was most missing. The client is now moving more toward underlying painful emotions and implicit maladaptive emotion scheme self-organizations centring around a sense of self as unloved, rejected, scared, and ashamed. This, however, needs to be further unfolded and differentiated. Core painful feelings have their nuances. They have to be attended to, and named, and underlying unfulfilled needs have to be articulated. This is the focus of the next step of the therapeutic process and will be elaborated on below. Before that, we will explore the accessing of core pain through the use of two-chair self-self dialogues.

Enacting the core pain in a two-chair self-self dialogue

The two-chair self-self dialogue is another chair intervention which can be used effectively in order to access underlying core painful emotions. The purpose of this task is to enact negative self-treatment. Within EFT, the task is traditionally referred to as a two-chair dialogue for conflict split (as one part of the self criticises the other, leaving the person feeling ashamed, worthless, etc.; see Greenberg et al., 1993; Elliott et al., 2004).

As with other experiential tasks, it is important that self-self dialogues be introduced when the intervention is an appropriate response to that which is most emotionally salient for the client at that point in time. The marker for a two-chair self-self dialogue is the presence of negative self-treatment within the session. Once this marker is present and the therapist judges the process of negative self-treatment to be sufficiently emotionally salient, both for the client at that moment, but also in relation to what is being addressed in therapy (what the client and the therapist agreed to work on in therapy), the therapist may suggest engagement in a two-chair task. Whilst one purpose of initiating this task is to highlight the way in which the client treats him- or herself, the primary purpose of the intervention is accessing the underlying core painful emotions which the problematic self-treatment evokes, in order that these core painful emotions can eventually be transformed.

Problematic self-treatment is normally enacted in the context of some other triggering situation, often difficult interpersonal treatment by the other. Therefore, it is not surprising that empty-chair dialogues with significant others (e.g., with a significant other who is experienced as rejecting the client) often lead to the client engaging in negative self-treatments (e.g., the client becomes self-rejecting). For this reason, it is often the case that empty-chair dialogue tasks are closely related to two-chair dialogue tasks and can overlap in therapy. For example, a client may have been demeaned by his or her parent and this treatment might have left him or her feeling rejected and ashamed. At the same time the client, at least in part, may doubt him- or herself, believing that rejection by others was merited (*I am angry with myself, as I must be doing something wrong if my mum treats me so badly.*). Alternatively, what appears initially to be sheer self-criticism may unfold in such a manner that it is clear that the self-treatment has an important interpersonal context (e.g., *I am angry at myself for disappointing my father who put so much hope in me, and put so much effort into helping me, and I cannot live with the shame of letting him down.*). In such instances self-self dialogues may give rise to self-other dialogue.

In the case of Tina, a client in her forties struggling with low mood and anxiety who was very self-critical, the therapist's invitation to engage in a negative self-treatment dialogue looked as follows:

Therapist: *If you come here? Yes? You can come. So you will be that critical, eh, critical, Tina because it seems like a part of you is always not happy with yourself. [The therapist is inviting the client into a chair that is traditionally in EFT referred to as the critic chair or the critic; cf. Elliott et al., 2004; Greenberg et al., 1993. The chair that the client is normally sitting in is referred to as the experiencer chair or the experiencer.]*

...

Therapist:	*So what do you do not like about yourself? Yes? What do you not like about Tina or what's your ...*
Tina:	*Don't like, em, the moodiness and ...*
Therapist:	*Ok, so you'll say to her. Yes? 'I don't like your moodiness'. [The therapist wants the client to enact the criticism to increase emotional salience and arousal.]*
Tina:	*I don't like you being moody and making other people in your family, em, unhappy. Probably doing similar things to what was done to me and ... You should be able to snap out of it and not be doing it. [The last sentence is an expression of a more superficial level of self-criticism in which the client is angry at the presence of secondary depressive emotions that were likely preceded by more primary painful emotions. The therapist's goal will be to differentiate this more superficial criticism to a more core targeted self-criticism aimed at particular personal qualities that are being criticised, see below; cf. Greenberg, 2011.]*
Therapist:	*Ok.*
Tina:	*If there are any problems, it'd be down to you.*
Therapist:	*Ok. Ok. So it's like ...*
Tina:	*Down to you.*
Therapist:	*Ok. So 'It's like all your fault'. Yeah?*
Tina:	*Yeah. It is all your fault.*

Once initiated, this self-criticism can then be further differentiated, with the therapist searching for what is at the core of the negative self-treatment. In other words, the therapist explores for those qualities in the self that the client does not like, cannot accept, or hates.

Therapist:	*'Because I am not happy with you?' Yeah?*
Tina: Yeah.	
Therapist:	*'I think it's all your fault'? [The therapist is amplifying negative self-treatment in order to increase the likelihood of accessing the core pain that it springs in the experiencer chair.]*
Tina:	*Yeah. That's right.*
Therapist:	*'And it's almost like I can't accept you'. Yes? 'I can't take you for who you are'. Yes?*

...

Tina:	*I don't like your weakness. You're very weak ... you just give in. You give in with people for ... [Here the negative self-treatment*

	is much more specific. The client dislikes her weakness, which is a personal, self-defining quality.]
Therapist:	*Yeah.*
Tina:	*To suit other people because ... you feel you should.*
Therapist:	*Yeah. So 'You're not adult enough', or something like that?*
Tina:	*No. Exactly.*
Therapist:	*Yeah.*
Tina:	*Don't feel grown up at all.*
Therapist:	*Yeah.*

The therapist highlights the nature and the manner of negative self-treatment in order to bring it fully to the client's awareness. The therapist may, for instance, highlight the level of self-disgust present or reflect a particular nonverbal behaviour that captures the level of self-hostility (e.g., *and you clench your fist and bite your teeth*). Typically, in the later stages of such dialogues, attention can also be focused on the function of negative self-treatment, as even seemingly negative self-treatments may have a protective function (e.g., *I am tough on you, so you can cope better and thus prevent experiences of further pain at being rejected by people who matter to you.*). The following excerpt illustrates what a focus on the nature and the manner of negative self-treatment can look like:

Client:	*You should be much more mature that you are.*
Therapist:	*Yeah and the feeling is like, like unforgiving, non-acceptance ...*
Client:	*That's right.*
Therapist:	*And kind of attitude of rejection or negative ...*
Client:	*Yeah. Like a ...*
Therapist:	*Judgment or something?*
Client:	*Yeah. Rejection really. Yeah.*

Once the negative self-treatment is highlighted and enacted fully, in particular its core message, the therapist can check for the impact of this criticism on the self, focusing on unfolding the pain it brings. So for example, the therapist might ask the client to come back to the experiencer chair and see 'What happens inside, when you get this criticism?' The underlying core pain needs to be systematically focused on and teased out by the therapist in a manner that balances empathic exploration with the communication of empathic understanding. The client's natural tendency may be to avoid the pain, as it is too uncomfortable. Alternatively, rather than access the core underlying pain, the client may collapse into secondary global distress, for example, hopelessness. When this global distress is worked through, however, it is almost invariably the case that the pain triggered by the self-attack and self-criticism is some form of maladaptive, unbearable shame.

Rather than disregard secondary emotions, the therapist facilitates access to the client's core pain by acknowledging these secondary feelings, by empathising with them, and by acknowledging the client's desire to avoid the pain. However, whilst empathising in this way, the therapist also maintains a focus on what lies beneath these secondary emotions, in other words on what it is that is so particularly painful and difficult that the client seeks ways to avoid it. The therapist enables the client to stay with the dreaded underlying feelings by naming these feelings and empathising with them, by facilitating the client's capacity to differentiate these varying feelings, and by helping the client put these feelings into language. Putting painful experience into words has been shown to have a regulatory function, which in turn helps the client stay with painful emotions (Lieberman et al., 2007).

With Tina, the work of assessing the core pain triggered by negative self-treatment (as enacted in the critic chair) took the following form:

Tina:	*I'm not happy with you. [The client here is still in the critic chair.]*
Therapist:	*Yeah. Ok. Could you come here [pointing to the experiencer chair]? See what impact it has on you? ... this is kind of part of you ... saying, 'I don't accept you. Too moody. Too weak. Behaving badly to your children'. Yes? 'Bringing all this tension that you have to them'. Yeah? ... Ok. So what's the sense like when you get this? How does, how does it feel inside? Take a breath and see how it feels.*
Tina:	*It doesn't really feel, it doesn't feel good being like that. It doesn't feel good but, it releases something in me but it's not a good feeling but I have to lose my temper or give out about something. You know?*
Therapist:	*What would you say to her? [The therapist is trying to keep the contact between the chairs—dialogue—so the client's engagement stays vivid and experiential.] How does it feel to get it? It's like 'I feel like I deserve it' or something? You're saying.*
Tina:	*I feel, yeah, like I deserve to be ... I deserve not to be happy or something ... That's all that I've known all, really else ... I realise that now. I didn't realise it. But I realise it. That's the way I've lived.*
...	
Therapist:	*It's almost like 'I'm used to it ...'. [The therapist is capturing secondary resignation here.]*
Tina:	*It's coming back to what I was like. Yeah.*
Therapist:	*'But I'm used to it. I expect it'.*
Tina:	*That's all I expect [secondary hopelessness].*
Therapist:	*Yeah. And how does it feel? Yes? You say that 'I got use to it. I almost feel like I deserve it'. But I assume that it must be also unpleasant. Yes? [The therapist is trying to unfold the experience and invites the client to stay with the felt quality of it.]*
Tina:	*It is very unpleasant.*
Therapist:	*It must be bringing this tension constantly. Yes? This is like constantly being slapped ... [The therapist is trying to build the experiential impact of the self-criticism.]*

...

Tina:	*It is. Constantly. And now I see my own children doing similar. Em ... Well yeah because like, me poor daughter like, she can't show any affection to anybody and I think that's terrible ...*
Therapist:	*Yeah.*
Tina:	*Cos I see her and that's coming from me I would say.*
...	
Therapist:	*So yes 'It's all your fault'. Yes? [aiming at the primary shame].*
Tina:	*Yeah. Yeah.*

In another self-self dialogue, Tina was able to access her underlying core painful experiences of shame:

Therapist:	*Can you sense what that rejection does to you?*
Tina:	*It just makes me feel very low and down and ...*
Therapist:	*Ok. Could you tell it to her?*
Tina:	*Yeah you put me down.*
Therapist:	*As if you ...*
Tina:	*You make me feel low.*
Therapist:	*Yeah.*
Tina:	*Worthless. [Worthlessness is typical label for shameful feelings.]*
Therapist:	*Yeah.*
Tina:	*Not able to just get on with anything.*
...	
Therapist:	*'So also when you do it? When you kind of criticise me ... '*
Tina:	*When you criticize me ...*
Therapist:	*'I feel like soft, or an eejit'. [Using the client's earlier words.]*
Tina:	*I just yeah, I just feel worthless, stupid ... I've felt like that for so long you see. I suppose. [This points at the chronic nature of painful feelings.]*
Therapist:	*Yeah and if you stay with this feeling stupid, worthless yes? Is it like that you even, I don't know, physically feel smaller almost or something? You know when you say like? [The therapist is trying to help the client to be able to stay with the experience without it taking control over the client.]*
...	
Tina:	*I just do whatever to keep the peace, to suit everybody but not me. I never sort of do what I really want to do ... I'm always trying to appease other people, you know? Just because I'm afraid of eh ...*
Therapist:	*The ...*
Tina:	*Confrontation, yet I'm getting all the confrontation.*

As mentioned in previous chapters, it is possible that negative self-treatment might historically in some way have fulfilled an adaptive function for the client.

For instance, children may attribute the reason for their negative treatment at the hands of caregivers, to own flaws or weaknesses, in order that they might have some perceived control over the other's behaviour (e.g., *If I improve, she will love me more.*). To a limited extent this makes sense, as the alternative may be even more intolerable (e.g., to have to live with the hopelessness that *my treatment at the hand of others is beyond my control*).

Negative self-treatment may also be an expression of care; for example, the self-critic may be attempting to ensure that the self does not get into situations where experiences of failure or rejection would be difficult to bear. For instance, a client might push him- or herself to be perfect in order to not be exposed to unbearable experiences of failure or rejection. The critic in such instances pushes the self in order to prevent an undesirable outcome. An EFT therapist may collaborate with the client to highlight this dynamic, and to bring it more fully into the client's awareness. However, the acquisition of insight is not seen as a central therapeutic goal; rather the core work from an EFT perspective is to access the underlying, unbearable emotional pain that the critic manages or contributes to, in order that this pain can be further worked on and eventually transformed through the generation of adaptive emotional responses.

Overcoming avoidance

Accessing the client's core painful feelings is also made difficult by a variety of client-idiosyncratic emotional and behavioural avoidance processes. Clients avoid underlying feelings because they are simply too painful to tolerate. Avoidance of such feelings thus serves a protective function. These processes need to be empathised with by the therapist. The protective function they serve needs to be highlighted and brought to the client's awareness. By helping the client to recognise that he or she is actively involved in such avoiding processes, the client is helped to develop a sense of his or her own agency in these processes. The therapist also helps (e.g., mostly through the use of imaginary chair dialogues) the client to feel the toll of these avoidance processes; typically tiredness, tension, resignation, or fearfulness. One important aspect of that toll which is brought to client awareness is that avoidance obscures the client's identification of, and pursuit of, own needs.

By focusing the client on the toll of avoidance processes, and on the unmet needs that avoidance obscures, the therapist facilitates a mobilisation of the client's resolve both to overcome avoidance and to seek to have his or her needs met. The client is coached to stand up to the avoidance; to take risks both in feeling difficult feelings and in engaging in previously avoided situations. In EFT, clients are typically aided in overcoming emotional and behavioural avoidance via, at first, enactments of the avoidance processes in self-interruption (Greenberg et al., 1993) or self-worry dialogues (Murphy et al., 2014; Timulak et al., 2012). We will now have a brief look at what these dialogues look like (for more details see Elliott et al., 2004; Greenberg et al., 1993; Murphy et al., 2014).

Markers of avoidance

Once avoidance is present in the session, the therapist has the option to make it a focus of the therapy. This may happen for instance, when the client engages in the worry process or complains about worry being one of the major problems he or she struggles with (a marker of worry). Alternatively, it may happen when the client, in the middle of an experiential exploration, suddenly feels stuck, tense, or unable to stay with emerging difficult feelings (a marker of self-interruption). The client might pull back from emotional expression, so for instance, in an imaginary dialogue where the client was about to stand up to the other and express protective anger, he or she might instead suddenly pull back, and be overcome with fear, panic, or tension (again, a marker of self-interruption).

Enacting the avoidance

Once the therapist and the client agree that they want to focus on the avoidance process, the therapist may suggest the use of one of a number of experiential chair dialogue tasks. The therapist may ask the client to first come to the other chair and enact either *the interrupter* (in the case of self-interruption) or *the worrier* (in the case of worry). The therapist will encourage the client to enact the particular avoiding process by saying something like 'How do you stop yourself from feeling?' or 'How do you worry yourself? Please do it'.

The following excerpt illustrates what the start of a chair dialogue in which the client enacts worry might look like:

Therapist: *So I'm going to ask you to be that part of you that worries ... to see how it impacts on you ... to see what happens ... You'll almost have a dialogue between the part of you that worries ... and the part that is then kind of scared.*

Client: *Yeah.*

Therapist: *... the part that of you that feels what it is like to be worried ...*

Client: *Yeah. [The client moves to the worrier chair.]*

Therapist: *So this is the part of you that worries ... is like ... almost saying 'You have to be ready' or something? Yes? 'You have to do this ... or do that ... or think about so and so ... You have to not to forget to do all these things'. Yes? So if you were that part? And you'll talk to you, to yourself? Yes? What do you say to him? How do you worry him?*

By enacting the worry (or interrupter in the case of self-interrupter work), the client is helped to become more aware of his or her own agency in the worry or interruption process. The client can see that it is not simply that worry just comes, or that emotions just disappear, but rather, that it is him or her who actively worries him- or herself, or interrupts his or her own emotional experiencing.

Highlighting the function of avoidance

At this stage the therapist can also point to the function of the worry or interruption. The therapist might simply ask, 'And what is the function of what you are doing? What do you want to achieve by it?'; 'What do you want to achieve by worrying?'; or 'What do you want achieve by making sure that he [you] does not stand up for the self and does not express any anger?' What typically comes to the surface at this point (and therefore into the client's awareness) is that the client's avoidance is motivated by an anticipatory fear. This might be a fear that something unbearable could happen; or it might be a fear in relation to the emotional experiencing which is starting to seep out to the surface. It is important that the therapist validate both this fear and the motivation it creates to avoid harm and pain. As the avoidance is essentially an effort to protect the self, the therapist empathises with this effort. Such empathic validation might look something like the following:

Therapist:	*But it's almost like a sense that something bad will happen? Yeah?*
Client:	*It has to happen.*
Therapist:	*So you better be ready?*
Client:	*Yeah.*
Therapist:	*Or something? Yeah?*
Client:	*Prepare yourself for it ... kind of ...*
Therapist:	*Ok. So it's very ... kind of eh ... Yeah. I mean it's to, to prevent anything bad from happening.*
Client:	*Yeah.*

This type of intervention shows the client that they not only have agency in their own avoidance processes, but that these processes are fundamentally both intentional and meaningful. It helps the client to become more aware of their avoidance processes, and to become more aware of their own role within those processes. Sometimes clients may spontaneously explore and reflect on the origins of their avoidance strategies. For instance, they may report that it is a behaviour learned from a significant other. Alternatively, they may report that it is a strategy they learned as a way to cope with a feared significant other; or a strategy that was developed after experiences of being traumatised, in an effort to avoid similar traumatic experiences.

Checking in for the impact of worrying or interrupting

Once the client enacts the worry or interruption process, the therapist asks the client to come back and sit in the experiencer chair. The therapist asks the client to see what impact the worrying or interrupting has on him or her, for instance, enquiring 'What is happening inside when you get that (referring the worrier/interrupter chair)? What does it do to you?' It is common for clients to struggle with this task, especially in early dialogues, and in such instances it is the therapist's task to help the client focus on his or her inner experience, and how this is impacted by the worry or interruption process. When the task is going well, however, clients are able to see how they feel obstructed, tense, or tired (in the case of self-interrupting processes); or tense, scared, and tired (in case of self-worrying processes). The therapist then helps the client to stay with these unpleasant feelings, in order that the client can feel the toll the avoidance processes has on the self. At this stage, the client may experience contact with hitherto avoided primary painful feelings (loneliness, shame, terror) as they begin to seep out into awareness (Murphy et al., 2014). When this is the case, the work of therapy will be to focus on these underlying, painful feelings.

If the client does not get in touch with underlying, primary painful feelings, the therapist simply stays with the client where he or she is at, and helps the client to fully feel the toll of the enacted worry or interruption on the self:

Therapist:	*It must take a lot of energy. Yes? To be getting it [take the worry message constantly]. Yes? It must be tiring. Yeah?*
Client:	*Exhausting. [The client expresses the toll of the worry.]*
Therapist:	*Yeah.*
Client:	*It's tiring.*
Therapist:	*Yeah.*
Client:	*And it's ... Sometimes you don't always get the head to stop rambling.*
Therapist:	*But if you go to that tiredness. Yes? [The therapist facilitates the client to stay with the experiential impact of the worry.]*
Client:	*If I go to that tiredness, I'll go asleep.*
Therapist:	*For the moment here. I mean it feels like you wouldn't wake up. Yes?*
Client:	*Yeah.*
Therapist:	*It feels like it's just never, never-ending tiredness. [The therapist empathizes with and evokes the felt tiredness.]*
Client:	*Yeah.*
Therapist:	*Yeah. Ok.*
Client:	*It's just twenty-four hours a day.*
Therapist:	*Just try it for ten seconds to feel that tiredness. Yes? Don't run away from it. [The therapist facilitates the client to sense fully the impact of the worry—tiredness.]*
Client:	*Don't have to try ... I feel it.*
Therapist:	*Ok. It's there. Ok.*
Client:	*It's here.*

This type of therapeutic process makes the toll of the avoidance process very tangible, allowing it to be fully felt by the client. The therapist then focuses on moving beyond the tiredness.

Identifying the obstructed need

Avoidance not only protects the client from feeling the core pain; it also prevents the client from meeting his or her need to live a freer life. At the moment when the client is able to feel the negative impact of the worry or interruption process, the therapist asks the client what it is he or she needs in place of the tiring, scaring, tensing worry or interruption. Typically, clients express a need to be more free, to be less obstructed, and to be less scared. The expression of such need is mobilising and prompts the client to challenge both the worry/interruption/avoidance, and the fear fueling those processes. The client may mobilise an inner determination to be less fearful and to live more freely. He or she might express an eagerness to take more risks, to feel his or her own feelings, and to pursue his or her own needs without fear, worry, interruption, or other forms of avoidance. As successful therapy progresses across sessions, accessing this agentic stance in the face of avoidance processes becomes increasingly easier for the client. In overcoming avoidance via the mobilising of unmet needs, fearfulness is transformed into a more free access to own emotions, to emotion-informed needs, and to adaptive action based on an awareness of those needs. The following excerpt illustrates the manner in which one client's mobilisation against the worry process unfolded.

Client:	*Be quiet. [This is expressed toward the worrier chair. The client is standing up to the worrying part of the self.]*
Therapist:	*Ok.*
Client:	*Just be ...*
Therapist:	*Ok. 'Let me be'. Yes?*
Client:	*Give my brain a break.*
Therapist:	*Yes ... 'Give my brain a break'. Yes? Tell her. [The therapist encourages expression that consolidates the protective anger felt by the client.]*
Client:	*Give my brain a break. [The client expresses a need to be free of the worries.]*
Therapist:	*Yeah.*
Client:	*Be quiet.*
Therapist:	*Yeah. 'Be quiet'. Yeah. And you stop yourself. Yes? There is some anger in 'Be quiet'. [The therapist is picking up on the client's anger becoming weaker.]*
Client:	*Yeah.*
Therapist:	*Tell her that you mean it. You know you're too nice almost. Because it costs energy to be nice. Yes? [The therapist is making sure that the client resolutely stands behind her needs, and coaches the client to express the anger.]*
Client:	*Yeah.*
...	
Therapist:	*That anger is very important as well. It's like 'Be quiet. Let me be. Let me take a breath'. Yeah? [The therapist coaches the client to express the anger.]*

Client: *Yeah. Just be quiet. Just stop talking. Leave me ... On my days off let me have a day off. [The client is able to harness the anger more.]*

Therapist: *Ok. Ok. 'So this is what I need'. Yes?*

This mobilisation of the need to be free from worry and tiredness helps the client to overcome his or her fearfulness, thereby allowing him or her to become more ready to explore and work on the problematic and painful aspects of their emotional experiencing. The client's emerging emotional freedom is also typically reflected in an increased capability to overcome behavioural avoidance. The client may thus, for instance, become less fearful of entering situations in which he or she may be criticised, situations in which he or she was historically afraid of entering for fear of feeling unbearable shame.

The more compassionate interrupter/worrier

Sometimes, when worry and/or self-interruption processes are central to a client's difficulties (e.g., in anxiety disorders), the worry or interruption is addressed more centrally in therapy, and dialogues between the worrier or interrupter on the one hand, and the experiencer on the other, are enacted more often. In such cases the therapist may check how the client responds in the worrier chair to seeing the impact or toll of the self-initiated worry process on the self (i.e., the felt experience in the experiencer chair). The therapist may, for instance, ask, 'So how is it to see her feeling tired, tense, scared, etc.?' If the toll and pain caused by the worry or interruption process has been acutely felt and expressed by the client in the experiencer chair, the client in the worrier chair may soften in their self-treatment/stance. Sometimes, this can be a prolonged process, and the therapist may need to use a variety of skilled interventions to facilitate it happening. (See Chapter 8 for a discussion on how therapists can work with the difficulty in experiencing compassion.)

Eventually, however, clients in well-progressing therapy do become more compassionate toward that part of their self, which suffers as a result of the avoidance process. This softening or self-compassion can take a number of forms. The client may express understanding of the pain he or she experiences as a consequence of worry and/or self-interruption. The client may express understanding for the needs (such as freedom from the worry) that he or she wishes to pursue. The client may also express in the worrier (interrupter) chair a willingness to not worry the self to the extent that he or she previously did; he or she might make a commitment to try to be less controlling; and he or she may directly express compassion to the experiencing self. Alternatively, the worrier/interrupter may ask the experiencer to ignore him/her as he/she is incapable of stopping the worry. Or the worrier/interrupter may simply acknowledge that he/she is weak and afraid, and reach out for, and seek some level of connection and support from the experiencer. This, in turn, can bring experiences of connecting sadness that is often somehow linked to the core pain, for example, to core painful feelings of loneliness.

As the client's avoidance processes are gradually overcome, the client has increased access to the underlying painful feelings which become the main focus of therapy. This process can be visible both within individual sessions, but also across a number of sessions. As already stated above, in successfully progressing EFT, clients become increasingly capable of accessing those hurts in need of healing and transformation. Again, this is not a straightforward or linear process; rather it is a two steps forward, one step back process, characterised as much by frequent setbacks as by its incremental gains (cf. Pascual-Leone, 2009).

EXPERIENCING THE CORE EMOTIONAL PAIN AND IDENTIFYING THE UNMET NEEDS

Once the core painful emotions are accessed in the session (e.g., with the help of the experiential tasks described above), it is important for the therapist to help the client become capable of staying with the accessed painful emotions. It is important to help the client tolerate painful emotions and differentiate their various facets and associated meanings, without succumbing to emotional avoidance or collapsing into secondary emotions such as hopelessness or helplessness. Differentiation of the painful core emotions can be helped primarily through a sensitive empathic responding that promotes emotional regulation (Greenberg, 2011). The therapist's sensitive empathic responding also counters feelings of shame, loneliness, and/or fear by promoting feelings of acceptance, safety, and an isolation-breaking connection and caring.

The therapist's empathic presence, however, may also need to be supplemented by guiding instructions and psychoeducation. Such interventions are important in order to explain to the client why it is good to stay with painful experiences; that painful feelings can be regulated and modulated via an exploration of their nuances and their symbolisation in narrative (Angus and Greenberg, 2011). Clients can be explicitly instructed to observe how the feelings feel. They can be encouraged to recognise that they are more than their felt uncomfortable feelings, even when those uncomfortable feelings feel all-encompassing and self-defining (as evidenced for instance, in the verbalised felt-sense *I am worthless.*). The therapist may encourage the client to stay with painful feelings (e.g., shame) and observe how those painful emotions feel, what action tendencies are in them (e.g., to shrink or hide), and what thought processes accompany them (e.g., thoughts such as *I am worthless, flawed.*). The therapist may encourage the client to observe that although those painful feelings are powerful, they are not all that there is to the client, that the client is more than those feelings, and that those feelings do not define who the client is, but rather contain important information for the client about his or her unmet needs. The client may also be taught that it is possible to change these feelings (see the next chapter), and the client can be taught that feelings can shift and be followed by other, differing emotional experiences that may be more comforting for the client.

At the moment of felt core pain, the therapist may also use psychoeducation and may point out to the client how certain feelings feel (e.g., the shrinking feeling of shame), why they are so difficult to bear (e.g., evolutionarily, they meant exclusion and thus lower chances for survival), or what are they informing us of (which needs are not being fulfilled—e.g., to be accepted). As the client accesses core painful feelings repeatedly in therapy, it is hoped that his or her capacity to bear difficult emotions increases. Correspondingly, it is hoped that there is a decrease in both the client's need to avoid these painful feelings and in the client's fragility with regards bearing them.

The differentiation of felt pain is emotionally very powerful and difficult for the client as in essence they are touching on what is the most painful in their experiencing. In Chapter 4 we looked at an example of a client first touching on core emotional pain (*I needed mum.*) in the context of a supporting and empathic therapeutic relationship. In the excerpt below we look at the same process from the perspective of how pain can be differentiated in an empty-chair dialogue between the client and her imagined mother:

Client: *But I know, from my kids growing up that we should have had that childhood. And we didn't (choking quality).* [The client is in touch with her sadness.]

Therapist: *I gave it to my children.* [The therapist is empathic and evocative through highlighting the contrast between the client's caring for her children and how she was cared for by her mom.]

Client: *I gave it to my kids (voice strained with emotion, words are almost inaudible).* [The client is overwhelmed by emotion here, showing that the experience is too painful and difficult to be with.]

Therapist: *Yeah.*

Client: *You should have given it to me (almost a whisper, crying).* [This is directed to her imagined mother sitting in the empty chair.]

Therapist: *There's pain in it, and anger, yes? It's painful what's missing yes when it was like this.* [The therapist is picking on the different aspects of the hurt (pain/sadness and anger) and thus attempts to differentiate it.]

Client: *My kids would never see what you put us through (crying). We'd tell them sometimes (sniff) but they can laugh about it, because they never had to live with it, and they never will.* [The client is unfolding the experience in further narrative.]

Therapist: *Yes, but it's not laugh, laughing for me yes.*

Client: *It was never laughing for me.*

Once the core primary emotions are accessed, differentiated, and stayed with, the therapist facilitates the client to focus on the unmet needs embedded in those core painful emotions. As explained in the introductory chapters, painful emotion informs the clients about unmet needs. The felt emotions reflect an interaction between the need and the individual's perceived response to that need (e.g., need—*I want to be accepted*; perception—*I am being put down*; emotion—*I feel deflated*). The unmet needs (e.g., to be accepted, loved, or protected) embedded in core primary painful feelings are articulated most easily when the client is fully experiencing the painful emotion. Therefore, when the core painful emotions are accessed by a client in therapy, when they are fully savoured by the client, differentiated, and put to narrative, the therapist moves his or her focus with the client on to what it is that the client needs, what is most missing, and so on. Such interventions facilitate the client to articulate what is needed as the felt experience will be guiding him or her. If the client, for instance, feels shame in the face of judgement and is guided to attend to what the felt shame indicates he or she most needs, the likely response from the client will be that he or she needs acceptance and approval.

The articulation of unmet needs helps to further differentiate the client's painful emotions as the articulated needs capture another aspect of the felt experience. Thus even a formulation of a sense of need contributes to the client's regulation of painful, dreaded emotions. The interplay between an unfolding differentiation of unmet needs and further differentiation of the felt pain is visible in the following example. (In Chapter 4, we looked at how the client Ann accessed core pain. Here, we look at a later section from that same dialogue, focusing on Ann's articulation of unmet needs and further differentiation of painful emotion.)

Therapist: *Yeah, yeah ... It's like full of pain. The pain that I can feel now, I can stay with it.* [The therapist is speaking on behalf of the client.] *Yeah ... So I need you, what would you need from her?* [The therapist is explicitly focusing on facilitating the client's articulation of an unmet need.]

Ann: *(sniff) Not an apology, but an explanation (voice collapses with emotion). And back then when we were kids, I needed a mother (tearful).* [The expression of need to have a mother—one can infer needs to be loved, protected, cared for, etc.]

Therapist: *Ok.*

Ann: *I didn't know it at the time. Cos I thought life would be better without you.*

Therapist: *Yeah.*

Ann: *And it was. God forbid me for saying it but it was.*

Therapist: *Yeah, yeah ... this is how it felt. I just wanted you not to be there, so I have, I can achieve some peace or something yeah?* [The therapist capturing different aspects of the client's experience in an empathic responding.]

Ann: *Yeah (crying) but I was still not getting the peace from her.*

Therapist: *But I know that I needed a real mother, yeah? For you to be there as a mother.* [Again, focus on the need.]

Ann: *Yeah, and I'd nobody to turn to (very tearful).*

Therapist: *So there was nobody for me there, yeah?*

Ann: *No (crying).*

Therapist: *It just aches.* [The therapist focusing on the experiential aspect of the painful emotional experience.]

Ann: *With things like that, when my kids are sick. I know I have [my husband] and I know he's there and he does everything he needs to do for me. But then I would have liked my own mother to be there (choking with tearfulness). Just to go and say, 'Ma, I need a cup of tea, sit and talk to me.' Try and help me deal with it. Instead of having to let me deal with it myself. Which I'm gonna have to keep on doing (with a lot sadness and sobing).*

Therapist: *Yeah.*

Ann: *But it would have been nice just to have her there.*

Therapist: *Yeah 'I needed you there'.* [Focusing on the unmet need and expressed sadness.]

Ann: *Yeah (crying).*

Therapist: *I was so on my own just to deal with all of it.*

Ann: *It's not even that. It's every now and then a girl needs her Mum.* [The client expressing her need.]

Therapist: *Yeah. Just to have you there.*

Ann: *The boys mightn't need them. But every now and again a girl does need her Mum (crying heavily).* [The client here is clearly accessing her core painful feelings of abandonment, rejection, and not feeling loved and articulates her unmet need for her mother's love.]

Therapist: *Yeah. Every girl needs it and I needed it as well. I needed you so much yes in my life.* [The therapist is empathically echoing the client's experience.]

Ann: *I did (crying) and it's only now that my own kids are growing up. I realise that because I'm there for them, and they know I am, and they know I always will be ... It's very annoying, and it is very hurtful that she wasn't there for us, or for me.* [More elaboration of the aspects of the pain.]

Therapist: *Yeah, you were not there for me.*

Ann: *She wasn't there for me.*

Therapist: *You weren't there for me. Yeah and this is just so painful. And it's just such a loss yea? And such a sense of being on my own in my life.* [The therapist is offering more empathic differentiation.]

Ann: *(nodding) Yeah. Even though I have [my husband] and I have the kids, I still feel lonely. You'd love to just go up to them and say 'I'm going to me Mam' (crying).*

Therapist: *Every girl needs it, and I need it and I needed it.*

Ann: *Yeah (sniff).*

An articulated need, in the context of a salient and powerful emotion, is a heartfelt need that naturally triggers compassion in the therapist, as was naturally the case in the therapy session described above. It increases the chance of the client being able to experience self-compassion (for instance, in a chair dialogue when the client is instructed to look from the other chair at their own self in pain), and it also increases the chances of the client experiencing a sense of entitlement to have his or her needs met.

It is envisaged that the accessed painful emotions are at the centre of problematic emotion schemes and self-organisations. These painful emotions and associated unmet needs have their origin in past or current salient emotional injuries. It is envisaged that the work on any particular powerful emotional experience is also work on the overall schematic structure and thus also on the dominating self-organisations (cf. Greenberg, 2011). In the next chapter we will look at how accessed core painful emotions can be transformed through the accessing, experiencing, and expressing of (self) compassion and protective anger. Before we move on to exploring this transformation work, however, we will first briefly look at how the core pain was accessed in the case of Ann, the case conceptualisation for whom was presented in Chapter 5.

Case of Ann—strategy for therapy

In the previous chapter we looked at the case of Ann. We could see her core sense of loneliness, her sense of not feeling loved, and her terror that those close to her might be hurt. We identified a core sense of shame that somehow her qualities were responsible for the lack of love from her mother. We could see her negative self-treatment and also her profound avoidance of felt experience, fuelled by a fear of potential triggers that could bring on pain. We will look now at how Ann's core pain and unmet needs were accessed in therapy. In the next chapter we will focus on how this core pain was transformed in therapy.

The therapist's first task in therapy, after building an alliance with Ann and after trying to help her to regulate the strong emotional arousal present in the session, was to distil Ann's core underlying pain. This aim was pursued by actively evoking and exploring painful situations. In the first instance, current pain-provoking situations were explored; later exploration moved on to memories of events that were formative in creating Ann's core pain and which resembled current pain-provoking situations. The link between the currently felt pain and historic similar experiences was established, for instance, by asking Ann at points when she felt feelings of profound loneliness in the session: 'When do you remember feeling like this earlier on in your life?'

Accessing core pain was difficult mainly because Ann often collapsed into states of global distress whenever core pain was touched on. The therapist responded to such collapses with a compassionate presence, but also with calming interventions such as clearing a space (Elliott et al., 2004), an intervention that tries to put upsetting and overwhelming issues aside for the moment (see above; also Chapter 8). The therapist also spent a lot of time at the end of the early sessions making sure that when leaving his office, Ann was emotionally regulated, and not overwhelmed with distress. The therapist also explored with Ann things she could do outside of sessions in order to support her developing capacity to regulate feelings of overwhelming distress (e.g., going for a walk). For some clients who collapse easily into global distress, the facilitation of protective anger may serve as a sort of steering rod; however, this was a limited option for Ann, as her experiences of anger typically came in the form of maladaptive, secondary reactive anger. Expressions of anger were also followed by feelings of shame at having become angry, thereby precipitating further collapses into the global distress.

Access to core pain was also obstructed by Ann's self-interruptive and avoidance processes. The emotional avoidance processes were mainly visible through a constant worry process that caused Ann to become emotionally flooded and exhausted. This process was eventually counteracted by asserting Ann's need for rest, and by increasing Ann's awareness of the impact of her worry process on herself (e.g., tiredness) as well as her attendant need to be free and playful. Eventually Ann became capable of accessing a protective anger that countered and opposed her self-worrying process (*I've had enough of you.*). In one worry dialogue, she imagined the worry-producing part of herself as a bush that was growing inside her, and she enacted throwing it away from her. She then practiced this standing-up-to-the-worry process at home and noticed that she became increasingly capable of stopping her worry.

Ann's core painful feelings were accessed mainly through the use of chair dialogues. For instance, Ann engaged in imaginary dialogues with her neighbour's children, who were growing up without their mother. She identified with the pain they believed they must have felt, openly admitting that she herself knew how they felt. She also engaged in imaginary dialogues with her father, whose potential loss she believed she would not be able to tolerate. Mainly however, Ann dialogued with her mother (see the excerpt above) and through these empty-chair dialogues, accessed her sense of abandonment, loss, feeling unloved, and craving for her mother's love. She also accessed core painful feelings of shame (*something in me is flawed and unlovable*) not only in imaginary dialogues with her mum but also in self-self dialogues, in which she attacked herself for who she was (in a manner similar to how her mother used to attack her). Enactment of self-attacks evoked feelings of shame and a sense of being flawed and unlovable. She also articulated hate for her own distress, anxiety, vulnerability, controlling behaviour, and the anger that came with memories of being neglected.

Once Ann's core pain was accessed, it was important to put it into language. This involved both consistently empathic responding, as well as a sustained effort to help Ann stay with her painful feelings. The therapist coached Ann both to stay with her painful feelings and to put them into a narrative that would allow her to make meaning from them (e.g., *Breath. Just see how loneliness feels. Try not to run away from it. You are more than that empty sense inside. It is just a powerful feeling. This is how the loneliness feels. If you were to put it to words how does it feel? Speak to you mum [imagined in the other chair] from that loneliness. What do you say to her?*). The most decisive task was, however, to help Ann articulate the needs embedded in her core painful emotions (cf. the description in the excerpt quoted above, e.g., 'I needed mum'.).

Ann's core painful feelings were regularly accessed in the middle part of therapy, where they were differentiated, put to language, and expressed in the context of imaginary dialogues. This usually happened in the natural flow format, when the feelings were first attended to, then labelled and finally expressed, so the emotion would be fully present in the room (Greenberg, 2002). Ann's unmet needs were similarly attended to, named, and expressed. Together, these therapeutic processes laid the ground for the transformation work outlined in the next chapter.

7 Strategy for therapy—transforming core emotional pain

The accessing of underlying pain (i.e., primary maladaptive emotions) in the session and the articulation of unmet needs leads naturally to a point where the work of therapy is to facilitate a response to that felt pain, and to those needs associated with it. This response is facilitated by the therapist when he or she compassionately responds to the client and justifies the client's entitlement to have unmet needs met. Even more importantly in EFT, the client is facilitated to enact compassionate and protective responses in imaginary dialogues with salient others and with the self. These enactments are important because the client is then not only the object of compassion or validation, but is also a subject, an active agent capable of generating self-compassion and a healthy anger-based self-protection.

The accessing and generation of these two (self-compassion and protective anger) primary adaptive emotional stances is transformative; alleviating pain, and countering and reducing the overwhelming and all-consuming nature of maladaptive emotional states such as sadness/loneliness/loss, shame and terror/fear. As these maladaptive emotions are increasingly followed, very closely in session, by experiences of compassion and protective anger, maladaptive emotions become less dominant and less central to the client's self-organisation. As compassion and protective anger are generated more regularly in the therapy process, the client becomes more emotionally resilient and flexible (Pascual-Leone, 2009) and learns to go swiftly from felt pain to a more soothing and protective, compassionate, and assertive stance. Analyses of successful cases of therapy show that as therapy progresses, successful clients become increasingly capable of accessing core painful feelings; articulating the unmet needs in those painful feelings; and responding to those painful feelings with self-compassion and protective anger (Crowley et al., 2013; Dillon et al., 2014; Keogh et al., 2013; McNally et al., 2014). The client's dominant and problematic self-organisations are thus transformed, becoming more flexible and resilient as the client gains increased access to primary adaptive emotions.

In therapy, both the enactment of compassion and protective anger, and the 'letting in' (i.e., the experience of being the beneficiary) of such experiences is important. For this reason, both need to be fully savoured by the client. Doing so contributes to the transformation of emotion scheme configurations as a significant amount of time is spent with the client feeling new experiences which are corrective and which balance painful experiences. Interestingly, research has shown that time spent in these healing experiences often leads to the client spontaneously grieving past hurts (Pascual-Leone and Greenberg, 2007; Timulak et al., 2012, etc.). Although such grieving is painful, it is not as hurtful or overwhelming as the distress previously experienced by the client. Rather it tends to contain a letting-go quality; while the client still feels sad, the grieving also brings a sense of relief.

This type of healthy, adaptive grieving appears in particular to be a response to expressions of compassion, whether from the therapist to the client, or from the client to him- or herself. On the other hand, validation provided by the therapist to the client and expressions of protective anger by the client, have both been shown to bring about experiences of empowerment. The experience of empowerment is a very resourceful emotional state, and such experiences are particularly visible in successful cases (e.g., Crowley et al., 2013; Keogh et al., 2013).

We will now have a detailed look at how transformation is facilitated in the context of both the therapeutic relationship and imaginary dialogues. Again, such dialogues can take place both with emotionally salient others who are linked to the client's pain, as well as with pain inducing parts of the client's own self.

TRANSFORMING EMOTIONAL PAIN IN IMAGINARY DIALOGUES WITH EMOTIONALLY SALIENT OTHERS

The basis of therapeutic change in EFT is the presence of a caring, compassionate, and validating therapeutic relationship. The therapist acknowledges the client's pain, communicating compassion and empathy toward the client. The therapist also provides validation for the client, both by the fact that he or she is a witness to the client's pain, and by communicating the belief that the client deserves to have his or her needs met. This therapeutic relationship in turn facilitates the emotional transformation work in EFT. This transformation work mostly occurs during experiential empty-chair and two-chair tasks: imaginary dialogues in which the client enacts painful triggers in order to access painful emotions, experience these emotions, and respond to the unmet needs contained in those painful emotions. The main difference between the compassion and validation provided by the therapist, and that enacted by the client, is that in imaginary dialogues, the client not only receives compassion, but becomes an agent capable of generating and expressing compassion and protective anger. The client thus learns to initiate internal self-processes that increase his or her emotional resilience and flexibility (cf. Pascual-Leone, 2009).

The most significant roles in imaginary dialogues are often those played by salient figures, either from the client's past or present, who in some way shaped the client's emotional injuries (for an overview of EFT work with imaginary dialogues, see Elliott et al., 2004; Greenberg et al., 1993; for an overview of the empirical work which led to the development of the model of working with the salient other, see Greenberg and Foerster, 1996; Greenberg and Malcolm, 2002;

Paivio and Greenberg, 1995). Inevitably, the salient other is evoked in the other chair because for some reason, features of that salient other trigger the client's pain. The previous chapter elaborated on how one client accessed feelings of loneliness in a dialogue with an unresponsive mother (*I feel so much on my own, I needed mum to be there for me.*). Once the evoked painful feelings are fully experienced by the client in a dialogue, and once the unmet needs are articulated and expressed to the other, the therapist typically checks whether the witnessing of such pain brings any softening in the stance of the enacted imagined other (i.e., whether the enacted other can in any way communicate a compassionate response to the present pain).

The manner in which the enacted imagined other responds to the pain expressed by the self in the experiencer chair varies greatly from client to client, and often can be dependent upon what the imagined other was like in real life. So for example, if in real life the imagined other was an individual who on some occasions was capable of being responsive to the client's needs, there is a chance that within the imaginary dialogue, the client may spontaneously enact the imagined other responding compassionately to expressions of pain and need. In other words, once the client in the role of the other sees the hurt expressed in the experiencer chair and the unmet needs contained in that hurt, he or she, enacting the other, is more likely to respond in a compassionate manner, if such a response was within the repertoire of the enacted significant person in real life. Therefore, while the therapist wants to access core pain, and thus instructs the client to enact the hurtful other (trigger) in order to evoke that pain, once this hurt is accessed, the therapist is also interested in checking for the client's response to that pain when he or she is in the role of the other. For example, the therapist can say, 'Can you see her hurt? She needs you to be a mum for her. What is your response to her? How do you feel like responding to her from inside?' In general, it has been observed that the greater the quality of the expressed raw hurt in the context of the heartfelt expressed need (e.g., poignancy; intensity), the greater the likelihood that the client will spontaneously enact caring or compassionate aspects of the imagined other (cf. Hughes, Timulak, and McElvaney, 2014).

It is important to note that EFT is an experiential therapy. Therefore, while the therapist checks to see whether the client in the role of the other is moved by the expressed pain to a spontaneous expression of compassion, when this is not the case, the therapist respects where the client is at, and respects what he or she is currently capable of. So if after being prompted for a compassionate response, the client as the imagined other instead responds with more rejection, the therapist acknowledges this. When the client as the imagined other says, 'I do not care about what you need', the therapist asks the client as the imagined other to express this directly to the experiencer chair. In such instances, however, the therapist also seeks to bring into the client's awareness what it is that is driving such rejection. The therapist may even ask directly, for example, 'So what is driving you to be so harsh on her? What are you trying to do by rejecting her?' Such enquiry can sometimes help to bring into awareness what it is that lies behind such a harsh stance. For instance, the imagined other might reply, 'I am unhappy in my life and just cannot care about anybody else;

I do not have any capacity for it; I cannot care'. When such rejection is expressed (although now perhaps somewhat more meaningfully), the therapist asks the client to change chairs. Once the client is sitting in the experiencer chair, the therapist asks the client to attend to the impact of this treatment on the self. The client is asked how it feels to be rejected in this way after expressing such vulnerability and need; for example, 'What happens inside when you get that rejection "I don't care"? What does that do to you inside? Leaving aside the fact that you understand she was unhappy and had no capacity to care, what does it do to you, inside, when she says "I don't care"?' At this stage, we have observed that clients typically respond in one of two ways. Either the client collapses into unbearable global distress, expressing feelings of hopelessness and helplessness (e.g., *She never loved me and she never will. There will never be anybody who would really care and love me.*) or, more adaptively, he or she can respond spontaneously with protective anger (e.g., *It is not acceptable what you are saying. I deserve love and care. I always deserved it. Your problems are your problems, but I was just a child, and I deserved to have my mom.*).

If the client spontaneously expresses protective anger, the therapist validates this, and checks with the client what it feels like inside to be assertive in this way. Typically, clients report feeling a sense of relief and a sense of empowerment. This is a markedly different experience to the rejecting anger felt and expressed by clients during experiences of global distress, when anger is typically mixed with sadness and hurt, and when the client is more likely to feel desperate and angry for not being loved. Protective anger is subtler. It is self-defining, providing the client with a sense of his or her own self; a sense of his or her own value; and a sense of his or her own strength. It is the opposite of the upset and despair typically present in states of global distress.

Although some clients respond spontaneously to further rejection by the other with anger, this is not always the case, and even with those clients who do, it can often take a substantial period of time before the client is able to generate a good quality of protective anger. Rather than being able to hold onto protective anger, clients often collapse back into a state of global distress characterised by hopelessness, helplessness, and despair (*She never loved me and she never will. Nobody will.*). Such collapses are an indication of the level of the client's distress and vulnerability. In such instances, the therapist is compassionate and empathic. He or she tries to enable the client to get back in contact with their hurt in order that they can again express the core pain and the related unmet needs. The therapist seeks to help the client articulate fresh aspects of the pain. Once this pain is again articulated in a poignant manner, the therapist may ask the client who *would* have responded to that pain and need (e.g., the client's father), and then asks the client to enact this imagined, more compassionate other. Alternatively, the therapist may suggest to the client that he or she simply be his or her present self. The therapist then invites the client as his or her present self to the other chair and asks him or her: 'What do you feel toward that girl who feels so uncared for, and who so much wants to be loved?' If the client is then capable of generating compassion, the therapist asks him or her to enact and express it to the imagined vulnerable self in the experiencer chair. In such instances, compassion often comes with a lot of sadness, as the client is impacted by witnessing the pain of the self in the other chair. Both sadness and compassion are very connecting, and experiences of both contribute to breaking the felt sense of isolation and rejection. The client may be very upset and say something like: 'I see your pain, and I love you so much. I want to protect you, and care for you'. The therapist may capitalise on these emerging feelings by asking the client how it feels inside as he or she says these things, doing so in order that the client can fully savour the feelings of compassion. The client may then perhaps respond: 'Very caring and very sad to see her like this'.

The therapist's next task is to help the client let in these feelings of compassion. Clients with emotional difficulties often do not allow themselves accept compassionate experiences as they often, as a consequence of negative self-treatment (see below). have the sense that they do not deserve love or care. In order to facilitate the client's letting in of compassion, the therapist may say something like: 'Come here [back to the experiencer chair]. How does it feel inside to get that carrying response? Can you let it in?' As already noted, the client may not be able to let the compassion in and may say: 'I do not feel anything'. The therapist then has to respect the client. He or she reflects the client's experience as it is: 'Nothing comes through, nothing gets to the despair you feel inside. Certainly not an imaginary response. Can you tell her, "I do not feel anything"?' As the client enacts this non-acceptance of compassion and as the therapist accepts and validates it, the therapist may also gently suggest to the client that he or she tries to let the compassion in, for example, 'I know nothing came in, but could you just for the moment imagine letting it in? Could you try it? (pause) What does it do to you? How does it feel inside?' We have observed that as therapy and sessions progress, even clients who initially struggle to allow in experiences of compassion eventually become able to do so (cf. Crowley et al., 2013; Keogh et al., 2013). Once this happens, the therapist wants to further capitalise on it, and seeks to bathe the client in the compassion and its impact. He or she may ask the client: 'So how is it inside when you let it in?' Clients usually respond by reporting that they observe a variation of relief, for example, 'I feel relieved'. The therapist may want to further expand the client's experience, so he or she might ask the client to express these feelings to the other chair: 'Can you tell her, "I feel relieved"?' When clients follow this suggestion, they often report feeling even more relieved. Once again, the therapist checks with the client as to how it feels to express what they are experiencing, in order that these changed and emerging feelings are further brought into the client's awareness.

Once compassion is generated and its acceptance facilitated, the therapist can focus on the development of protective anger. With the client, the therapist might revisit the rejecting other's behaviour (trigger) in order to explore how the client might protect him- or herself against it: 'So when she says "I don't care", what will you do with it? Will you let it destroy you inside? What do you want to do with it now at this moment [stressing the present moment of strength rather than returning when the client was not able to stand up for the self]?' The therapist asks questions like this with the hope that the client will be better able to support him- or herself. The therapist is hoping that the client will speak from a stronger inner sense, in other words, that a more assertive self will emerge. Such a position might be represented in statements such as 'I deserved to have a caring mum, but if I get this type of treatment, I will not allow it to destroy me'; or 'I am a good person inside and I deserve(d) love'. Once the client is able to generate some anger (if therapy progresses well), the therapist facilitates the client to embody and enact this anger fully, for instance, by asking the client to express this anger to the imagined other: 'Tell it to her'. Again, as the client does so, the therapist checks: 'And how does it feel?' Clients typically respond by describing some variation on a sense of empowerment, for example, 'I feel strong'. The therapist can further consolidate this emerging sense of empowerment by asking the client to enact that sense of empowerment, and to express it to the other: 'Tell her, I feel strong'. As the client does so, the therapist once again checks how it feels inside to express this sense of strength, and once again, doing so usually brings about an even more solid feeling of empowerment. To consolidate this emerging sense, the therapist may ask the client to say 'I am strong' directly to the therapist: 'Could you say it to me?' This is often quite difficult for clients who are not typically very assertive in their day-to-day lives. Expressing one's own sense of strength directly to the therapist—a living, breathing human being who is present in the room—is a qualitatively different exercise to expressing such feelings to an imaginary other. The client may, therefore, first express the words 'I feel strong' with some shakiness, but after more encouragement and coaching from the therapist (who may ask the client to repeat the expression a few times), the client is usually able to own the solid sense of self more and more.

While the generation of compassion and protective anger becomes progressively easier for clients in successful therapies (Crowley et al., 2013; Keogh et al., 2013), the facilitation of such processes is a very complex task that occurs across multiple sessions. Indeed, it is most evident in long-term therapies, in which contrast and change across time are more visible. Initially, it may be very difficult for the client to access any compassion or protective anger, and the therapist has to work hard to get at least some of these experiences during the session. However, in successful therapy, as sessions progress, clients become capable of generating more and more of these experiences. Such experiences are also generated more quickly in response to experiences of distress, and as therapy progresses, they also improve in terms of quality of their presence.

What may also happen is that the client in some cases may be able to get compassion from the 'imagined' person who triggered the injury. This usually happens if in reality the relationship with the person also had positive aspects to it. Whilst the reasons for this are not fully established, we can speculate that as hitherto avoided aspects of the other's hurtful behaviour are expressed, eventually, caring memories of the other that were inaccessible due to emotional avoidance of the injury-related issues also spontaneously come to the surface.

Whilst compassion is elicited through expressing and witnessing one's pain, protective anger is stimulated by highlighting the hurtful aspects of the other's behaviour. Once accessed, protective anger requires repeated validation from the therapist and repeated experiencing by the client, in order that he or she becomes capable of generating a resolve to protect him- or herself. As experiences of protective anger emerge in therapy, and as the client learns to stand up for the self, without fear of being attacked or without collapsing into self-judgment (e.g., self-criticism; that assertiveness is not acceptable), this part of the client's self becomes increasingly available to the client when needed outside of the therapy session. One must, however, be aware that building self-compassion and protective anger often depends on resolving the negative self-treatment processes that block or hinder the easy generation of such adaptive emotional experiences (see section on negative self-treatment transformation below).

Let us have a look at an example of how self-compassion and protective anger can be built in a therapy session in the context of an imaginary dialogue of the client Laura, who fought her depression and anxiety with an emotionally salient hurtful other (her unresponsive and often blaming mother):

Laura:	*Well she never loved me.*
Therapist:	*Try to say it. Yes? I mean it's very hurtful. Yes? 'But you never really loved me'.* [The therapist encouraging ownership of the core pain, its experience and expression.]
Laura:	*She never did.*
Therapist:	*... was sense inside. Yes? 'You never really loved me'.* [The therapist using evocative empathic responses.]
Laura:	*You always made me feel like I wasn't ...*
Therapist:	*Yeah.*
Laura:	*... I wasn't worth it. Or I wasn't ...* [The client touching on primary shame.]
Therapist:	*Yeah.*
Laura:	*I was an inconvenience.*
Therapist:	*Yeah.*
Laura: `	*You always made me feel like that.*
Therapist:	*Yeah. But it's almost like: 'What's there to life?' Yes? 'If my Mum doesn't love me.' or something? Yes? It's like, 'I just want some small thing'. Yes?*
...	
Laura:	*All I ever wanted when I was a kid was for her to stop.*
...	
Therapist:	*Because this is how it felt. This is how I saw it. Yes? And it's almost ... And it's almost like 'I will ... I hold you accountable for it'. Yes? 'It was all your responsibility'.* [The therapist fostering protective anger.]
Laura:	*Yeah.*
Therapist:	*'It wasn't ok. I shouldn't have gone through it'. Yes?*
Laura:	*Mmmm.*
Therapist:	*'Regardless of how you suffered or how bad it was for you. You shouldn't have ...'*
Laura:	*Yeah.*

Therapist: *'... take me through it. To take me ...'*

Laura: *She ... She ... You were ... She ... You were the mother ... you should have done it. You should have been there for me.* [The expression of need in the context of protective anger.]

...

Therapist: *Could you switch now? So now, as Mum in your head. Yes? Just ... It's just in your head. Yes? What does she say to this? 'I shouldn't have gone through it'.*

Laura [as the imagined mother]: *'I'm sick. You ... You have to get up and do these things for yourselves. I'm not able to be doing it. You're going to have to get up and look after yourself now'.* [The client enacts the imagined mother and as she does so, she can connect with her mother's unresponsive behaviour. The enacted mother stays unresponsive, although she is not directly attacking anymore, which can be seen as a slight softening.]

...

Therapist: *But is it really like 'I'm unresponsive'. Yes?* [The therapist highlighting the manner of remembered mother's treatment.]

Laura: *Yeah.*

Therapist: *'I can't understand what you're talking about'. Yes? 'I have no energy. I have no willingness'.* [The therapist respects where the client is and goes with the enactment of mother as unresponsive.]

Laura (as mum): *Yeah. 'I'm not able'.*

Therapist: *'I'm not able'.*

Laura (as mum): *'Go down and get me cigarettes'.*

Therapist: *Yeah. Yeah. 'So you're just here to serve me' or something 'and I really can't be bothered by you'.*

...

Laura (as mum): *'And don't lose the money'.*

...

Therapist: *Yeah. Ok. Could you swap now? What do you say to her when she says 'Don't lose the money. Don't ...'*

Laura: *'Get up off your arse and go yourself'.* [Rejecting anger mixed with protective anger appears.]

...

Laura: *And I know I make mistakes with me own kids and I know I'm not perfect. But I wasn't ... I wasn't as bad as her.*

Therapist: *Yeah.*

Laura: *I wasn't.*

Therapist: *Tell her. 'I wasn't as bad as you'. Yeah?*

Laura: *'I wasn't as bad as you'.* [This is a self-worth supporting expression that contains a flavour of protective anger and empowerment.]

Therapist: *'And I know I was'. Yeah?*

Laura: *And it gets me down that I get so angry at her.* [This is a good example of self-criticism that stops the experience and expression of adaptive anger. This now needs to be focused on in the work. We will have a look at working with negative self-treatment later in this chapter.]

After a digression into self-criticism for feeling angry at her mother (which we will focus on further below), the therapist and the client manage to get back in contact with the client's vulnerable experiences of not feeling loved and being rejected. The therapist can then probe for a compassionate response to the witnessed pain.

Therapist: *So it's like ... 'I was so lonely that I, I became a loner' or something? Yes? 'Because they* [siblings], *kind of withdrew further' or something?*

...

Laura: *Mmm. So that's the way it's always been.*

Therapist: *Yeah. 'I had to deal with the big world immediately ...'.*

...

Laura: *... deal with the big bad world since I was about ten.*

Therapist: *Yeah. Yeah. Could you swap now? Yes? We'll try first as her. We'll see. What's the response from within her* [mum]*? Yes? I mean her in your head. Now. Yes? 'I stayed on my own'. Yes? 'I had nobody. No one'.*

Laura (as mum): *'I was here. I was sitting in the chair. I was here'.* [The client says this in a dismissive tone.]

...

Therapist: *... It's still 'I'm not taking it'.* [The therapist highlights and respects that the client when enacting the mother can connect only with this dismissive, uncaring part.]

Laura (as mum): *'I was here'.*

Therapist: *Yeah. But it's really 'I don't hear you'. Yeah? I mean what is the real message? ... 'I, I'm not listening'. Yes? Or 'I ... I don't take anything ...'.* [The therapist is highlighting the message given to the client.]

...

Therapist: *Could you come here now? So what do you say to that dismissive attitude? It's like, 'It's not a big deal. You should ... I was here. Whatever'.* [The therapist is probing for protective anger by highlighting the mistreatment.]

Laura: *You only hear, hear what you wanted to hear.* [More protective anger is emerging.]

Therapist: *Yeah.*

Laura: *And you only seen what you wanted to see.*

Therapist: *Yeah.*

Laura: *And if it wasn't about you ...*

Therapist: *Yeah.*

Laura: ... *it didn't happen.*

...

Therapist: *So it's like ... It's almost like 'It's no ... There's no worth in pouring my heart out because you're just not listening'. Yes?*

Laura: *No.*

A short while later, the therapist again probes for compassion toward the vulnerable experiences of not feeling loved and being rejected. This time the therapist tries to employ the current self and probes for whether the client as her adult self can be more caring toward her younger self that was so hurt.

Therapist: *Yeah. Ok. Could you come here? And I'll ... As you. Yes? Now as you. As adult you now. Yes? If you see yourself, I don't know, this ten year old. And she's saying: 'Alone in the world'. Yes? What would you say to her? What would you want to say to her? As an adult. Yeah? Or if you even imagine if it wasn't you but somebody else in that situation. Yes? A girl in that situation. Yes? What do you feel toward her? What would you tell her?* [This client is very self-reproaching; therefore, the therapist suggests that she imagine some other girl in order to mitigate for a potential self-rejection. The client is very caring to her children in real life, which suggests that she should be able to show that care to somebody who is vulnerable. She might also be less harsh toward a stranger than she might be to herself.]

Laura (as an adult self speaking to her younger self): *Now. I'd say 'Go tell the teachers'.* [Self-compassion starts to seep in.]

...

Therapist: *Yeah. 'You'll find somebody'. Yes? 'You'll ...'*

Laura: *'... tell my Dad'.*

Therapist: *Yeah. 'Tell your father. Tell the teachers'. Yes? 'It's not ok to stay alone with it'. Yeah?*

Laura: *No. It's not alright.*

Therapist: *Yeah.*

Laura: *'You need to ... stand up or try and ... Try your best to make yourself be heard. Try your best to ...'*

Therapist: *Yeah. 'Somebody will hear it'. Yeah?*

Laura: *'Someone eventually will hear it'. Yeah.*

Therapist: *Yeah.*

Laura: *'Or make ... Try and make them listen even though you're only a kid'.*

...

Therapist: *But it's like what? 'I wouldn't leave you alone in it. Or I would make sure that somebody listens. I'll make sure*

	... '[The therapist tries to promote agency and ownership in the client's compassion.]
Laura:	*And I'll be there for you to just come and talk or just ...*
Therapist:	*Ok.*
Laura:	*... come and have a cry or just come and ....*
Therapist:	*Yeah. 'I would be there for you'. Yes?*
Laura:	*Mmm. Just come and I give you a couple of hours' peace.* [The client now experiences compassion toward own wounded, vulnerable self.]
Therapist:	*'So I would create a safe haven for you'. Yes?*
Laura:	*Yeah.*
Therapist:	*'I would protect you'. Yes? 'From it'.* [The therapist further promotes the client's compassionate experience. The therapist wants the client to fully savour it.]
Laura:	*Mmm.*
Therapist:	*'As much as I could have'. Yeah. Because ...*
Laura:	*As much as I was ...*
Therapist:	*Yeah.*
Laura:	*... able to. I would just ...*
Therapist:	*Yeah.*
Laura:	*Stay, sit there. And just be a kid.*
Therapist:	*Ok. Tell her. Yes? 'Come and stay with me'.*
Laura:	*Come and stay with me. Just be a kid and have a childhood and not have to worry for a few hours ...*
Therapist:	*Ok.*
Laura:	*... before you had to go back to the madness.*

At this point, the therapist could also focus the client on how it feels when she provides a caring, compassionate, and protective presence to her imagined vulnerable younger self. The therapist could say: '*And how does it feel inside when you are there for her?*' This would be done so that the client could become more fully aware of the experience, could savour it, and might therefore more readily consolidate it. This is the type of experience the therapist wants the client to be capable of spontaneously generating after therapy ends.

As discussed above, many clients find it difficult to accept compassionate responses. Therefore, as the therapist helps the client to access compassion, he or she also checks with the client how it feels to receive compassion.

Therapist:	*Yeah. Yeah. Ok. Ok. Could you swap now. Yeah?*
Laura:	*Mmm.*
Therapist:	*See how it feels inside. Yes? Be the kid. Yeah? 'I have a safe place here. Don't worry about anything. Do whatever you want'. Yes? How does it feel?*
Laura:	*I'd still have to go back to the madness.* [The client has a difficulty letting in compassion. It could perhaps undermine

the full acknowledgment of adversity she went through if she admitted that an imagined caring other would heal the hurt.]

Therapist: *Yeah.*

Client: *'I'd still have to go back to them'.*

Therapist: *Yeah. 'I can't stay here forever' or something? Yeah?* [Therapist validates the client's despair.]

...

Therapist: *'I will have to go home there'. Yeah? 'And nothing will be good enough' or something? Yeah?*

Client: *Yeah. 'No matter what we do, it won't be good enough'.*

A minute later the therapist probes again to see whether the client can let in the compassion:

Therapist: *Yeah. Yeah. And how is it to hear 'Be a kid'. Yeah? 'Stay with me as much as you can'. How is it to hear it?*

Laura: *'Is it possible?' 'She'll come and get me'.* [The client is still not capable of letting compassion in, and instead hopelessness sets in.]

...

Therapist: *It's like: 'My life is so desperate that it won't be possible' or something? Yes? 'It won't be possible to get that safe space here'. Yeah.*

Laura: *Yeah.*

Therapist: *'So I need ...'. What would you need from her? From that adult self? Yes? That you see here. 'I need from you ... 'what? 'To have understanding for how difficult it really is for ...'.* [The therapist mobilises the unmet need.]

Laura: *Probably understanding. Yeah. And to make it go away. To make it stop happening. And to ... When I ... When I was a kid, for people to listen.*

Therapist: *'Make it safe for me. I need you to make it safe for me'. Yeah?*

Laura: *Yeah.*

Therapist: *Ok. Could you swap? Yeah? As an adult, yes, how do you respond to it? Yes? 'Make it safe. I will need you to make it safe for me. I will need you to listen'. Yes? 'Make the others listen'. What's your response from inside to her?* [The therapist wants to further facilitate any compassionate presence that the client can provide for herself.]

Laura (as an adult self speaking to her younger self): *Powerless.* [The client is not capable of being agentic and compassionate in the face of her own despair and suffering.]

Therapist: *Ok. Ok. But just see her need. Yeah. I mean it's heart-breaking in a way. Yes? Tell her, Yeah? 'I feel so powerless but if I had a power what would it be?'* [The therapist acknowledges powerlessness, but also probes for potential compassion.]

Laura: *I'd take her and run away.*

Therapist: *Ok. Tell her. Yes? 'I will take you and run away with you'. Yes?*

Laura: *I'll take you and run away and you wouldn't have to go through it.*

Therapist: *Yeah. 'So I would make a new life for you'. Yes? 'Somewhere ...*

Laura: *Yeah.*

Therapist: *... in family. New school. New friends. Somewhere safe.*

Laura: *Make you happy.*

...

Therapist: *Yeah. But it's like: 'I'm powerless but this is in my heart, yes, that I would do for you'. Yes? 'If I wasn't powerless. But I am powerless. This is what I wish for you'. Yes?*

Laura: *Yeah.*

Therapist: *'This is what you deserve'. Yeah? Yeah?*

Laura: *This is what I think you deserve.* [The client here is validating herself.]

Therapist: *Yeah.*

Laura: *This is what it should be like.*

Therapist: *Yeah. Yeah. 'It's really heart-breaking that I'm so powerless to do anything about it'. Yes? 'Because I would so much want to do it'. Yeah?*

Laura: *I would ...*

Therapist: *Yeah. No. I know. I know. But now this is the part that would do it for her. Yes? Ok. Could you come here? Yes? So how is it to hear it? Yes? It's like 'I would do, in my heart, yes, I would want a different life for you. I would run away'.* [The therapist is again probing the client to let in the compassion.]

Laura (in the experiencer chair where she was speaking as small her): *Impossible.* [The client still cannot let in any of the compassion.]

Therapist: *I know. But how is to hear it? Yes? I mean this is powerless but how is it to hear it? Yeah?* [The therapist persistently probes whether the client can let in the compassion.]

Laura: *Hopeful.* [The client starts tentatively let in some of the compassion.]

Therapist: *Ok. Ok. 'So it's ... It brings hope to hear it from you'. Yes?*

Laura: *Yeah.*

Therapist: *So it feels: 'I can feel it. I can feel what you're saying'.*

Laura: *Kind of.* [The client is still hesitant but lets some of the compassion in.]

Therapist: *I know it's difficult to let it in. Yes? But it's almost like 'I don't want to invalidate how difficult it was' or something? Yes? I mean how difficult it was at home. That's why it's so difficult to bring, to let anything like this in.* [The therapist highlights the struggle of letting the compassion in and guesses that the hopelessness experienced in reality makes it difficult to believe in the effects of an imaginary compassionate response.]

Laura: *Yeah. And I didn't want to get anybody into trouble.* [The client spontaneously reveals that she also expects that she could be blamed if she accepted some compassionate treatment—perhaps this is based on memories from childhood.]

Therapist: *Ok. Tell her. 'I don't want to get you in trouble'.*

Laura: *I don't want to get anybody into trouble.*

Therapist: *Yes? 'I don't want to burden and bother anybody'.*

Laura: *No. I don't want to get anybody into trouble. I don't even want to get me Mum into trouble.*

...

Therapist: *Yeah. But ultimately it shouldn't have happened. Yeah*? [EFT is a relational therapy, and the therapist now speaks authentically for himself as he is moved by the client's suffering and wants to express his caring.]

Laura: *No.*

Therapist: *I'm telling you. Yes?*

Laura: *Yeah.*

Therapist: *I see and I hear it. Yeah? And I'm powerless to go back in time. Yes?* [The therapist authentically responds from inside of him. He is genuinely moved and feels very caring toward the client].

Laura: *Mmm.*

Therapist: *But you shouldn't have gone through it. Yeah? Nobody should. Not a girl, small girl.*

Laura: *No one should have.*

Therapist: *Yeah.*

Laura: *No one should have. And I'd love to be able to turn back the clock ...*

Therapist: *Yeah.*

...

Laura: *It'll never happen.*

Therapist: *Yeah. But you have it in your heart. Yes? When you sit here. You gave it to your children as well. Yes?*

Laura: *I hope so.*

After an exchange like this, the therapist helps the client to savour the experience of relief (e.g., the emerging hopefulness that can be seen in the above example). The client is, therefore, helped to access and experience his or her core painful emotions (e.g., being rejected, unloved, worthless), adaptive emotional responses to those painful feelings (e.g., feelings of being protected, cared for, or loved), and the feelings of relief that these adaptive emotional responses give rise to. Similarly, experiences of protective anger are important to savour, as they offer a firm anchor against feelings of self-deprecation, and lead to a sense of empowerment. In general both of those processes, (1) the transformation of core pain through compassion, and (2) the transformation of core pain through protective anger, are equally important. Clients vary in their capacity to engage in these processes. Some clients have difficulty accessing self-compassion whilst others may struggle more with allowing themselves to be angry at mistreatment they have experienced. Generally speaking, the therapist seeks to balance both processes, within the overall therapy, and also within individual sessions.

Hurt and unmet needs are the opposite sides of the same coin, and both need to be responded to with validation and the sense of deservedness that is explicit in protective, empowering anger. Although imaginary dialogues are pivotal in this process, as they allow the client to experience painful and transformative emotions more fully and realistically, hurt and need can also be accessed and responded to through other forms of enactment, and through the real relationship between the therapist and the client. In the family and couple versions of EFT, these goals are achieved through enactments between the actual client participants in the session (cf. Greenberg and Goldman, 2008; Johnson, 2004).

The process outlined above, namely a compassionate responding to need backed by protective anger, has been observed to lead, naturally, to a process of grieving (cf. McNally et al., 2014; Pascual-Leone and Greenberg, 2007). Clients typically proceed to recount the difficulties and adversities that they encountered; however, while this recounting brings sadness, the sadness is rarely upsetting or overwhelming. Instead, it has typically been observed to have a calm, letting-go quality, the client often speaking in a manner indicating a degree of reconciliation with what has happened. In the case of Laura, the exchange detailed above was followed by a period of reflection where Laura compared her and her children's childhood, and expressed thankfulness that her children did not fully understand what she had gone through in her own childhood. Again, whilst Laura's sadness and grief were evident as she spoke, her emotional expression was much calmer and composed than during initial stages of therapy.

Transformative emotional experiences in EFT are typically experienced in dialogues with emotionally salient others, or in dialogues with parts of the self. If core painful feelings, like in the example above, stem from a specific relationship with a significant other, it is often particularly powerful if the enactment of care and validation comes from the imagined other. However, in EFT such dialogues are never scripted; rather, the therapist checks for spontaneous emotional experience and expression of that experience. That said, it should be evident at this stage that the EFT therapist does intentionally facilitate the imaginary dialogue and does seek to facilitate specific processes. For instance, the therapist actively probes for compassion by helping the client to witness their own accessed and expressed pain in the other chair; he or she encourages the client's protective anger by highlighting the mistreatment that the client is getting from the hurtful person, now imagined in the other chair; or he or she probes for the client's resilience through the use of paradoxical interventions. (In this last instance, for example, a client who cannot stand up for the self might be instructed, 'So tell him I will be your slave forever' with the hope that the client will reject such subjugation, and instead stands up for the self by saying, 'I do not want to be your slave, I will not be your slave'.).

Clinical experience suggests that people who in reality, had a mixture of both negative and positive experiences with the salient other can, as therapy progresses, often access a more positive other in the later stages of imaginary dialogues. This typically happens after the core hurt has been fully expressed and unmet needs articulated (cf. Greenberg and Malcolm, 2002). It appears that many clients can then enact the imagined significant other as compassionate, protective, and/or validating. Hughes et al.'s (2014) small study showed that a sequence of several dialogues can be decisive in this respect, and the 'softening' of the imagined (remembered) significant other can come, not in the first, but rather in later dialogues/sessions. In the above quoted excerpt for example, Laura was not capable of enacting a compassionate response from her imagined mother. Enacted in the other chair, Laura's imagined mother remained dismissive and unresponsive. The therapist, therefore, asked Laura to respond from her current adult self to her small, younger, hurt self (thus eliciting and enacting the compassionate response Laura's hurt needed.)

As EFT is an experiential therapy, it is the experience of compassion that is of primary importance; not who the compassion is expressed by. In this sense it is not that important which role the client enacts the compassionate response from. For this reason, the compassion expressed by Laura as her adult self in the excerpt above is as effective as if this compassion was expressed by Laura's enacted mother. That said, when the pain-provoking other is enacted in as powerful a way as in Laura's case, any compassion enacted as coming from that imagined other will perhaps be especially powerful and persuasive at undoing experiences of hurt triggered by perceptions of that other (e.g., see the dialogue between Tina and her imagined mother in Box 1). Indeed, although she was not capable of doing so in the therapy session quoted above, in one of her later sessions, Laura did become capable of spontaneously expressing compassion in the role of her mother. Our observation has been that the likelihood of this happening increases as successful therapy progresses, and this may perhaps be explained by a corresponding increase in emotional flexibility as therapy progresses. Greater emotional flexibility across therapy is visible in the manner in which successful clients become more capable of achieving higher-level emotional processing of problematic experiences, for example, achieving more easily and for longer periods of time, experiences of compassion, protective anger, relief, and empowerment (Pascual-Leone, 2009). Our studies have also shown that clients in successful therapies collapse into global distress less and less, can tolerate core pain more and more, and can more easily access compassion and protective anger (e.g., Crowley et al., 2013; Dillon et al., 2014; Keogh et al., 2013; McNally et al., 2014, see also original in-session work of Pascual-Leone and Greenberg, 2007; Pascual-Leone, 2009).

BOX 1 AN EXAMPLE OF A DIALOGUE IN WHICH THE CLIENT ENACTS REPARATORY EXCHANGE WITH THE IMAGINED SIGNIFICANT OTHER

This is an excerpt from the fourth dialogue between Tina and her mother, who had died a few months previously, and with whom Tina had a very difficult relationship. In childhood, Tina's mother put her down a lot and did not show her any love. Her mother never expressed any positive or warm feelings toward her. In the previous three dialogues, Tina enacted her imagined mother was not capable of expressed any softening. On the contrary Tina, as her imagined mother, responded with contempt to expressed vulnerability (*You are needy, weak.*). The current excerpt is from session 13. Therapy is progressing well, and as a consequence, Tina reports that things are going well for her in her life. In this session, she recalls that when she visited her paralysed mother shortly before her mother's death, Tina could see helplessness in her mother's eyes, but also a wish for connection. She even had a sense that her mother had tried to say that she loved her. The following is an excerpt from the dialogue that ensued in session 13 between Tina and her imagined mother.

Therapist: *If you picture her (mother) there yes, I mean what picture comes in mind, when she was old or some previous one or ...*

Tina: *The picture that just comes into mind now is of her just lying in the hospital bed there and being so helpless after being so domineering, to see her like that you know, and putting her hands out to me and looking at me and she didn't want me to go.*

Therapist: *Okay so can you sense that knot if you picture her there, yeah?*

Tina: *Yeah.*

Therapist: *So if you spoke from it, yes, what is it that you'd like to say to her or what's kind of going through your mind, yes, ...?*

Tina: *I kind of, I'm looking at her face pleading with me and in a way I feel I suppose guilty that I didn't, I couldn't get her out of there and do something for her ...*

...

Tina: *Helpless and you actually looked as though you really cared something for me in the hospital and I think maybe you did but it was, I feel sad that it was on your death bed really, that it was too late for me.*

Therapist: *... Okay so if you were her now yes* [nonverbally asking the client to change the chairs and sit in the imagined mother chair], *you are your mum and you see Tina, yes, there, what would you say to her? What would you like to say to Tina?*

Tina (as her imagined mum): *I love you. You know I do really don't you ...*
Therapist: *Yeah, so can you sense that love?* [The therapist wants the client to savour the feelings.]
Tina (still enacting her imagined mother): *Yeah ... I know, I know I've been wrong to you. I know, I know I was wrong to you in a lot of ways but you know I love you really, don't you?*
Therapist: *Yeah okay so it's like I'm really sorry yes about how I was.*
Tina: *Yeah, I'm really sorry for the way I was with you. Just, that's what I feel, you know, she would, she was like that at the end.* [The client is elaborating on the therapist's responses, which shows that she is fully immersed in the experience of compassion.]
Therapist: *So it's really I love you and I'm sorry, these are the things yes, and I so much want to be with you yes and I'm so sorry for everything that I did or that I didn't, yes, that we missed out on or something.*
Tina: *Yeah, Yeah, Yeah.*
Therapist: *And it's this sadness yes and love that comes across somehow yeah.*
Tina: *Mmmhmm yeah. She was as sad as what, mother's sad, like I wa—, I'm sad, she's sad but I made you sad Tina ...*
Therapist: *Yeah so I feel bad about this yes that I did?*
Tina: *Yeah, and I'd like to put it right before I die. Because you know she knew she was.*
Therapist: *So it's almost like forgive me for it yes or something.*
....
Tina: *Don't, don't leave me ... don't leave me, you know I love you, you know you're very special, you're the o—, you know you're my main thing in life.*
Therapist: *Yeah come here yes* [the therapist nonverbally pointing to the client to change the chair]. *How is it to hear it?*
Tina (in the experiencer chair): *Yeah it's good. I don't actually feel that anxious now you know.*
Therapist: *Okay, can you let it in yes? Like I love you, I'm sorry, forgive me yes, I should have done it differently, I missed you yes, I'm proud of you.*
Tina: *I think that you, mother, were a bit of a control freak, you, I actually think you were a, you were acting like, you're my mother but you seemed to always be a bit jealous of anything that I had. You never thought anybody was good enough for me, nobody ever would be and yet you didn't seem to like me but nobody was ever good enough.*
Therapist: *Yeah okay. So it's almost like you had your faults or something yes?*
Tina: *Yeah ... I see your faults.*
Therapist: *Okay and she's saying here forgive me yes so how is it?*
Tina: *Well yeah, of course, of course I forgive you.*
Therapist: *Can you yeah?* [The therapist is checking whether this expression is truly authentic.]
Tina: *Yeah, ah yeah.*
Therapist: *Can you say it to her?*
Tina: *I can forgive you, of course I can.*

(*Continued*)

Therapist:	*Okay. So, It's like, I'm fully aware of all those faults yes, but I can kind of now put it aside for a moment or something.*
Tina:	*I can come to terms with it. And I know by probably what's gone on in your own life has made you a bit like that you know.*
Therapist:	*So it's like it's a pity that those things were there yes but it's ...*
Tina:	*She'd buy you things and buy you ... but couldn't be nice do you know that kind of a way.*
Therapist:	*But it's almost like I have no need now to hold it against you yes or something even though I'm fully aware of it, yes and I won't kind of ...*
Tina:	*I've no need at all.*
Therapist:	*... forget about it or something yes but I've don't need to kind of punish you now.*
Tina:	*That's right but I do wish you had been a bit better with your grandchildren because you were even a bit, you were even very nasty with them on several occasions. You did the same to them as what you did to me ...*
Therapist:	*So you missed out there as well yes.*
Tina:	*Yeah, that's your loss really because you missed out, you know.* [The last few utterances show the grieving and sadness that is often visible after compassion is expressed and let in.] A portion of the transcript previously appeared in Witnessing client's emotional change in psychotherapy: An emotion-focused therapists experience of providing therapy. Timulak, L. *Journal of Clinical Psychology, 70,* 741–752. © 2014 John Wiley and Sons doi: 10.1002/jclp.22109

The transformation of emotional pain in imaginary self-self dialogues

As Chapter 5 on case conceptualisation showed (see Figure 1), the client's experience of the triggers of core pain is closely intertwined with efforts on behalf of the client to in some way shape or prepare the self for those triggers (e.g., to be stronger in the face of triggers; or to have some control over them). Often, this self-protective effort takes the form of a negative, hostile self-treatment; an urging of the self to toughen up, to be more vigilant, more clever, harder working, and so on. The bottom line within such self-treatments is almost inevitably self-blame and self-rejection; for example, 'If I was different, then I would not be pained by the situations or I would not encounter them'. In the previous chapter I showed how self-self dialogues are used to access core painful emotional experiences, often primary feelings of shame and worthlessness. Here I will focus on how that accessed core pain is transformed, focusing specifically on how this takes place within two-chair self-self experiential dialogues.

In the self-self dialogue (traditionally referred to in EFT as self-critic dialogue; Greenberg et al., 1993; Elliott et al., 2004—for empirical work on this task, see Greenberg, 1979; 1980; 1983; Greenberg and Dompierre, 1981; Greenberg and Higgins, 1980; Greenberg and Webster, 1982), the client is first asked to explicitly enact the self-criticism (or self-rejection; self-judgment), after a marker for this process arises during the client's self-exploration and recounting of upsetting experiences. For the enactment of the criticism, the client sits in the other chair (in EFT literature referred to as the critic chair) and expresses the criticism toward the self, imagined in the original client chair (referred to as the experiencer chair). This enactment is used to activate the core pain (see previous Chapter 6). Once the core pain is activated (e.g., shame at being inadequate), the therapist always facilitates the client, in the experiencer chair, to first be aware of the painful feelings; then to name them; and finally to express them to the critic (Greenberg, 2002). As the pain is unfolded and differentiated, the therapist asks the client to attend to the painful feeling and to see what that feeling needs, in other words, what the client needs from his or her own critical part. Frequently, articulated needs from the experiencer to the critic include a need to have a break from the criticism, or a need to be accepted rather than judged by the critic.

Once the pain is accessed, differentiated, and expressed, and the unmet needs articulated, the transformative work begins. First of all, the therapist asks the client to sit back in the critic chair and witness the expressed pain and unmet need(s). The client is instructed to see what his or her immediate experienced response is to the heart-breaking pain and the unmet needs expressed by the self from the experiencer chair. High-functioning clients who are capable of being self-compassionate in their day-to-day life often show signs of softening here. They are moved by the pain and try to respond in a caring way, for example, 'I am here for you, I understand you, I do not want you to feel put down, and so on'. More typically however, clients who present with anxiety, depression, or trauma have greater difficulty with self-compassion in their day-to-day life, and at this stage of the task are therefore often unable to be moved by the expressed pain and the unmet needs voiced by the self from the experiencer chair. Although at times such clients may show a partial softening, more typically they are non-accepting of the expressed vulnerability, instead escalating their own self-attack, accusing themselves of being weak, moany, or unable.

Such responses often help highlight the function of the critic. Although self-attacking, the critic may be so with the clear purpose of making the client more worthy, either in the here and now, or in the future as a consequence of the present treatment (e.g., *If I punish you, you will be tougher next time* other times position can be *You deserve punishment and nonresponsiveness.*). Clinical experience shows that clients who are so self-judgmental are often this way as a consequence of negative treatment by an authoritative significant other whose love they craved. In some instances, clients who did not feel the love of the significant other turned on themselves and blamed themselves for the other's (perceived) unloving treatment of them. Some clients appear to be self-punitive out of a fear that if they were to soften in their position toward the self, then that self would become even more unable, shameful, weak; in other words, a softening of the critical position might result in the self resigning from its efforts to meet the critic's (and implicitly perhaps the significant other's) demanding standards. It would often appear to be the case that clients hope that an escalated attack by the critic will stop the vulnerability expressed in the experiencer chair. The therapist's role in this escalation is to highlight the functions of negative self-treatment, and to help the client become aware of these functions (e.g., the therapist may say: 'It is like I have to punish you cause otherwise … what would happen otherwise?').

When the escalated negative treatment is expressed, the client is asked to move chairs, and to sit once again in the experiencer chair. What usually follows at this stage is very similar to the process which has already been described with reference to the empty-chair dialogue with a significant other. Asked how he or she feels in response to this attacking/critical treatment, the client typically either collapses into a state of global distress, expressing resignation, hopelessness, and helplessness (e.g., *I will never be accepted.*) or begins to stand up for him- or herself, experiencing and eventually expressing protective anger (e.g., *I do not deserve to be treated like that. I have a value.*). In the case of clients presenting with depression, anxiety, and/or a history of complex trauma, such protective anger is often not that easily available, and at this stage it is more typical for such clients to collapse into global distress. The therapist's role is then to empathise with the client's collapse, to help differentiate the felt pain, and to help unfold the underlying hurt that is evoked as a consequence of the escalated attack from the critic.

The therapist is doing two things here. First, he or she is trying to help the client to distil, and articulate, a sense of the toll of this attack on the self. This toll is typically a sense of worthlessness, isolation, or shame, and a corresponding action tendency to want to withdraw and hide. Second, the therapist attempts to foster the sense that this type of negative treatment is particularly harsh, and violates the client's natural needs to be acknowledged, accepted, recognised, loved, and respected. The therapist thus conveys to the client that he or she has a value which is being denied/demeaned/obliterated by the critic. In highlighting the harshness of the treatment, the therapist hopes to spontaneously trigger/evoke in the client, a rightful and just self-defence.

As the exploration of painful vulnerability continuous, the therapist asks the client to sit in the critic chair, witness the further unfolded painful experience, and notice what he or she feels toward the vulnerable self. As the dialogues progress across sessions, and as obstacles to a softening of the critic are highlighted (e.g., *If I soften then you will be even more problematic, because there will not be anything to toughen you up; you will just become more and more vulnerable and shameful.*), clients generally become more capable of softening and being self-compassionate. The therapist needs to watch for signs of such softening and compassion, and nurture these emerging capabilities in the client. Sometimes, the possibility of a softening stance shows in the manner in which the client is less critical. In such instances, the therapist needs to explore the feeling inside the client toward the expressed feelings of vulnerability in the experiencer chair. If there are any signs of compassion in the critic chair, the therapist has to highlight the nuances of this emerging self-compassion, and how the compassion feels for the client. Once compassion is expressed, the client is asked to sit back in the experiencer chair and is invited to attend to how it feels to receive this compassion. Again, it is often the case that a client may have difficulty letting compassion in, and in such instances, the therapist may encourage the client to experiment and endeavour to try letting the compassion in.

On the other hand, expression of further criticism or hesitation by the critic in accessing self-compassion both serve as a good basis for the generation of protective anger in the experiencer chair. Therefore, when the client in the critic chair is harsh or hesitant at showing any compassion, the client is asked to sit in the experiencer chair and see whether he or she will allow the critical part of the self to rule over the self as accessed in the experiencer chair. Sometimes, the therapist has to exaggerate the drama in order to provoke protective anger. If the client in the experiencer chair cannot find the strength to stand up for the self, the therapist may paradoxically demand that the client tell his or her critic: 'I will be your slave from now for ever'. Clients typically respond to such interventions by saying something like 'I cannot say it'. The therapist may then use this as an opportunity to encourage the client toward an expression of protective anger. For example, the therapist might ask: 'Do you want to be his (her) slave?' Clients will most likely respond to such a question by saying: 'No'. The therapist then may suggest to the client, that he or she state this to the critic: 'Tell him (her)—"I do not want to be your slave".' As the client expresses this, the therapist may ask the client 'And how does it feel when you say it?', thereby facilitating the client's noticing, and savouring the experience of standing up for and protecting him- or herself (for more on how to overcome difficulties with generating protective anger, see Chapter 8).

The building and receiving of compassion, and the building of protective anger, are cornerstones in the emotional transformation of those aspects of core emotional pain linked to negative self-treatment. Again, as with interpersonal dialogues, the goal is to build an emotional resilience and flexibility (Pascual-Leone, 2009), so that the client is not only self-judging or self-rejecting, but also self-compassionate and assertively self-protective.

An example of a transformative self-self dialogue can be seen in the following excerpts, which are taken from a dialogue in the latter stages of therapy. The client Laura has already engaged in a number of self-self dialogues; however, up until now she was not able to be either compassionate toward the vulnerable part of herself, or assertively protect her vulnerable self against harsh criticism. She was, however, able to access and express compassion in empty-chair dialogues, including dialogues with significant others such as her mother, with whom she had had a particularly difficult relationship. In the excerpt here, the client expressed how vulnerable she feels when she judges and condemns herself. The therapist initiated a two-chair self-self dialogue, and asked the client to enact her critic. In the critic chair, the client blamed the self in the experiencer chair for being weak. The following extract picks up the exchange after this first attack and begins with the therapist exploring with the client in the experiencing chair what it feels like to be blamed and attacked by her critical self in this manner.

Therapist (to the client in the experiencer chair): *... Speak from the vulnerable small. How does it feel when you feel weak and embarrassed and ashamed? 'I feel like ... ' what?*

Laura: *I feel like a kid ... I feel like I shouldn't be ... I shouldn't be here.*

Therapist: *I should disappear. Yeah?*

Laura: *Yeah. Because I can't handle things.*

...

Laura [speaking to the critic in the other chair]*:* *She does. She does have that right* [to criticise the client].

Therapist: *Ok. Tell her. Yes? It feels like you have a right.* [The therapist promotes direct expression between the parts of self in the dialogue].

Laura: *You do have that right. ... Yeah. Because I am weak and because I've let myself get so far to this point ... so you have ... She has* [speaking to the therapist] ... *She has got the right to give out to me. She has got the right to ...*

Therapist: *You have the right ... This is how it feels. Yeah?*

Laura: *Yeah ... Because without ... without you I won't sort myself and I won't.*

Therapist: *Yeah. Yeah. Ok. Could you come here* [inviting the client to the critic chair]*? ... When you see her like this here? Yes? This is the critical part, do you feel like you would want to kind of judge her even more ... or to be even harsher? For her feeling vulnerable even ...* [The therapist is trying to elicit compassion by highlighting vulnerability in the other chair and by confronting the client with the toll of her self-criticism. The EFT model for two-chair self-critic work assumes that this step would normally be preceded by the client in the experiencer chair expressing what the shamed part of her self needs from the critical part (cf. Elliott et al., 2004). Expression of need is particularly powerful at eliciting, or pulling, for compassion. In the flow of the session, this step may sometimes occur later, as is the case here.]

Laura: *Yeah.* [The client stays unforgiving and punitive.]

Therapist: *Ok. Do it a little bit.*

Laura: *Look at you* [with contempt in her voice].

Therapist: *Yeah.*

Laura: *Reduced you to tears again ... You just ... You just haven't got it in you. You just ...*

Therapist: *Yeah. You'll just crumble or something?*

Laura: *... You haven't got it in you so ... No ... I'm not going anywhere.* [I will not stop the criticism.]

Therapist *Yeah. Yeah. I'll be like this to you. Yeah. Where does it come from? I mean is this how you remember you treated yourself or somebody else kind of had this type of you know, dismissive attitude or ...?* [The therapist explores the function and roots of the negative self-treatment. If the therapist wanted to focus on the function, he could ask for instance *'And what do you achieve by being harsh on her?'*]

Laura:	*Growing up. If you couldn't do something they'd just say 'Well go away and leave it and we'll do it ourselves' ... The brothers and sisters and ... teachers in the school and my Mum.*

Sometimes, as was the case with this client, clients who struggle to stand up to their own self-critic may have the capacity to stand up to the other. At this point, therefore, the therapist decided to initiate an imaginary dialogue between Laura and her imagined cousin. In the course of this dialogue, the client was also put down; however, although she was scared of her cousin, she accessed protective anger and a capacity to stand up for the self. Wishing to capitalise on this emerging capacity to stand up for the self, the therapist then asks Laura to direct that assertive part of the self toward her own critic.

Therapist:	*Yeah. But say it to him* [imagined cousin in the other chair]. *It would be right to ignore you. Yes?*
Laura:	*It would be ... It would be right to ignore you.*
Therapist:	*Yeah.*
Laura:	*It would be. I resent you ... I do resent you doing it and ...*
Therapist:	*But even here when you picture him giving you that order.* [The cousin required her to fetch something for him in a particularly humiliating way.]
Laura:	*That he's actually roaring at me and that he can ... That he thinks he can do it. Well he could cos he did. But ...*
Therapist:	*Yeah. But you can't do it. Yes? It's not right. Tell him. Yes? As if he was here now. Yes? It's not right to do it. Yeah?*
Laura:	*It's not right to do it.*
Therapist:	*Yeah. And what's the sense inside as you are saying it?*
Laura:	*I feel strong sitting here saying it.*
Therapist:	*Yeah. But you know it kind of ... It's the opposite of the fear. Yeah?* [The client was initially scared of the cousin.]
...	
Therapist:	*... Yeah. 'I do not deserve to be put down and be treated like this'.*
Laura:	*No. I don't and ... No.*
Therapist:	*Yeah. But somehow when you criticise yourself. Yes? And I understand over years you were criticised by many people. Yeah? You somehow go down to that shame, vulnerable, weak ... and you don't stand up for yourself. Yes? Like I do not deserve to be treated like this. Yeah? Even though that contempt* [self-contempt] *is beyond reasonable. I mean it's very strong. Yeah.*
Laura:	*Yeah. Yeah.*
...	
Therapist:	*Come here and be that critic. Again. You. We'll see whether you can stand up for yourself or not. Put her* [self in the experiencer chair] *down again. Yes? How you're doing it. Yes?*

Laura (in the critic chair speaking to the experiencer chair): *You're wrong.*

Therapist: You're wrong. Yeah. You're too weak or something?

Laura: *You're wrong. You're ...*

Therapist: *You're too small. Too childish. Yeah?*

Laura: *Yeah. Too childish ... You ... You behave like a child sometimes that it's just ridiculous ...*

Therapist: *Yeah. Yeah. But it's like: I'll be always here and judging you and making sure that you feel miserable about yourself because you'll never measure up or something? Yes? I'll be always more powerful than you or something? Yes?* [The therapist is highlighting the strength of the criticism.]

...

Therapist: *I'm the powerful one here.* [The therapist is speaking on behalf of the critic highlighting its crushing power.]

Laura: *I'm the strong one and you are just there. That's it. I'm the strong one.*

Therapist: *Ok. Tell her again. I'm the strong one and you are ...*

Laura: *I'm just ... You're just there ...*

Therapist (nonverbally invites the client to sit in the experiencer chair): *Ok. I'm the strong one. You're nothing. Yes? You are just there. Yes? What's your response to that?*

Laura (from the experiencer chair, speaking to the critic): *You're right.* [Laura is collapsing again, resigning in the face of criticism.]

Therapist: *Yeah. So I'm just awful upset. When I face you I'll just collapse. Tell her. Tell her. Yes? Tell that voice over there. I always collapse when I face you.* [The therapist stays close to Laura's experience even when it is not adaptive, thus respecting the client's experience.]

Laura: *I do always collapse. I always crumble ...*

Therapist: *Yeah. But now ... How is it now? Do you want to collapse in the face of this?* [The therapist prompts for protective anger by pointing at what the client would want (wish) if it was in her power.]

Laura: *No.* [Laura is starting to stand up for the self.]

Therapist: *Ok. So tell her what you want? I want you ... what? I don't want to collapse. Yeah?* [The therapist supports protective anger through the assertion of the need to be strong.]

Laura: *I don't want to collapse. I ... I don't ...* [Laura client starts to stand up for the self even more.]

Therapist: *Yeah.*

Laura: *... I don't want to feel like that kid anymore. I don't want to feel ...*

Therapist: *Yeah. Ok. Tell her.* [The therapist facilitates expression of protective anger.]

Laura: *I don't want to feel vulnerable all the time and I don't want to ... be second guessing myself. I want to take this ...*

Therapist: *Yeah. So if she says ... She says: Just ... You're just there. I'm strong. What do you say to her? To that?* [The therapist uses this intervention to see whether Laura will take ownership and control over her own well-being, and whether she will stand up to the critic.]

Laura: *You are strong but I want that strength a different way. I want that strength to be able to be seen as a person and not ... and not to be walked on all the time ... and not to be a doormat.*

Therapist: *Yeah. I want to be seen as a person. Say it.* [The therapist empathically highlights the gist of the client's statement. The client's statement is not only empowering, but also gives rise to self-esteem.]

Laura: *I want to be seen as a person.* [...and Laura owns it.]

Therapist: *Yeah.*

Laura: *As a ... fully fledged adult.*

Therapist: *Yeah. And I am a fully fledged adult. Say it to her.* [The therapist promotes the further ownership of the assertive stance that the client is touching on.]

Laura: *I am an adult.* [This is a clear expression of protective, boundary-setting anger. It is not expressed aggressively, yet it conveys power and ownership of own value.]

Therapist: *Yeah. You are an adult.* [The therapist validates Laura.]

Laura: *I am ... I am an adult.*

Therapist: *You are. Yes?* [Further validation.]

Laura: *Mmm.*

Therapist: *And you are a fully fledged adult. Yes?*

Laura: *Yeah.*

Therapist: *Tell her. Yeah?*

Laura: *I am an adult. I'm a fully fledged adult ... I don't think I can be classed as a kid anymore.*

Therapist: *Yeah. And I can put people in their place. Yes?* [The therapist wants to consolidate emerging protective anger and empowerment further.]

Laura: *I can.*

Therapist: *So I can face you as well. Yes?*

Laura: *Yeah.* (A portion of this dialogue appeared previously in Witnessing client's emotional change in psychotherapy: An emotion-focused therapists experience of providing therapy. Timulak, L. *Journal of Clinical Psychology, 70,* 741–752. © 2014 John Wiley and Sons doi: 10.1002/jclp.22109)

A short while later, Laura goes even further, expressing trust in herself, and a sense of self-esteem.

Laura:	*So I know I've done something ...*
Therapist:	*So ... Ok. Yeah. So tell her. Yes? I know I did some things right.*
Laura:	*I know I did some things right and I know ... I done ... I've done my best.*

The client in the excerpt was able to face her own critic, which is an important part of the process of emotional transformation. Equally important is when the client can relate to the pain caused by negative self-judgment. Indeed further on in this transformative self-self dialogue, Laura states that even her negative self-treatment (self-judgment) comes from a caring and protective place:

Laura [back in the critic chair]:	*It was me who helped you achieve it.* [This is now said in a soft voice.]
Therapist:	*Ok.*
Laura:	*It's me who kept the fight in you.*
Therapist:	*Ok.*
Laura:	*It's me who made you have that strength.*
Therapist:	*Ok.*
Laura:	*But now ... It's me who made you have that strength years ago to cope with it. But it ... It's me now trying to build back up your strength or trying to ...*
Therapist:	*Yeah. I see. I see. I see what you say. But it's almost like I come across as contemptuous. Yes? 'But I basically want to make you stronger' or something? Yes? It's trying to build you. Yes? So it's actually, 'I care'.*
Laura:	*Yeah.*
Therapist:	*In a kind of strange way.*
Laura:	*I ... I care because if I don't push you and if I don't criticise you ...*
Therapist:	*Yeah.*
Laura:	*... you won't take it off anybody else ...*

The dialogue then continues with Laura in the experiencer chair expressing that such care from the critic has to come in a different form, if it is to be of help.

Embedding transformative work in the overall therapy process

Compassionate responses to the unmet needs contained in core painful experience, and empowering assertion of one's right to have those needs met are both experiences which directly heal core pain. This is particularly the case when the compassion and assertion are generated by the client. Thus, it is important that the therapist guides the client to stay with these experiences, savour them, and to reflect on them. Although it is typical for EFT that transformative work happens mainly in vivid experiential dialogues with either those imagined others who originally triggered the client's painful experiences or with parts of the self that contribute to the experienced pain, such transformative work is firmly embedded in the therapist's overall strategy for therapy. This strategy assumes that transformative work is preceded by empathic work focused on the unfolding and differentiation of the client's core pain, and that such work takes place within the context of a therapeutic relationship characterised by the therapist's compassionate and validating presence.

The therapist can consolidate the impact of transformative experiences by encouraging the client to consider actions that would reinforce these in-session experiences, in his or her life outside of the therapy room. Actual transformative work is thus followed by reflection on both the transformative experience within session, but also on the strategic place of such transformative experience in the client's overall life. Transformative experiences are thus reflected on and consolidated by action in the real world outside of the therapy session. As with other therapies, EFT may utilise the idea of providing the client with homework (Greenberg and Warwar, 2006). In the case of EFT, such homework is typically focused on a broadening of the client's awareness of self-functioning or actions that would consolidate the emotional flexibility or resilience achieved within the session. For instance, the work illustrated in the above-presented excerpts might be followed by work exploring how the client's emerging self-protective stance might be supported in the client's life outside of the therapy session. Similarly, if the client feels experiences of love, acceptance, or self-protection; and a sense of entitlement to such positive experiences, within the session, therapy might then focus on practical ways in which the client may have similar adaptive experiences supported in life outside the session.

The therapist may also use psychoeducation (so-called 'hot teaching'; Greenberg, 2002), that builds on emotional experiences within the session. For instance, the therapist may explain to the client parts of EFT theory, illustrating this with what just happened in the session. For instance, the therapist may explain to the client how he or she may be avoiding emotional pain, and how this avoidance then contributes to having that pain unprocessed. The therapist may explain how compassion and protective anger undo painful experiences that are difficult to bear, and so on. The therapist may encourage the client's reflection on the overall emotion scheme dynamic (see Figure 1), for example, the role of triggers, negative self-treatment, emotional and behavioural avoidance, core pain, unmet needs, as well as the importance of compassion and protective anger. Reflection might focus on the past experiences that led to the development of the problematic schemes, but also on current emotional functioning. Such endeavours consolidate therapeutic work on emotional processing by facilitating the client's construction of a coherent, authentic, personal narrative (see Angus and Greenberg, 2011).

On an emotional level, empirical work shows (Dillon et al., 2014; Pascual-Leone and Greenberg, 2007; Pascual-Leone, 2009; McNally et al., 2014) that compassionate responses to the hurt self and to unmet needs, together with protective anger backing those needs, lead to a grieving of both current hurts, but also those past hurts which led to the development of maladaptive emotion schemes centred around the core emotional pain. This grieving is the grieving of shame-related, loneliness-related, and fear-related experiences. However, this grieving is a higher order emotional process, which is notably different to both the unbearable distress of global distress, and the extreme pain of core pain, in that it is both better regulated and characterised by a letting-go quality. The client spontaneously recounts his or her hurts; however, while he or she is sad, this sadness is not all-consuming, but rather is characterised by a sense that those distressful memories are being let go. The therapist at this point is simply an empathic, understanding, interested, and engaged witness who sees, hears, and acknowledges what the client went through. The time can thus naturally be spent in reflecting and recounting those difficult memories, in a way that allows for the building of a coherent, personal narrative that the client can use in understanding the story of his or her life (cf. Angus and Greenberg, 2011).

Transformative work on core emotional pain is followed not only by reflection on the emotion schemes (and on the work of their transformation), narrativisation, and grieving, but also is typically followed by the appearance of client experiences of agency, empowerment, and growing personal strength or resilience. As a result of transformative work, the client can find him- or herself with the greater sense of maturity and resilience that comes with overcoming adversity. This does not only mean personal strength, but also includes sensitivity to both own pain and to the pain of others. In summary, the transformation of core pain and the re-scripting of core emotion schemes centred around that pain lead to greater emotional flexibility, greater emotional resilience (Pascual-Leone, 2009), the development of an authentic personal narrative, the growth of an own sense of agency and maturity, and to increased emotional perceptivity (see also Figure 1 in Chapter 5).

CASE OF ANN

In Chapter 6 we looked at how Ann accessed her core painful emotional experiences in therapy, for example, her sense of abandonment and loss, feeling unloved, craving for her mother's love; the core painful shame—*something in me is flawed and unlovable*; and her sense of being unprotected and not resilient enough to cope with life. Once the core painful emotional experiences felt by Ann in response to enacted interpersonal triggers were evoked, and the unmet needs in these painful feelings articulated, the therapist tried to bring about compassionate responses to the expressed pain. The therapist typically facilitated this by one of the following interventions; either by asking Ann to enact a remembered responsive other (e.g., she enacted compassionate responses from both her husband and her father); by probing for compassionate responses from Ann as her adult self toward her younger hurting child self; or by probing for compassionate responses from Ann's enacted imagined mother to the heard heart-breaking hurt that she as a child felt. All of these proved to be difficult as any vulnerability expressed by Ann was typically met with contempt, whilst the needs embedded in the expressed pain were dismissed. Although Ann could enact a compassionate stance toward her hurt child self when doing so as her imagined father or husband, these responses were somewhat limited in depth as Ann had a sense that neither her father not husband fully understood her. The best source of compassion was thus Ann's compassion for her own children, as enacted in certain dialogues in which she witnessed the pain of her own children. Eventually, Ann became capable of expressing compassion toward an unknown, imagined child facing conditions similar to those Ann herself experienced in her own childhood. Toward the end of therapy, Ann was also able to be compassionate toward her hurt child self, in the context of repeated empty-chair dialogues, primarily with her imagined mother.

It was somewhat easier for Ann to access anger backing her right to have had what she deserved to have had in childhood (e.g., love and support from a caring mother), although she easily collapsed into reactive and rejecting anger which she then blamed herself for feeling. The therapist therefore sought to help Ann focus her anger on establishing a protective boundary in the face of her imagined mother's unresponsiveness, for example facilitating statements such as 'I deserved to be cared for, regardless of what you say, it is just a fact'. Such expressions of protective anger were, however, often followed by sadness and a collapse into global distress.

Work on boundary setting with regard to her mother's dismissive unresponsiveness was paralleled with work on establishing a boundary in the face of a tiring and intrusive worry process. Eventually, as a consequence of these efforts, Ann became clearer in her view of what it was she needed, clearer in her perspective on the situation, and firmer at standing up for her own perspective and her own needs.

Work on developing a capacity to stay with the underlying and all-consuming loneliness, shame, and trauma-related fear showed gradual progress over the course of therapy. Ann became capable of staying with these experiences for longer periods of time without collapsing into global distress. She gradually became more capable of putting her distressing experience into a detailed narrative, and became quicker at identifying what it was she needed. Ann's painful experience centred not only around pain in relation to her unresponsive mother, distress as a consequence of her own self-contempt (to a great extent introjected from mom), and distress as a consequence of her own worrying and overprotective behaviour, but also stemmed from a variety of situations in which her or her children (with whose pain she easily identified) were caught up. These emotionally charged situations were typically enacted in chair dialogues, during which she enacted the emotional response of the various characters in the given situations. Ultimately, Ann became more readily able to develop a self-compassionate and protective stance to expressions of pain and unmet need. She became more capable of bouncing back, reorganising herself more quickly from states of global distress, and instead accessing empowering, assertive anger. The process was far from linear, taking place in a slow and painstakingly gradual way over the course of around twenty sessions. The non-linear process was in keeping with observation by Pascual-Leone and Greenberg (2007) and Pascual-Leone (2009) that therapeutic change is often a two steps forward (into healthier emotional processing), one step back process.

Ultimately, going by conventional outcome measures, the course of therapy was successful. During therapy, Ann reflected that for the first time in her life she felt heard and understood (she said to therapist: 'You get me'.). Toward the end of therapy, she reported an increased sense of inner confidence, that she felt capable of facing any potential difficult issues that she or those close to her might encounter on a day-to-day basis. She was visibly less upset about the neglect and mistreatment she experienced in her relationship with her mother. She was able to grieve and express sadness at what was not present and at what should have been present, but demonstrated a capacity to do so with a letting-go quality, and without becoming overwhelmed. She developed a capacity to allow her children more independence, no longer needing to be as enmeshed in their dealings as she previously insisted on being. For example, she was able to allow them to attend medical treatments without instructing them how to go about it, and without phoning constantly to check how it was going. Finally, she found herself a new hobby (a course for women in a local community centre) and was capable of taking time for herself without feeling self-reproach that it was selfish and bad to do so.

8 Overall treatment strategy and working with difficulties in therapeutic process

The process of emotional transformation in well-progressing therapies presented in the previous chapters is naturally non-linear. This means that in some sessions there may be more progress than in others. It also means that in some sessions there may be regression. The therapist directs the pace of therapy on the basis of the client's responses and experiences during the session. Thus, with some clients the therapist may spend more time building the therapeutic alliance and creating a sense of safety; with other clients the therapy may move more quickly to the work of accessing core pain and attempting to transform that pain. The therapist's strategy is also inevitably shaped by environmental variables, such as the context in which he or she sees the client. For instance, the therapist's strategy may be different in a time-limited context than it might be in a therapy that is open ended.

TREATMENT STRATEGY AND THE LENGTH OF THERAPY

Research studies investigating the application of EFT are often limited to EFT conducted over the course of twenty (or fewer) sessions of therapy. This number of sessions represents a common upper limit in therapies examined in Randomised Controlled Trials (cf. Timulak, 2008). When the therapy is conducted within this limit, the establishment of a therapeutic alliance is usually the primary goal of early sessions. If there are no relational complications, this process may take up to three sessions (cf. Greenberg and Watson, 1998). During this time, the therapist refrains from suggesting engagement in experiential tasks aimed at accelerating access to core painful emotional experiences. After the first three sessions, however, and once a therapeutic alliance has been formed, the therapist typically uses the presence of task markers (e.g., lingering painful feelings in salient interpersonal relationships; Elliott et al., 2004), to initiate appropriate experiential tasks (e.g., unfinished business dialogue for interpersonal emotional injury). If the client appears to be more emotionally fragile or interpersonally withdrawn, suspicious, or hostile, more time will need to be spent on exploring what would help him or her settle into therapy. It will be necessary to help such a client become capable of tolerating a focus on vulnerable emotional experiences. It will be important to help the client see that work on these painful emotions is relevant; and that the offered therapeutic approach is a plausible and useful way to carry out this work. To achieve collaboration in such cases, the therapist needs to communicate a considerable degree of empathy, to be non-defensive, and to be open in his or her enquiry as to why the client is reluctant to engage in therapy. A tailored case conceptualisation that can be shared with the client in a language that makes sense to him or her can also help to build collaboration on the goals, tasks, and bond in therapy (Bordin, 1979), as the sharing of such a conceptualisation may help the client better understand the therapist's suggestions and plan for therapy.

In therapies that are not constrained by external limits (e.g., in private practice), the therapist has naturally more space to establish both safety and the focus of therapy. While in time-limited therapies, the focus may be limited to the most pressing emotional problems, in long-term therapies the focus may shift. Thus issues that appear to have been overcome may recede to the background, whilst other issues may come to the fore. Newly emerging issues are typically linked to those issues already worked on in therapy; this is as would be expected as the client's emotion schemes (emotional processing) are intertwined. For instance, once the client makes progress in therapy with regards to his or her emotional experiencing of a complicated parental relationship, the therapy may shift focus to difficulties the client might be experiencing in his or her relationship with a current romantic partner. While this new relationship inevitably brings different emotional experiences, there are often also shared elements. This is because our emotion schemes and self-organisations are based on our previous experiences; our emotional memories inevitably shape our current emotional processing.

Let us go back for a moment to the early stages of therapy and imagine that a therapeutic collaboration has been established. The goal of the therapist will now be to focus on the core painful aspects of the client's emotional experience (see Chapter 5 on case conceptualisation). These painful aspects are first identified through a process of empathic exploration. They are then focused on, and accessed, typically through the use of experiential tasks such as an empty-chair and two-chair dialogues in which the client enacts situational triggers or problematic aspects of self-treatment. These triggers are then used to elicit inner painful emotional experiences, primarily those most problematic emotions that are at the centre of problematic emotionally laden self-organisations (Greenberg, 2011). The therapist may need to make a judgment as to which core painful emotional experiences he or she should focus on in a given session. For instance, with a client who is reluctant to engage in therapy, the therapist may initially focus on less threatening problematic issues, as judged by the client's willingness to stay with these issues, and by his or her lesser avoidance of them. By contrast, with a client who more openly accesses painful experiences, the therapist may focus more quickly on the most painful aspects of the client's emotional experiencing.

Once the core painful emotional experiences are present in the therapy session(s), the goal of the therapist is to differentiate the core painful emotional experiences, to facilitate the client in articulating these painful experiences in language, to help the client overcome avoidance or feelings of being overwhelmed, and to facilitate the client in developing a capacity to bear these emotional experiences. As Chapter 7 on emotion transformation pointed out, the therapist is ultimately trying to facilitate an articulation of unmet needs (e.g., for closeness, acceptance, or safety) as well as a healing response to both the core pain and unmet needs (i.e., compassion and protective anger). Once the core painful emotional experiences are accessed in the session, the therapist facilitates a transformative response to them. This is what the therapist is trying to achieve in every single session. For instance, when the client feels loneliness, shame, or traumatic fear in the session, the therapist does not wait until the next session, but rather tries to facilitate experiences of soothing connection, validation, and protection (or feelings of deservedness and resolve) in that same session.

Thus, in principle, the therapist seeks in every session to facilitate responses to core pain and unmet needs that bring about experiences of self-compassion and protective anger. As elaborated on in previous chapters, these two types of experiences are antidotes to the felt experiences of vulnerability, loneliness, shame, and fear. With any given client and in any given session, the therapist may focus strategically on one or the other of these experiences, seeking to promote either protecting anger or compassion. For instance, if the client is naturally capable of self-compassion, it may be good for the therapist to start by promoting self-compassion, and then helping the client to savour this compassion, in terms of generating it, expressing it, and receiving it. However, if such a client has significant difficulty accessing protective anger and is scared to stand up for him- or herself, the therapist's ultimate strategy may rather be to focus on the promotion, generation, ownership, and expression of protective anger, and the capacity to overcome fear of standing up for the self. Therefore, while the default position is to promote both compassion and protective anger in a given session or phase of therapy, focusing on one or the other of these strategies may be more central or important in a given moment.

While the therapist is trying to facilitate self-compassion or protective anger, he or she cannot push the client to those experiences. The EFT therapist respects the client's experience and operates within the client's 'zone of proximal development'. Put simply, the therapist cannot push the client where the client is not. In cases where the client is not able to experience self-compassion or protective anger, the therapist goes back to the client's experience and acknowledges it. The therapist may highlight the wished-for experience, while acknowledging that it is not felt currently. Often, this highlighting of the wished-for response can be enough to bring a glimpse of it, as the client engages with the wished-for response on at least some level.

Again, within a time-limited framework, the therapist may be under pressure to (work at an accelerated pace, in order to) generate some transformative experiences, for example, to facilitate the client gaining some experience of feeling both entitled to his or her needs, and entitled to have these needs met through feelings of compassion and/or protective anger. However, as transformative experiences are transformative precisely because they are authentic and spontaneous, this creates a seeming paradox for the therapist. One way for the therapist to deal with this seeming paradox is to try and increase the likelihood that such experiences would appear by encouraging the client's enactments in the experiential imaginary dialogues. However, despite the effort, time-limited work may have its limits.

Short-term work requires that the therapist uses every single transformative experience as an opportunity to promote the client's self-reflection and planning outside the therapy room. The therapist may regularly use transformative experiences (or any other emotionally salient experiences in therapy) as opportunities for psychoeducation and/or collaborative reflection, working together with the client to construe an understanding of the client's problematic emotion schemes and self-organisations. Together with the client, the therapist may plan homework on how to support transformation of problematic emotion schemes outside the therapy sessions, in the client's everyday life (Greenberg and Warwar, 2006).

In longer-term therapies there is a natural flow, a rise and ebb, of salient emotional experiences. The experiences of pain and its transformation are worked on in the context of a variety of triggers and situations that are typically enacted across a number of imaginary dialogues. Emotional experiences of pain are accessed, enacted, experienced, and transformed, periodically over the course of therapy, as and when they arise. These in-session processes are interspersed with real-life situations outside the therapy sessions, in which the client attempts to enact self-compassionate or self-protective stances. The client's attempts are also brought back to, and reflected on, within the therapy sessions.

Whilst longer-term therapy may contain the same elements as time-limited therapy, the focus may be more on in-session, experiential (emotional) work rather than psychoeducation, with situations outside of the therapy room providing natural opportunities for the client to apply 'emotional learning' from sessions. Outside therapy events are then reflected on, in collaboration with the therapist, after they have occurred naturally in the client's life. For instance, a client who battles with experiences of unbearable shame in social situations (stemming from being shamed by his mother during childhood and from being bullied by peers during adolescence) may, in short-term therapy, experience a sense of empowerment by facing up to and challenging the imagined bullies during in-session imaginary dialogues. This experience may happen on two or three occasions, and the therapist and client can draw on these pivotal experiences in order to try and plan how this strong part of the self could be available to the client during difficult social situations. In longer-term therapy, that same client might experience a sense of empowerment ten or fifteen times, and in a variety of dialogues. Furthermore, over the course of a longer-term therapy (e.g., of one-year duration), he may also have plenty of opportunities in real life to use this more confident part of the self. Successes and setbacks, with regards to relying on/drawing on these emergent, confident self-organisations in the real world, are then brought back to the therapy office where they are reflected on and reworked, and where once again, a resolve to try them out in the real world may be built.

Differences between short- and long-term work exist not only in the assessment of what can be accomplished in therapy (i.e., which core painful emotional schemes can be focused on, and to what extent), in the goals of therapy, in the more prescriptive nature of short-term work, or in the use of psycho-education, reflection and planning; they also exist in the way in which the therapeutic work comes to an end. The short-term therapy ending is often predetermined by an external structure. The therapist thus constantly focuses on this imminent ending. From early on in therapy, the therapist focuses on the prevention of difficulties and setbacks that might come when therapy finishes. The therapist uses collaborative reflection and psychoeducation to plan with the client for those times when the client will be on his or her own.

By contrast, endings in long-term work may be determined more by the client's own self-determined state of readiness and independence. As such, emerging states of readiness and independence are collaboratively assessed for over the course of therapy. This is not to say that the fostering of client independence is still not a primary target of therapy. As with short-term therapy, the ultimate goal of longer-term therapy is not only to provide support, but also to build the client's independence. For this reason, the therapist has to remain mindful of the potentially adverse consequences of allowing therapy to continue for too long. The point at which therapy should end can be regularly renegotiated between the therapist and client, and when necessary (e.g., toward the end of therapy) made a therapeutic focus. The process of ending therapy (whether short- or long-term) is particularly important to clients with a lot of anxiety and avoidance issues, as such clients may be particularly fearful of being on their own, facing the dangerous world without the support of a therapist.

Therapeutic strategy does not depend only on whether the number of sessions is unlimited or finite. Strategy also depends upon whether the client is capable of accessing certain emotional experiences; and whether he or she is able to tolerate these experiences without collapsing into further states of emotional dysregulation. Therapeutic strategy may also depend upon whether the client is capable of accessing important transformative experiences. The next section will explore a number of common pitfalls that can occur when working with clients presenting with depression, anxiety and traumatic experiences, and suggest a number of possible strategies for addressing such obstacles to a healing therapeutic process.

WORKING WITH EMOTIONALLY OVERWHELMED CLIENTS

Some clients come to therapy very emotionally distressed with an overflow of painful (secondary) emotions such as despair, hopelessness, and helplessness. For such clients this overwhelming state of global distress is omnipresent both in and outside of therapy. Such clients can cry uncontrollably and may not be able to articulate their distress in a coherent narrative. In other words, while emotional arousal may be high (Warwar and Greenberg, 1999), the articulation of the meaning implicit in the painful experience may be poorly differentiated. This may be how the client presents generally; alternatively, it may be a state into which the client collapses when focused on something that is particularly painful.

When working with this type of upset, the therapist has to first try to help the client to become capable of staying with painful emotions without becoming overwhelmed by them. This can be attempted in several ways. For instance, the therapist's empathic presence may in and of itself be calming and regulating. In particular, by his or her constant focus on naming and verbally clarifying the client's experience, the therapist can help to make an otherwise overwhelming experience lacking in meaning, more clear, more understandable, and more coherent and thus also, somewhat more regulated (cf. Lieberman et al., 2007). The therapist may also explicitly instruct the client to take some calming distance from the overwhelming experience, for instance by breathing calmly in the session. Outside the therapy session, the therapist may suggest calming activities, such as going for a walk.

EFT also uses a specific task (or technique) to help clients regulate overwhelming emotional experience and keep some experiential distance from it. This task, called clearing a space, is based on the work of Gendlin (1996) and is well-described in other EFT publications (e.g., Elliott et al., 2004). In this task, the therapist first asks the client to pay attention to the middle of their body (where clients often feel the most upsetting feelings). The client is then instructed to label the felt feeling (e.g., feeling rejected). It is desirable that this labelling also references the perceptual element or trigger in the environment that evokes the feeling (e.g., I feel rejected *by him*). Finally the client is instructed to imagine putting this now named upsetting feeling at some distance from him- or herself, for instance next to the self, in the corner of the room, into a box, outside the room, and so on. Having thus put the feeling aside in their imagination, the client is then directed to once again pay attention inwards to the middle of the body, to see how he or she is now feeling inside. Usually, the above exercise gives rise to some shift in the felt feeling. The client may report some relief; alternatively, temporarily they may report a worsening of the upsetting feeling. The process of paying attention, naming the feeling (and its trigger), and imagining putting it aside is then repeated, until a significant degree of relief is experienced by the client.

Some clients may have difficulty putting the named feeling away in the imagination, in part because they may see some benefit to the feeling. For instance, an apprehensive anxiety (e.g., I have to be ready for the attack) may be seen by the client as functional, as it prepares the client for potential catastrophe. Thus the client may be resistant to seek relief from such a feeling. In such a case the therapist may instruct the client to imagine putting the upsetting feeling aside, but within reach, and for a while only, not forever. With the reassurance that the feeling is within reach and can be accessed at will, or as needed, the client is then asked how it feels to have even that little bit of distance (indeed, it is most likely that the feelings will come back quickly just by the client thinking about the issues linked to those feelings). In some cases, clients who are not used to using their imagination may struggle with the concept behind this task. In such cases, the therapist has to work hard in order to embellish the imagined picture, for example, by offering various suggestions as to how the client may push away the feeling in his or her imagination (e.g., *imagine that the wind is blowing it away*). Effectively, in these instances, the therapist has to help the client build his or her capacity for imagination.

The following is a brief excerpt from a clearing a space task with a client Catherine, overwhelmed with anxiety, whose level of distress was such that she could not engage in the session.

Therapist: *It's like a traumatic, complicated situation that you have to be sorting ...*
Catherine: *Mmm.*
Therapist: *So you are totally aroused, prepared to be sorting it or something ...*
Catherine: *Mmm. Or at the back of ... not even at the back of my mind ... I just want to keep walking.*
Therapist: *Yeah. Cos you are so aroused and agitated and everything.*
Catherine: *Yeah.*
Therapist: *Ok. So you say that it's here. Yes?* [Pointing to the middle of the body.]
Catherine: *Yeah.*
Therapist: *If you put a, some label on it. Yes? ... It's not one thing. Yes? It's like all of those things that you have to look after. Or, or label maybe just I need to be walking or whatever. Because it sounds like there are too many problems that you have to attend to. Yes? So what is some of it?* [The therapist is trying to differentiate upsetting triggers and respective feelings as several issues overwhelm the client.] *... I have to do this. I have to do ... So what's one of them? What's the biggest of them that comes to mind now? It's like this sense ...*
Catherine: *The husband gone away.* [The client is naming an upsetting trigger.]
Therapist: *Ok. So it's like ... And what comes with it? It's like husband going away meaning it's all on me or something? Or less secure.* [The therapist is trying to help to name the respective feeling that goes with the trigger 'husband away'.]
Catherine: *He's just not there.*
Therapist: *Ok.*
Catherine: *He's just not there.*
Therapist: *Ok. So if I need it, yes, or something ...*
Catherine: *I ... He's just not there.*
...
Therapist: *Ok. Ok. But it's almost like 'My peace is disturbed because something is missing from my everyday situation'.*
Catherine: *Mmm.*
Therapist: *That I rely on or that it's a part of everything.*
Catherine: *Yeah.*
....
Therapist: *Ok. So we label it 'husband away'. Yes? So see how your body reacts when you kind of put that label as though you*

know portion of my upset is husband being away. Yeah? Gets it ... Does it get more agitated or? [Initially when the clearing a space is started and the first feeling named, the client may start to feel worse.]

Catherine: *Mmm.*

....

Therapist: *... We'll try to put it aside. Yes? That, almost that feeling or. Or ... the upset husband being away. Yes? So a portion of my agitation is husband being away. Where would you put it? ... It won't disappear fully cos it would be very easy.* [The therapist reassures the client that he understands that the distress is so strong that it may not be that easy to put it aside.] *But it may be a way of trying to calm a little bit. Yes? Could you imagine that you are putting that feeling 'husband being away' somewhere? Where would you put it?*

Catherine: *On the windowsill where we sit in the kitchen.*

Therapist: *In your house? Yes?*

Catherine: *Yeah.*

Therapist: *Yeah. So try ... to imagine putting it there. Yes? That feeling. Yes? Almost. Yeah? Does it go ... the imagination? Yeah? Can you put it there?*

Catherine: *Yeah. I can see it.*

Therapist: *Ok. So it's there. Yes?* [The therapist is highlighting the distance.]

Catherine: *Mmm.*

Therapist: *So a portion of your upset is there almost. Yes? How does it feel inside now? Yes? When we put a portion of it there? How is it inside? It's like you know that it's there. Whenever you think about it you'll get upset again.* [The therapist highlighting that the distress may easily come back just by thinking about it.] *Yes?*

Catherine: *Mmm.*

Therapist: *But now for a moment you're putting it aside. You can take a breath as well.* [The therapist is further enhancing regulation by pointing to regular breathing.]

Catherine: *Yeah. I know it's there. The window is there and I've put it on the window.* [The client's spontaneous expression suggests that she is fully engaged with the imagination.]

Therapist: *Yeah. And how is it inside now? Here? Yes? It's there. How do you feel now inside?*

Catherine: *A bit, a ... Yeah. I, I can get on with doing things.* [The client indirectly reports some positive shift.]

The therapist and the client then continue and focus on other aspects of the client's feeling of being overwhelmed, identifying the other feelings and issues that are contributing to the upset. In response to the question *'So what else is in there? Yes? What else is this upset about?'*, the client identifies other upsetting feelings/triggers, including her son being away (something bad could happen to him), her elderly mother's ill-health, and the feeling that something bad would happen that weekend because the last time her husband was away, a family member got really sick. As the client names each feeling and the issue it relates to, she is asked by the therapist to put it aside, and then after doing so, to check how it feels inside. The client imagines that she is putting the distressing feelings (and the issues that they are connected to) in different places in her house, e.g., she imagines placing the feeling labelled '*Something bad will happen*' into the rubbish bin in her house:

Catherine: *... in the bin.*
Therapist: *In the bin ... but in the bin in here?*
Catherine: *In the house.*
Therapist: *In your house? Ok. So imagine it. Imagine, yes putting it in the bin. Yeah? It won't go away for, because it's a real worry yes? But for a moment.*
Catherine: *Mmm.*
Therapist: *Yes? Put it to the bin. Yeah? Ok. Can you imagine it?*
Catherine: *Mmm.*
Therapist: *Yeah? So it's in the bin there in your house. Yes? But you are here. Yes? So you put some distance between you and that upsetting thing. Yes?*
Catherine: *Yeah.*
Therapist: *Ok. What's the sense inside now? Yes? When you put it away?*
Catherine: *It ... I know it's in the bin and ... But it's not fully gone till I take the bin out.*
Therapist: *You want to put [the bin] somewhere ... Yeah. Throw it away or something.* [The therapist wants to support the client in getting some distance from the upsetting feeling.]
Catherine: *It's not fully gone till I take the bin out.*
Therapist: *Take it out. Imagine that you are taking it out.*
...
Catherine: *It's at the top of the yard. Yeah.*
Therapist: *Yeah. Ok. You can even push it as far as possible up the yard. Yeah?*
Catherine: *Yeah.*
Therapist: *Ok. So it's there. Yeah? You're here.* [By pointing at the distance 'you are here' and the bad feeling 'is there', the therapist is trying to support an experiential distance between the client and the upsetting feeling.] *The, the kind of bad thing during the weekend is there. Yeah?*
Catherine: *Yeah.*
Therapist: *So how is it inside now? Yeah? I mean in your body. Yeah? How is it?*
Catherine: *Sort of ... a bit warm alright. Yeah. I can feel the warmth.*

The therapist then further focuses on how Catherine is inside, and the client reports feeling tense in her chest. As she unpacks the tension and what it is connected to, she realises that she is weighed down by her *daughter's unhappiness*, which is then labelled as another feeling. Again, the therapist instructs Catherine to put the feeling aside. Next the therapist focuses not only on what is felt inside the client's body, but also on what it is that the feeling needs. (This is one of the options used in the *clearing a space* task; Elliott et al., 2004). The client reports a need to be able to lie down.

Therapist:	*And when you say this 'I, I need to switch off'. Yes? When ... Can you sense in your body some kind of representation of that feeling 'I need to sleep'. I mean how is it inside now? Yeah? Is it eh?*
Catherine:	*It's so warm.*
...	
Therapist:	*But it's still not, kind of you, you do not feel fully relaxed or something? Yes?*
Catherine:	*I'm getting there. ... But I know now it's ok to put it aside for a few minutes.*
Therapist:	*Yeah. Yeah. Yeah.*
Catherine:	*What am I trying to say? I know that it's there and ...*
Therapist:	*Ok.*
Catherine:	*But it's not in my face ... at the moment.*
Therapist:	*Ok. Ok. So this is good? Yeah?*
Catherine:	*Yeah. So if it's not in my face or it's not coming at me ...*
Therapist:	*Yeah. Ok. You feel kind of more calm or something? Less overwhelmed by it or something? Yes?*
Catherine:	*Yeah.*

Apart from the clearing a space task, the already mentioned empathic holding, and breathing, what particularly helps easily overwhelmed clients are the strategies used in transformative work. For instance, experiences of compassion (self-compassion) enacted in the imaginary dialogues are often especially calming. Thus at one point in a later session, when Catherine was particularly upset, the therapist asked her whose presence would help her to bear the upset. Catherine nominated her husband, and the ensuing enactment of her imagined husband in an imaginary dialogue had a very calming effect. Strictly speaking, such experiences are not necessarily fully transformative as the elicited compassion is targeting a general, global distress, rather than primary underlying painful experiences and unmet needs. Nonetheless such experiences can help to build the emotional capacity to bear pain. Eventually they bring the client closer to being able to access the underlying primary painful emotional experiences that need to be articulated in order that they can be responded to and transformed.

In a manner similar to soothing compassion, experiences of protective, empowering anger also build the client's capacity to bear upset. Empowering experiences serve as a steering rod for the client and build the client's resilience, confidence, and resolve to be able to access and stay with painful experiences. The combination of compassionate and self-affirmation promoting experiences increases the likelihood that the client develops the capability for healthy, emotional self-regulation. Nevertheless, as our studies show (e.g., Dillon et al., 2014), for some clients, despite huge progress in emotional transformation, vulnerability to becoming overwhelmed, and to emotional collapse may still be present. However, as several studies are showing (e.g., Pascual-Leone, 2009; Dillon et al., 2014; McNally et al., 2014) even in such instances where clients continue to collapse into states of distress, in successful cases the duration of such collapses shortens as therapy progresses. Similarly, the likelihood that the client will be capable of bouncing back from the collapse also increases, if and as therapy progresses well.

WORKING WITH EMOTIONALLY AVOIDANT CLIENTS

Some clients present problems in EFT work that are just the opposite of the ones described above. Since emotions can often be unpleasant, people develop strategies to avoid, control, over-regulate, and/or interrupt their emotional experiencing and expression. Some of those strategies are acquired through socialisation at a young age, as emotions may not only be difficult to bear for the affected individual, but also for those adults who look after him or her. Clients who avoid, over-control, or over-regulate their emotional experiences typically present with a lack of emotional arousal (although other strategies are also present; e.g., distraction, dismissal, deflection, inappropriate humour, use of secondary emotions [e.g., anger instead of hurt], etc.; see O'Brien et al., 2012).

In Chapter 6 we looked at working with emotional avoidance through the use of a chair dialogue, in which the part that interrupts the emotion is enacted in one chair and the suppressed part in another (see also below). For some clients the issue of avoidance may be more global and general than just a specific avoidance of a specific painful emotion. In such cases the therapist needs to attempt to address the issue of avoidance and emotional over-regulation on an every session basis. To this end, the therapist uses typical EFT evocative strategies and interventions, doing so with patience and persistence as the client may not access emotions easily.

The primary condition that increases the likelihood of freer emotional experiencing and expression is the presence of a trustworthy and safe therapeutic relationship. Safety is promoted by the therapist's empathic presence. The safety is also promoted by an explicit client-centeredness, in other words, through the therapist's check-in about how the client feels about different aspects of the therapeutic work. An important part of building a safe environment for emotional experiencing and expression is the provision of a rationale for why accessing painful emotions may eventually be good for the client. The therapist provides a rationale for the therapeutic work in language that is easy for the client to understand. He or she explains that difficult emotional experiences first have to be accessed and felt, in order that they can be transformed by accessing countering feelings that bring relief or a sense of personal confidence and empowerment. Painful emotional memories are thus activated, in order that they can be re-stored together with the adaptive emotional experiences generated in therapy.

Access to emotional experience is built not only through the relational nature of EFT, or through the provision of a rationale, but also through the therapist's moment-to-moment manner of interacting. The typical EFT therapist's manner of responding is very evocative, thus increasing the likelihood of sparking an emotional experience in the client. The therapist focuses constantly on emotional experience (e.g., *What is the most painful part of it all?*). He or she empathically resonates with the client's emotion (e.g., *It aches inside.*), and uses highly evocative, metaphoric language (e.g., *It just leaves a hole inside.*). The therapist also coaches the client to experience and express emotions (e.g., *Say it again: I really resent your laugh.*). The therapist attempts to help the client become more aware of his or her inner experiencing (e.g., *What happens inside when you stay with the picture of your mother?*). The therapist invites the client to stay with the feeling of the emotion and to pay attention to its bodily experiencing (e.g., *Can you stay with that sadness? How does it feel in your body?*). As typical ways of working in EFT, these interventions are used with most clients; however, many of these interventions can be particularly useful with clients who struggle in accessing their emotions. As said before, such clients may simply require more patience from the therapist, and more tenacity, in trying to bring about emotional arousal in a gentle, empathic manner.

An important aspect of working with clients who have difficulty accessing their emotional experience is for the therapist to provide permission for emotions as they appear. For instance, in a situation where the client is on the verge of tears, the therapist may encourage him or her to cry, to let the tears come (e.g., *If you let the tears come, what would they be saying?*—cf. Greenberg, 2002; 2007). The therapist may also encourage the client to observe how he or she stops him- or herself from experiencing emotions (e.g., *How do you make sure that you will not cry?*). Furthermore, the therapist may encourage the client to experiment with emotional experiencing and expression. For instance, with one client who presented as unable to cry within the session, I asked her whether she cried outside the session. When she confirmed that she did, I then suggested that she select a film that she knew would move her to tears. I suggested that she watch the film, observing as she did how her eyes welled-up with tears during particularly moving scenes. I instructed her to deliberately try to refrain from stopping herself crying. We then discussed this exercise in the following session. When asked if she had been able to cry, the client reported that she had been. This provided useful material to work on in therapy, the two of us exploring how the client used deliberate control to stop emotions. We explored the differences between therapy and other social situations, thus identifying what it was that actually lead the client to stop her own emotional experiencing and expression, namely interpersonal embarrassment and a sense of being exposed or unprotected if she cried in front of others.

Another way of working with emotional over-regulation is through the evocative use of the two-chair dialogue task (e.g., self-interruption dialogue) described in Chapter 6 (see Elliott et al., 2004; Greenberg et al., 1993). Just to remind the reader, in this task the client is asked to sit in the chair opposite the one he or she usually sits in, and enact the interrupting, emotion-suppressing part of the self (see Elliott et al., 2004; Greenberg et al., 1993). The point of the technique is that the otherwise automatic emotion-supressing activity is brought into the client's awareness. For instance, the client may become aware of how he or she tenses his or her muscles, or forces his or her gaze downwards, in order to silence the self. Once the interrupting activity is enacted toward the imagined self in the experiencing chair, the client is asked to change chairs, and the therapist instructs the client to see how the interruption makes him or her feel inside. This usually leads the client to become aware of the toll (the emotional or physical cost) of the self-interruption. Clients often report feeling squashed, or describe having headaches, neckaches or tense muscles. The therapist asks the client to stay with the experience and express it to the interrupting part (the self-interrupter) in the other chair. As the unpleasant experience caused by the interrupter is felt, differentiated, named, and expressed to the interrupter, the therapist asks the client what he or she needs from the interrupter, or needs for the self in relation to the interrupter. Clients typically identify a need for freer experiencing and expression. The therapist encourages the client to express this need to the interrupter. As the dialogue continues, the client in the interrupter chair is asked to respond to this need. In well-progressing dialogues the interrupter typically softens and offers support to the newly asserting, experiencing self. However, in some cases the client is simply unable to stop interrupting the self, and in these instances, this needs to be acknowledged. A continuing dialogue between the two parts of the self is facilitated. One common outcome is that the experiencer, confronted with a continuing inability of the interrupter to soften, but supported by the therapist, becomes more assertive of his or her need. A more detailed description of the use of two-chair dialogues for overcoming emotional avoidance in the form of emotional interruption or self-worrying processes is described in Chapter 6.

In EFT, the self-interrupter task is often conducted in the context of other tasks such as empty-chair dialogues for unfinished business (cf. Greenberg et al., 1993), in which the client typically expresses some core interpersonal injury to an imagined significant other (this task is described in greater detail in Chapters 6 and 7). Again, just to remind the reader, it is postulated that when emotional experiencing and its expression are stopped in imaginary dialogues with salient hurtful others, it is because the client, on some level, feels that it is too scary to express him- or herself or to allow him- or herself feel certain feelings toward the significant other. In such cases the self-interruption task is then initiated and worked through until the disowned feelings are felt, and the need to be allowed express these feelings to the significant other, is responded to (cf. Greenberg et al., 1993). In well-progressing therapies, this need for freerer emotional experiencing and expression (as well as an additional implicit need to be free from the cost of the interruption, i.e., the unpleasant, uncomfortable feelings that the interruption itself gives rise to) is generally responded to. Occasionally, for very over-regulated clients, the self-interruption task can become quite a central part of therapy, with the therapist offering this type of work repeatedly throughout the therapy process. In such cases the work on mobilising the need for allowing one's own feelings and their expression may have to be enacted several times, and repeating this process may become quite a central part of the overall therapeutic strategy.

Obviously, clients who over-regulate their emotions may struggle with chair dialogues precisely because these tasks are emotionally evocative. Requests that they engage in such tasks may thus lead to even more protective interruption. The therapist, therefore, needs to work on the therapeutic alliance, and on building a sense of safety in the work for the client. He or she needs to have a collaborative understanding with the client as to how they will be working in therapy. The therapist has to also perhaps be somewhat more active in order to keep clients on-task, and in order to maintain the pace of tasks, as without such supportive direction, the clients may tend to interrupt or avoid the tasks (for instance, by talking to the therapist about the imagined other rather than talking directly to the imagined other). The therapist's active pace thus provides necessary scaffolding that helps the client engage in the task.

When using these above-mentioned strategies to help the client feel and express emotions, the therapist needs to always be aware that meaningful progress for clients varies from one individual to another. It is important to always judge a client's emotional accessibility on the basis of his or her initial baseline (Greenberg and Warwar, 1999). Clients who are very regulated may appear to be making very little progress if compared to emotionally less-regulated clients. The same over-regulated clients may, however, be seen to be making significant progress in relation to their emotional accessibility, when compared to themselves at the beginning of therapy.

INTERPERSONAL DIFFICULTIES

As suggested in Chapter 4, the quality of the therapeutic relationship is a crucial factor underpinning any therapeutic, emotion-focused work. However, with some clients the formation of a trusting therapeutic alliance may be more challenging than it might be for others. For good reasons, certain clients may be cautious in any relationship and especially in any relationship that requires them to disclose personal wounds, sensitive content, fears, or anything else that might evoke a sense of shame. In other words, the client's cautiousness in forming a therapeutic relationship has to be considered through the lens of that client's particular vulnerability. A person who was repeatedly betrayed or abused may be naturally suspicious of contact with any new individual. Furthermore, many clients have had experiences with health professionals, whereby they have felt dismissed, patronised, or not taken seriously (see for instance, Timulak, Buckroyd, Klimas et al., 2013). Such experiences make it difficult for clients to trust, and these difficulties need to be understood and empathised with.

Furthermore, in the context of emotion-focused therapy, some clients may feel particularly cautious given the explicit focus on emotion. It is unsurprising that some clients may be apprehensive that evocative emotion-based work may bring (hitherto avoided) painful vulnerability easily and quickly to the surface. The client has to trust not only that the therapist is non-judgmental, acceptant, and sensitive, but also that he or she is skilful enough to handle the difficult feelings in a way that limits the difficult feelings to as short a time as possible. For some clients who have never had the experience that feeling painful emotions can lead to feeling better, this can be a particularly difficult concept for them to negotiate. In such instances, the therapist does not have any option other than to try earning trust moment-by-moment, and step-by-step.

The main skill needed by the therapist in order to negotiate difficulties in the therapeutic relationship is for the therapist to be able to recognise when the client is hesitant about the progress of therapy. As many clients are quite deferential (cf. work of David Rennie, 1990; 1994) and do not always communicate their reservations about therapy, the therapist has to be particularly sensitive to any signs of hesitation and dissatisfaction. Client dissatisfaction can often be expressed indirectly (e.g., by complaining about the time the sessions are held at, by complaining about the way the therapist's room looks, etc.; cf. Safran and Muran, 2000). Some clients are more direct (e.g., they may disclose how they do not trust health professionals) whilst others even explicitly express distrust (e.g., expressing a wish to finish therapy prematurely, or sharing with the therapist that they feel damaged by him or her, etc.). In some cases, a client's reservation with regards to the relationship may simply be an expression of his or her hopelessness and suffering, and in such instances, client expressions of reservation or criticism may represent a desire to see whether the therapist is capable of bearing such hopelessness and whether is him- or herself more hopeful for the client than the client can be for him- or herself (cf. the psychoanalytic concept of testing the therapist, in which the client exposes the therapist to the experiences that the client struggles with; Weiss and Sampson, 1986).

Jeremy Safran and Christopher Muran (2000) have devoted a significant part of their research career to studying therapeutic ruptures and the best possible ways to respond to them. According to them, one of the major premises of working with ruptures is to understand that there is a particular client vulnerability that is being activated by the therapeutic interaction, which makes the client protectively withdraw from the relationship and/or defend him- or herself by criticising the therapist. Therefore, it is imperative that the therapist understands that any apparent rupture signals hurt which needs to then be focused on.

To focus on vulnerability is, however, challenging. The therapist has to remain emotionally stable and available for the client, and not become scared of emerging or existing conflict (something that is sometime easier said than done). The therapist will need to be able to accept that he or she may not reach all clients, at all times, and that in some cases, the collaboration may not work out. Admitting this may help the therapist to let go of the need to be perfect at all times (a need often based on the therapist's own self [related] difficulties and insecurities). Letting go of the need to be perfect may increase the quality of the therapist's presence when focusing on a particular client's vulnerability. The therapist will be better able to show his or her understanding of the client's struggle, and may be better able to negotiate with the client as to how their work together could be tailored to the client's need for greater safety. For instance, it may be negotiated that chairwork will be used only after the client feels ready to take greater risks and/or when he or she feels able to access feelings in a more evocative way. An important issue here may be the therapist's transparency about his or her inner processes in relation to the work, and his or her perceptions of the client. Equally important (and already elaborated on) will be the provision of a rationale for the particular way the therapist is working, for instance, explaining why accessing pain is so crucial if we want to transform it.

Nevertheless, despite the therapist's best efforts, therapy may not always work out (Barlow, 2010). Some clients may simply be too scared to engage at this particular point in their life (Lipkin, 1948). The client's self-assessment in this respect may often be quite accurate, as they may know that they do not have the resources outside of the therapist's office to help them cope with whatever is happening in therapy. In some cases, the client's suffering is just so overwhelming that he or she simply has no control over his or her own engagement in therapy. In such circumstances, the therapist may endeavour to refer the client to other potential avenues of help (e.g., medical treatment, social work support, etc.), in part hoping that by broadening the range of professional support available to the client, the likelihood of the client accessing the help they need at that point in time will increase.

OVERCOMING SECONDARY ANGER

Some clients have difficulty accessing the underlying hurt triggered by interactions with emotionally salient people in their lives. Instead, they are staying in a state of secondary anger (in EFT literature, also referred to as rejecting anger; Pascual-Leone and Greenberg, 2007; Pascual-Leone, Gilles, Singh, and Andreescu, 2013) in relation to those people. Whilst irritability and anger may in such instances serve a self-protective function, these feelings also prevent the client from processing and transforming the underlying injury. Often such secondary anger serves as protection against unbearable experiences of shame. For instance, some people have a particular intolerance of rejection and respond to experiences of rejection with aggression (Eisenberger, 2011).

With some clients, this presentation of secondary anger is what appears most of the time in therapy. In such cases, the therapist has to first validate the anger and its protective function, but then he or she also needs to focus on what is being avoided by the anger and what is so difficult to tolerate. For instance, a client named John, who had particularly extreme experiences of being shamed by his father in childhood, as an adult expresses an unending rage toward a boss who regularly smirks at him and humiliates him. Initial therapy sessions were spent with John primarily venting anger at the boss, whilst any hints by the therapist that they focus on the underlying hurt caused by the boss's treatment of John were rejected. While John was able to engage in an empty-chair dialogue with his boss (during which he did not go beyond expressing rage toward the boss, e.g., expressing an urge to physically attack him), John became very avoidant when the idea was suggested that he engage in an unfinished-business dialogue with his father. Exploration of his feelings in relation to his father revealed that he essentially did not see the point in engaging in a dialogue with his imagined father. In real life he had always felt 'broken' by his interactions with his father and thus could not imagine any conciliatory reaction from his father in the therapy room. Furthermore, he did not want to enter into any imaginary dialogues with his father because he anticipated that such dialogues would simply evoke a relentless rage aimed at his father, and he stated that he did not feel good about himself for being so full of hatred. In a scenario like this, the therapist's strategy is first to validate the anger, but then, gradually, to suggest to the client that he pay attention to the experience inside, just before he gets angry. For instance, if in a chair dialogue the client enacts a particularly hurtful behaviour of the other, such as shaming by his boss or father, the therapist may say: 'So he is saying "you are nothing". What does it do to you inside as you get this?' Most likely the client will respond by getting angry and shouting back. However, the therapist may say: 'See what happens inside just before you lash out? How does it feel to be put down like this?' Obviously, a client with chronic anger and rage may struggle to recognise feelings of shame (being put down) even after such prompting; therefore, the therapist may need to offer conjecture in order to help the client recognise and name what it is he or she is feeling, for example, 'See how it feels? It must be hurtful or difficult. It may be particularly uncomfortable. See where you can sense it in your body'. The therapist can then listen for any indication of experiences of hurt or shame, and empathise with and validate them. For instance, the client may say: 'I do not want to go there, I am just enraged', to which the therapist may respond: 'It is so difficult to be with those hurtful feelings of being put down; it is just so much better to fight for yourself, the anger comes'.

The focus on underlying hurt has to be a repeated one. The therapist may even teach the client how his or her fight reaction may function to prevent experiences of hurt and humiliation. The client may be taught how shame feels (e.g., a shrinking feeling of wanting to hide and disappear) and informed that it can be quite subtle and difficult to recognise. The therapist may need to use the language of hurt, vulnerability, shame, and humiliation in order to build the client's vocabulary for vulnerable experience. Initially it may be difficult for the client to use such language, as doing so results in the articulation of feelings that are unpleasant. However, as the therapist and client work with the client's painful feelings, that pain may become more regulated, thus leading to the identification of unmet needs, a process which in turn can provide a stepping stone in the generation of transformative experiences of compassion and healthy, protective anger.

HELPING TO DIFFERENTIATE CORE PAIN

The central work with a majority of clients is to help them to differentiate the aspects of their felt core painful feelings. Since these feelings are so painful, it is difficult for clients to stay with these feelings, to explore them, and to symbolize them in a coherent and meaningful narrative. Putting distressing feelings into a comprehensible narrative not only increases clarity; it also helps to regulate affect (Lieberman et al., 2007). Furthermore, achieving clarity in narrative leads almost inevitably to an articulation of the unmet needs that the pain points to (e.g., being accepted, feeling connected to, protected, etc.). The articulation of unmet needs is, as we have already seen, an important step in generating an adaptive response to these needs and the pain they are related to.

The strategies used by therapists to help clients stay with their pain and 'story it' (Angus & Greenberg, 2011) vary from client to client. The therapist may teach the client how feelings feel. The therapist may explain that although it can often feel as if feelings will never shift, feelings are actually transient in nature. The therapist may guide the client to see him- or herself as more than what he or she is feeling at a point in time. For instance, the therapist may say something like: 'It is so painful to stay with shame. Just pay attention to how it feels in the body. It may feel as if you are shrinking. See what action it urges you to take, for instance, to hide. See how it feels. This is a feeling, it feels as if it would never shift ... that it would be so defining. However, you are more than that feeling. It is just very uncomfortable'. The therapist may also help the client to regulate upset if he or she becomes distressed or overwhelmed (e.g., suggesting that the client takes a deep breath), thus helping the client to see that he or she has some control over the unbearable and fear-provoking feelings.

When facilitating the differentiation of core pain, the therapist needs to be patient with the client. He or she may choose to stay silent at times, so as to allow the client to stay with and savour difficult aspects of their feelings: 'How does it feel inside? Just stay with it'. The therapist may actively facilitate symbolisation of the felt quality by asking things like: 'If you were to put the feeling into the words, what words, descriptions, fit?' (this is a process similar to focusing; Elliott, et al., 2004; Greenberg et al., 1993). The therapist may also encourage the client to put the felt experience into a narrative (story), and he or she may facilitate expression of this narrative through the use of tasks such as empty-chair and two-chair dialogues: 'How does it feel inside? Speak from that feeling. Tell him what it does to you inside, tell him how it feels. What do you say back when you get it?' and so on. Eventually, after the client stays with the painful feelings and puts them into a coherent narrative, the therapist focuses on the articulation of the unmet or violated needs, helping the client to name and express these needs, for example, 'And what is it you most want when you feel so ashamed? What is it you needed most from your partner when he ridiculed you like this? Tell him'.

Obviously, all of these interventions are embedded in an empathic, therapeutic relationship. The therapist is empathically present, and he or she collaborates with the client in an empathic exploration of the client's experiencing. As a therapeutic relationship characterised by compassion and caring is also soothing and calming, the client's approach to, and experience of pain, is thus also regulated relationally. Hence it is crucial that the therapist has this caring and soothing presence, and that he or she actively, relationally, and warmly expresses this during the session (Timulak, 2014).

DIFFICULTIES IN GENERATING SELF-COMPASSION

Once the core painful feelings are differentiated and the unmet needs in them articulated, the therapist facilitates transformative experiences by bringing about adaptive healing emotional responses to the pain and unmet needs for the client. This is achieved by the generation of self-compassion and protective anger (see Chapter 7). However, as already pointed out in Chapter 7, for many clients these can be particularly difficult processes. With regards to self-compassion, many clients are so self-critical and self-attacking that it is difficult for them to access a more compassionate stance toward the self. The therapist has a number of options when it comes to trying to facilitate self-compassionate experience and expression. A number of these have been highlighted in Chapter 7, and these will be briefly reviewed here.

For instance, the therapist can communicate compassionate and validating responses from him- or herself toward the client (e.g., *You deserve to be accepted; I am not judging you.*). The therapist can facilitate the client's self-compassion by facilitating the client's enactment of a compassionate stance by a remembered, caring other. For instance, in the middle of a chair task, once the client has expressed need, the client may be asked who would have responded to that need. Once the client nominates a person, then the client may be asked to enact that person's compassionate response. The therapist may also prompt for a compassionate response as part of an unfinished-business dialogue. For instance, if a male client expresses hurt caused by a significant other (e.g., shame felt as a consequence of negative judgment by his father), the therapist will ask the client to express what he needs in the context of that shame, and direct this expression to his imagined father in the other chair (e.g., *I need you to accept me for who I am.*). The client will then be prompted to respond to that need as the imagined other (*Come here, be your father, how does he respond to that need?*).

Another option for generating self-compassion arises when the client expresses a developmentally significant hurt. In such instances the client can be asked to sit in the opposite chair and can be prompted to respond from his or her adult self, now, to the imagined, younger, hurting self. The therapist instructs the client to look at his or her younger self, to see how it feels to witness that vulnerable self in need, and to notice how he or she now, as an adult, is inclined to respond to that need. Whilst this strategy usually brings a compassionate response, some clients who are very self-condemning do have difficulty with it. Clients who have difficulty expressing compassion to their younger self can be instructed to imagine a child other than themselves, who might have had an experience similar to their own. So for example, they might be asked to imagine a child who grew up in the same neighbourhood (or also had an alcoholic father) and see how they would feel toward, and respond to, that child.

Another option that the therapist has when working with a client who struggles to generate self-compassion is to explore the reasons behind the client's difficulty with self-compassion. For instance, after the client has experienced and expressed their pain in the experiencer chair, he or she might be asked to move to the other chair. If the client is unable to respond compassionately to the pain expressed by the experiencing self, the therapist might ask the client to see why it is so difficult to witness and acknowledge the pain: 'Somehow you cannot relate to that pain. What would happen if you responded to it more softly? What is so unacceptable about it?', and so on. This intervention often facilitates awareness of the function of self-judgment and self-rejection. Sometimes this is a fear that 'if I were nicer to you (self), I would just be fooling you … because nobody will ever like you'. Sometimes, this self-treatment arises out of a profound disappointment in the self. For instance, if the client feels a genuine guilt, he or she might perceive a compassionate, softer stance as somehow betraying the standards that he or she wants to follow. In other cases, this unwillingness to express self-compassion reveals itself as a form of self-protection, for example, 'If I beat you constantly, then you will not be that hurt if somebody else attacks you; you will be prepared for it'. Obviously these are just examples, and the actual function of self-criticism and self-attack will be highly idiosyncratic for individual clients. The above examples, however, illustrate that self-criticism, which is usually seen as being entirely negative, can in fact have some self-protective function, which in its own right can be viewed as representing a sort of softening and self-compassion. This may be pointed out to the client: 'So you do it out of protection', or 'You are harsh on the self because you do not want to forget the things that happened'. At the same time, and somewhat paradoxically, therapist validation of the client's (i.e., the client's inner critic's) need to remain self-critical often results in the client spontaneously adopting a softer stance. It is as if the client gives him- or herself permission to let down the protective guard, once this guard's self-protective function is recognised and respected.

The potential for self-compassion in some highly self-rejecting clients shows in the fact that they can be caring toward others (e.g., toward their own children). In such cases it is helpful to work on self-compassion by facilitating scenarios in the session where the client expresses compassion toward others. Clients thus learn to generate compassion, to feel it, to savour it, and to express it. Clinical experience suggests that the capacity to feel compassionate toward others appears to be a good predictor of a client's capacity to eventually be able to feel compassion and express it toward the self. Differences between the compassion the client feels capable of feeling toward others and the difficulty he or she has in expressing such compassion for the self can also be used therapeutically, with the therapist highlighting and exploring this paradox with the client.

There are clients who have never had an experience of somebody being compassionate to them. In such cases, generating and expressing self-compassion may be a highly complicated process. In such instances, the therapeutic work may need to be much more gradual. The therapist may work with the hope that his or her sustained compassionate presence may help to heal the client's wounds, and that his or her modelling of compassion may facilitate the client in developing a capacity to relate to their own self in a more caring way.

DIFFICULTIES IN GENERATING PROTECTIVE ANGER

As we have elaborated, the experiencing of compassion is one of the two primary transformative and healing responses to painful emotions and unmet needs. The other is to experience a protective anger that validates unmet needs (and backs the right to have those needs met) (e.g., *I deserve to be accepted, acknowledged, approved of, etc.*). Chapter 7 highlighted various ways in which protective (or self-assertive) anger can be facilitated by the therapist. For some clients, however, accessing self-protective anger, and expressing an entitlement to have needs met, can be especially difficult. Individual clients may be too timid or too terrified to stand up for themselves. Alternatively, they may too easily feel guilt when they do attempt to stand up for the self. Such difficulties are usually a consequence of a client's past experience, typically experiences whereby he or she was undermined, bullied, or blamed, if and when he or she attempted to stand up for him- or herself. Sometimes it may also be the result of broader social influences (e.g., girls are often expected to be nice, polite, and acquiescent—in other words, non-assertive). Therapeutic work with clients who experience difficulty being assertive, therefore, needs to especially focus on building and supporting the assertive part of the self, as this part is the bearer of confidence and self-esteem, and the source of a sense of personal power and competence.

As with compassion, the baseline therapeutic response facilitating the generation of protective anger is the therapist's own validation of what the client needed and deserved (e.g., *You were not treated fairly, you deserved acceptance from your father.*). However, while it is important that the client experience such validation from the therapist, it is also important that he or she become capable of generating his or her own protective anger, his or her own sense of entitlement to have needs met, his or her own determination to live life freely, and so forth. Chapter 7 highlighted the way that EFT therapists facilitate protective anger through the use of chair tasks in which the client is confronted with the hurtful or undermining behaviour of the other (or of a part of the self) and asked whether he or she will continue to allow that hurtful behaviour, or alternatively, whether he or she will fight back.

Often clients who struggle with self-assertion will find it difficult to stand up for the self, and are instead collapsing in the face of such attack, and withdrawing. In such cases, the therapist can focus the client on whether he or she likes to be attacked. Usually it is quite clear to the client that he or she does not want to be attacked. The therapist then encourages the client to express these sentiments to the attacking other (or self) and the process of doing so becomes a building block in the development of a future, more assertive self. Similarly, the therapist may ask the client what he or she would want to do in the face of such attack if they had more power. Clients are often much better at identifying what they would want to do (which is, in its own way, a formulation of need) than they are at actually doing it. However, once a client can identify what he or she would want to do, or what he or she needs to do, the therapist encourages the client to express this to the imagined attacker in the other chair. This expression of what the client would want is again a stepping stone in the building of a more assertive self. Every expression of self-assertion, however tentative, is then further validated and encouraged by the therapist. Ultimately, the building of a more assertive self is a long-term process, and the steps outlined above are repeatedly worked on within and outside of sessions.

Sometimes it emerges that a client can be somewhat more assertive in certain particular contexts. For instance, a female client who struggles to be assertive of her own needs might spontaneously express protective anger in support of her own children. Such particular contexts (in which the client is not so terrified or guilt ridden) can then be brought into the session, and in this imagined context, the client can be encouraged to assertively stand up for him- or herself. The client is then directed to savour the experiences of being more powerful and of standing up for the self: 'See how it feels inside when you say that … "I will not let you do that to my children". Say it again. "You will not hurt me or my children". How does it feel inside to say that?' If the client recognises that they feel more personally powerful, and shares this realisation with the therapist, he or she is encouraged to express this to the imagined other: 'Say it to him, I feel stronger and it feels good'. The therapist thus helps the client to generate and savour feelings of entitlement and empowerment, and helps the client to consolidate awareness of how liberating and self-supporting these feelings are. Once it becomes possible for the client to feel confident in some contexts, the therapist may quickly seek to facilitate the client's capacity to draw on this emerging self-assertion in more challenging and scary contexts. So, for example, after feeling the power of self-assertion in the context of protecting her children, the therapist may facilitate the client in standing up for herself, and setting boundaries, in relation to her dismissive and intrusive father: 'So you are able to stand up for your children, when they are being harmed. Let's imagine your punitive father in the other chair. How do you, as an adult, protect yourself. What do you say to him? How do you set up a protective boundary?'

As described in Chapter 7, sometimes the EFT therapist may need to use a paradoxical intervention in order to evoke client assertiveness. For instance, when the client is scared, resigned, or deferring, the therapist may empathically acknowledge what the client is feeling, before suggesting that the client tell the attacker that he or she is unable to be assertive in a particularly embellished way: 'You just feel weak. So tell him … I feel weak. I will always feel weak. I will just be here and I will tip-toe around you, and I will be silent, never contradicting you … just serving you. So tell it to him'. Faced with putting this into words, some clients refuse to do so, and instead, spontaneously begin to assert themselves (e.g., *I will never say that.*). Other clients, however, are so resigned that they actually express these sentiments as suggested. In such cases, the therapist may enquire: 'Do you like saying it?' To which the natural and typical response is 'No'. The therapist then encourages the client to express this dislike to the attacker: 'Say it. I do not like saying that I will always tip-toe around you'. This then can be followed with: 'What would you like to be able to say?' As the client reveals what he or she would like to be able to say, the therapist encourages him or her to say this to the attacker. Thus, again, a more assertive part of the self begins to emerge, and as it does, the therapist focuses the client on noticing and savouring how it feels inside to be assertive. The therapist also encourages the client through the above processes repeatedly, building and validating the client's emerging capacity for self-assertion.

As mentioned in Chapter 7, work on accessing protective anger can be more difficult for clients whose anger was often invalidated or judged as inappropriate. As these clients may be profoundly avoidant of their anger, the therapist's strategy aimed at supporting its emergence will need to be especially sophisticated. The therapist may, for instance, ask the client to enact the suppression of anger in a two-chair dialogue (*Come here* [pointing to the other chair]. *How do you stop him* [pointing to the self chair] *from being angry? Stop his anger. Do it!*). The client can then be instructed to observe what impact such suppression has on him- or herself. (*Come back* [to the self chair]. *What happens inside when you are stopped, when your anger is stopped?*) Clients typically describe experiencing an unpleasant tension in response to this suppression. Clients report a sense of being obstructed and a sense of having their own needs obstructed. At this point, the therapist instructs the client to see what he or she needs when feeling this sense of obstruction. Often clients respond by voicing a need to let out their anger (*I need to say how I see things, I need to express what I like and dislike.*). The therapist then can instruct the client to express this need to the significant other (or self) in the other chair e.g., 'Now say it to your father in the other chair'. The therapist may ask the client to sit straight, to put his or her feet firmly on the floor, to look at the eyes of the [imagined] person that they are standing up to, and to express his or her own perspective in a clear and assertive way (cf. Greenberg, 2002).

As mentioned above, the process of accessing and expressing protective anger has to be worked on continuously in therapy, particularly in the case of clients who avoid expressions of anger, or are over-compliant and over-accommodating of others. Work on anger may also focus on the origin of this suppression. For instance, it may transpire that a client's difficulty with self-assertion originated, to some degree, in childhood messages from the client's parents, for example, 'You are mean if you are angry'. The work of therapy may then involve a shift in focus in order to address the shame experienced by the client in connection with their anger.

Another significant problem with accessing assertive anger arises with clients who are by nature very angry, and who respond to negative treatment with a form of anger, defined by EFT theorists as *rejecting anger* (Pascual-Leone and Greenberg, 2007; see the section above on secondary anger). Rejecting anger has an experiential quality, similar to that of global distress. Typically, the client is upset; however, rather than collapsing into despair, he or she presents with reactive rage and anger (*You bastard*). For clients who have difficulty allowing themselves to feel and express any anger, early expressions of anger, even in its rejecting form, can be viewed as adaptive. For these clients, reactive anger may therefore be a good midpoint on the road to self-assertion and protective anger. However, in the case of clients for whom reactive rage is a default position, such anger may be maladaptive, constituting as it often does an avoidance of underlying hurt (cf. Pascual-Leone et al., 2013). In such instances, anger expressed by a client usually has a reactive quality, whilst any reminder of the hurtful trigger (e.g., betrayal) simply brings more anger. As already described in the above section elaborating on the work with secondary anger, when working with such habitually angry clients, it is therapeutically important to access the client's underlying hurt (e.g., being let down, rejected, or abandoned). The shaping of protective anger (e.g., *I am setting a boundary. Your betrayal cannot hurt me anymore.*) is strategically postponed until after the client's core pain and related unmet needs have been accessed. In order to help clients distinguish between protective and rejecting anger, the therapist can adapt a psychoeducative approach, for example, pointing out that the reactive element in rejecting anger reveals vulnerability rather than strength, whilst simultaneously highlighting the implicit strength or power in a protective anger stance (*It is different to be mad at somebody, and to set an appropriate boundary; to say: I am not going to accept that treatment from anybody.).*

As highlighted above, any adaptive experiences of appropriately expressed assertive anger can be further supported by instructing the client to pay attention to how it feels to assert oneself in this manner. The client is repeatedly facilitated in attending to his or her sense of developing strength, in articulating and expressing this strength, and in observing his or her inner experience whilst articulating and expressing his or her sense of emerging strength. The therapist may also instruct the client to express these assertive feelings directly to the therapist: 'Tell it to me: I feel strong'. This anchors the client's experience in reality, as it is more real and also more difficult to say things like this to the therapist than to the imagined other (or part of the self) in the empty chair.

As with overcoming problems in developing client experiences of compassion, building protective anger requires the therapist to be very patient, and to repeatedly set up tasks that can be used for building client strength. This work can be supplemented by work reflecting on the client's difficulty in generating healthy anger in the context of his or her personal history and current personal circumstances. The therapist may also review with the client the extent to which a more assertive stance is emerging outside of the therapy sessions, and reflect on those occasions. The hope is that eventually the client will be able to use this more assertive part of the self as a support for the self. Client experience and awareness of personal power brings a healing quality that not only transforms particular injuries, but also enriches the client's emotional repertoire when experiencing similar painful emotions. The capacity to generate protective anger is an important component in increasing the client's emotional flexibility (Pascual-Leone, 2009), with the client ultimately learning that accessing something painful at first can later lead to experiences of empowerment.

Afterword

This book provides a particular perspective on an emotion-focused way of working with clients who present with depression, anxiety, and traumatic experiences. This perspective looks at the therapeutic process through the lens of *emotion transformation,* as originally captured in Pascual-Leone and Greenberg's (2007; Pascual-Leone, 2009) work, and as subsequently developed in a programme of studies carried out in collaboration with my students at Trinity College Dublin (e.g., Crowley et al., 2013; Dillon et al., 2014; Keogh et al., 2011; Keogh et al., 2013; McNally et al., 2014).

To fully appreciate the nuances of an emotion-focused, theoretical understanding of human distress and its treatment in clinical work, I would however, encourage the reader to refer to what is a lengthy and growing list of outstanding EFT contributions. For instance, the reader may find a very useful theoretical outline and initial conceptualisation of EFT in the classic work by Greenberg et al. (1993), *Facilitating Emotional Change*. This book provides an overview of EFT theory and its clinical applications (particularly experiential tasks). This book is well-supplemented by an account of how to work differently, with different emotions, in Greenberg's and Paivio's (1997) classic *Working with Emotions in Psychotherapy*. A detailed exposition of the use of various experiential tasks is provided in a reader-friendly way, in Elliott et al.'s (2004) *Learning Emotion-Focused Therapy.* A succinct summary of EFT can also be found in Greenberg's (2011) *Emotion-Focused Therapy,* whilst a guide to working with emotions, regardless of the therapist's theoretical orientation, can be found in Greenberg's (2002) book *Emotion-Focused Therapy: Coaching Clients to Work Through Their Feelings.*

Emotion-focused therapy has also been developed for specific difficulties. These developments are captured in several theoretically and clinically rich manuals, such as Greenberg and Watson's (2006) *Emotion-Focused Therapy for Depression* and Paivio and Pascual-Leone's (2010) *Emotion-Focused Therapy for Complex Trauma*. Drawing on a number of intensive case studies, Watson et al.'s book (2007) compares successful and unsuccessful EFT treatments for depression. EFT for couples is also captured in a number of books (e.g., Greenberg and Johnson, 1988; Greenberg and Goldman, 2008; Johnson, 2004). Finally, I would recommend to the reader a forthcoming book on case formulation in EFT, by Goldman and Greenberg (forthcoming).

I hope that this book makes a contribution to EFT, further promoting its development as a coherent though still evolving therapeutic approach. I also hope that it will encourage the professional reader's interest in EFT as a relational therapy which works with the client's pain in a direct, but also respectful, caring, and empowering way. Finally, I hope that it enriches the reader's ways of working with clients, enabling them, together with their clients, to draw on the hidden potential in human vulnerability; the potential for connection, care, and love; but also fairness, freedom, and empowerment.

References

Angus, L. E., & Greenberg, L. S. (2011). *Working with narrative in emotion-focused therapy: Changing stories, healing lives*. Washington, DC: American Psychological Association.

Arseneault, L., Bowes, L., & Shakoor, S. (2010). Bullying victimization in youths and mental health problems: 'Much ado about nothing'? *Psychological Medicine, 40*, 717–729. doi: http://dx.doi.org/10.1017/S0033291709991383.

Barlow, D. H. (2004). *Anxiety and its disorders: The nature and treatment of anxiety and panic*. Guilford Press.

Barlow, D. H. (2010). Negative effects from psychological treatments: A perspective. *American Psychologist, 65*, 13–20. doi: 10.1037/a0015643.

Barrett-Lennard, G. T. (1998). *Carl Rogers' Helping System: Journey & Substance*. London: Sage Publications.

Bateman, A., & Fonagy, P. (2004). *Mentalization-based treatment for borderline personality disorder: A practical guide*. Oxford: Oxford University Press.

Baumeister, R. F., Twenge, J. M., & Nuss, C. K. (2002). Effects of social exclusion on cognitive processes: Anticipated aloneness reduces intelligent thought. *Journal of Personality and Social Psychology, 83*, 817–827. doi: 10.1037/0022-3514.83.4.817.

Bordin, E. S. (1979). The generalizability of the psychoanalytic concept of the working alliance. *Psychotherapy: Theory, Research & Practice, 16*, 252–260. doi: 10.1037/h0085885.

Bouton, M. E. (2004). Context and behavioral processes in extinction. *Learning & Memory, 11*, 485–494. doi: 10.1101/lm.78804.

Bradley, B., DeFife, J. A., Guarnaccia, C., Phifer, J., Fani, N., Ressler, K. J., & Westen, D. (2011). Emotion dysregulation and negative affect: Association with psychiatric symptoms. *Journal of Clinical Psychiatry, 72*, 685–691. doi: 10.4088/JCP.10m06409blu

Brown, J. L., Sheffield, D., Leary, M. R., & Robinson, M. E. (2003). Social support and experimental pain. *Psychosomatic Medicine, 65*, 276–283. doi: 10.1097/01.PSY.0000030388.62434.46.

Cacioppo, J. T., Hughes, M. E., Waite, L. J., Hawkley, L. C., & Thisted, R. A. (2006). Loneliness as a specific risk factor for depressive symptoms: Cross-sectional and longitudinal analyses. *Psychology and Aging, 21*, 140. doi: 10.1037/0882-7974.21.1.140.

Cacioppo, J. T., & Patrick, W. (2008). *Loneliness: Human nature and the need for social connection*. New York: WW Norton & Company.

Caspi, A., McClay, J., Moffitt, T. E., Mill, J., Martin, J., Craig, I. W., … & Poulton, R. (2002). Role of genotype in the cycle of violence in maltreated children. *Science, 297*, 851–854. doi: 10.1126/science.1083968.

Caspi, A., & Moffitt, T. E. (2006). Gene–environment interactions in psychiatry: Joining forces with neuroscience. *Nature Reviews Neuroscience*, *7*, 583–590. doi:10.1038/nrn1925.

Castonguay, L. G., & Beutler, L. E. (Eds.). (2006). *Principles of therapeutic change that work*. New York: Oxford University Press.

Chen, Z. & Williams, K. D. (2011). Social pain is easily relived and prelived, but physical pain is not. In G. MacDonald & L. A. Jensen-Campbell (Eds.), *Social pain: Neuropsychological and health implications of loss and exclusion* (pp. 161–178). Washington, DC: American Psychological Association.

Coan, J. A., Schaefer, H. S., & Davidson, R. J. (2006). Lending a hand: Social regulation of the neural response to threat. *Psychological Science*, *17*, 1032–1039.

Cohen, R. A., Grieve, S., Hoth, K. F., Paul, R. H., Sweet, L., Tate, D., … & Williams, L. M. (2006). Early life stress and morphometry of the adult anterior cingulate cortex and caudate nuclei. *Biological Psychiatry*, *59*, 975–982. doi:10.1016/j.biopsych.2005.12.016.

Courtois, C. A., & Ford, J. D. (Eds.). (2009). *Treating complex traumatic stress disorders: An evidence-based guide*. New York: Guilford Press.

Crowley, N. & Timulak, L. (2013, November). *Emotion Transformation in Generalised Anxiety Disorder: A Case Study of Emotion-Focused Therapy*. Annual Conference of Psychological Society of Ireland, Sligo.

Damasio, A. (2012). *Self comes to mind: Constructing the conscious brain*. Chicago: Random House LLC.

De Bellis, M. D., Hooper, S. R., Spratt, E. G., & Woolley, D. P. (2009). Neuropsychological findings in childhood neglect and their relationships to pediatric PTSD. *Journal of the International Neuropsychological Society*, *15*, 868–878. doi: 10.1017%2FS1355617709990464.

DeWall, C. N., & Baumeister, R. F. (2006). Alone but feeling no pain: Effects of social exclusion on physical pain tolerance and pain threshold, affective forecasting, and interpersonal empathy. *Journal of Personality and Social Psychology*, *91*, 1–15. doi: 10.1037/0022-3514.91.1.1.

DeWall, C. N., Pond, R. S., & Deckam, T. (2011). Acetaminophen dulls psychological pain. In G. MacDonald & L. A. Jensen-Campbell (Eds.), *Social pain: Neuropsychological and health implications of loss and exclusion* (pp. 123–140). Washington, DC: American Psychological Association.

Dickerson, S. S. (2011). Physiological responses to experiences of social pain. In G. MacDonald & L. A. Jensen-Campbell (Eds.), *Social pain: Neuropsychological and health implications of loss and exclusion* (pp. 79–94). Washington, DC: American Psychological Association.

Dickerson, S. S., & Zoccola, P. M. (2013). Cortisol responses to social exclusion. In C. N. DeWall (Ed.), *The Oxford handbook of social exclusion* (pp. 143–151). New York: Oxford University Press.

Dillon, A., Timulak, L., & Greenberg, L. S. (2014). Transforming Core Emotional Pain in a Course of Emotion Focused Therapy for Depression: A Case Study Investigation. Manuscript under review.

Eisenberger, N. I. (2011). The neural basis of social pain: Findings and implication. In G. MacDonald & L. A. Jensen-Campbell (Eds.), *Social pain: Neuropsychological and health implications of loss and exclusion* (pp. 53–78). Washington, DC: American Psychological Association.

Eisenberger, N. I., Taylor, S. E., Gable, S. L., Hilmert, C. J., & Lieberman, M. D. (2007). Neural pathways link social support to attenuated neuroendocrine stress responses. *Neuroimage*, *35*, 1601–1612. doi: 10.1016/j.neuroimage.2007.01.038.

Elliott, R. (2013). Person-centered/experiential psychotherapy for anxiety difficulties: Theory, research and practice. *Person-Centered & Experiential Psychotherapies, 12*, 16–32. doi: 10.1080/14779757.2013.767750.

Elliott, R., Bohart, A., Watson, J. C., & Greenberg, L. (2011). Empathy. *Psychotherapy, 48*, 43–49. doi:10.1037/a0022187.

Elliott, R., Greenberg, L. S., Watson, J., Timulak, L., & Freire, E. (2013). Research on humanistic-experiential psychotherapies. In M. J. Lambert (Ed.), *Bergin & Garfield's handbook of psychotherapy and behavior change* (pp. 495–538). New York: John Wiley.

Elliott, R., Watson, J. C., Goldman, R., & Greenberg, L. S. (2004). *Learning emotion-focused therapy: The process-experiential approach.* Washington, DC: American Psychological Association.

Feder, A., Nestler, E. J., & Charney, D. S. (2009). Psychobiology and molecular genetics of resilience. *Nature Reviews Neuroscience, 10*, 446–457. doi: 10.1038%2Fnrn2649.

Ford, J. D. (2009). Neurobiological and developmental research: Clinical implications. In C. A. Courtois & J. D. Ford, J. D. (Eds.). *Treating complex traumatic stress disorders: An evidence-based guide* (pp. 31–58). New York: Guilford Press.

Geller, S. M., & Greenberg, L. S. (2012). *Therapeutic presence: A mindful approach to effective therapy.* Washington, DC: American Psychological Association.

Gendlin, E. T. (1996). *Focusing-oriented psychotherapy: A manual of the experiential method.* New York: Guilford Press.

Goldman, R. N. & Greenberg, L. S. (forthcoming). Case formulation in emotion-focused therapy: Co-creating clinical maps for change. Washington, DC: American Psychological Association.

Greenberg, L. S. (1979). Resolving splits: Use of the two chair technique. *Psychotherapy: Theory, Research & Practice, 16*, 316–324. doi: 10.1037/h0085895.

Greenberg, L. S. (1980). The intensive analysis of recurring events from the practice of Gestalt therapy. *Psychotherapy: Theory, Research & Practice, 17*, 143–152. doi: 10.1037/h0085904.

Greenberg, L. S. (1983). Toward a task analysis of conflict resolution in Gestalt therapy. *Psychotherapy: Theory, Research & Practice, 20*, 190–201. doi: 10.1037/h0088490.

Greenberg, L. S. (2002). *Emotion-focused therapy: Coaching clients to work through their feelings.* Washington, DC: American Psychological Association Press.

Greenberg, L. S. (2007). *Emotion-focused therapy for depression (DVD).* Washington, DC: American Psychological Association.

Greenberg, L. S. (2011). *Emotion-focused therapy.* Washington, DC: American Psychological Association.

Greenberg, L. S., Auszra, L., & Herrmann, I. R. (2007). The relationship among emotional productivity, emotional arousal and outcome in experiential therapy of depression. *Psychotherapy Research, 17*, 482–493. doi: 10.1080/10503300600977800.

Greenberg, L. S., & Dompierre, L. M. (1981). Specific effects of Gestalt two-chair dialogue on intrapsychic conflict in counseling. *Journal of Counseling Psychology, 28*, 288–294. doi: 10.1037/0022-0167.28.4.288.

Greenberg, L. S., & Elliott, R. (2012). Corrective experience from a humanistic–experiential perspective. In L. G. Castonguay & C. E. Hill (Eds.), *Transformation in psychotherapy: Corrective experiences across cognitive behavioral, humanistic, and psychodynamic approaches* (pp. 85–102). Washington, DC: American Psychological Association.

Greenberg, L. S., & Foerster, F. S. (1996). Task analysis exemplified: The process of resolving unfinished business. *Journal of Consulting and Clinical Psychology, 64*, 439. doi: 10.1037/0022-006X.64.3.439.

Greenberg, L. S., & Goldman, R. N. (2008). *Emotion-focused couples therapy: The dynamics of emotion, love, and power*. Washington, DC: American Psychological Association.

Greenberg, L. S., & Higgins, H. M. (1980). Effects of two-chair dialogue and focusing on conflict resolution. *Journal of Counseling Psychology, 27*, 221–224. doi: 10.1037/0022-0167.27.3.221.

Greenberg, L. S., & Johnson, S. M. (1988). *Emotionally focused therapy for couples*. New York: Guilford Press.

Greenberg, L. S., & Malcolm, W. (2002). Resolving unfinished business: Relating process to outcome. *Journal of Consulting and Clinical Psychology, 70*, 406–416. doi: 10.1037/0022-006X.70.2.406.

Greenberg, L. S., Rice, L. N., & Elliott, R. (1993). *Facilitating emotional change: The moment-by-moment process.* New York: Guilford Press.

Greenberg, L. S., & Paivio, S. (1997). *Working with emotions in psychotherapy*. New York: Guilford Press.

Greenberg, L. S., & Safran, J. D. (1987). *Emotion in psychotherapy: Affect, cognition and the process of change*. New York: Guilford Press.

Greenberg, L. S., & Safran, J. D. (1989). Emotion in psychotherapy. *American Psychologist, 44*, 19–29.

Greenberg, L. S., & Warwar, S. H. (2006). Homework in an emotion-focused approach to experiential therapy. *Journal of Psychotherapy Integration, 16*, 178. doi: 10.1037/1053-0479.16.2.178.

Greenberg, L., & Watson, J. (1998). Experiential therapy of depression: Differential effects of client-centered relationship conditions and process experiential interventions. *Psychotherapy Research, 8*, 210–224. doi: 10.1080/10503309812331332317.

Greenberg, L. S., & Watson, J. C. (2006). *Emotion-focused therapy for depression.* Washington, DC: American Psychological Association.

Greenberg, L. S., & Webster, M. C. (1982). Resolving decisional conflict by Gestalt two-chair dialogue: Relating process to outcome. *Journal of Counseling Psychology, 29*, 468–477. doi: 10.1037/0022-0167.29.5.468.

Gunnar, M. R., Sebanc, A. M., Tout, K., Donzella, B., & van Dulmen, M. M. (2003). Peer rejection, temperament, and cortisol activity in preschoolers. *Developmental Psychobiology, 43*, 346–368. doi: 10.1002/dev.10144

Hawkley, L. C., Burleson, M. H., Berntson, G. G., & Cacioppo, J. T. (2003). Loneliness in everyday life: cardiovascular activity, psychosocial context, and health behaviors. *Journal of Personality and Social Psychology, 85*, 105. doi: 10.1037/0022-3514.85.1.105.

Heim, C., & Nemeroff, C. B. (2001). The role of childhood trauma in the neurobiology of mood and anxiety disorders: preclinical and clinical studies. *Biological Psychiatry, 49*, 1023–1039. doi: 10.1016/S0006-3223(01)01157-X.

Holt-Lunstad, J., Birmingham, W., & Jones, B. Q. (2008). Is there something unique about marriage? The relative impact of marital status, relationship quality, and network social support on ambulatory blood pressure and mental health. *Annals of Behavioral Medicine, 35*, 239–244. doi: 10.1007/s12160-008-9018-y.

Horvath, A. O., Del Re, A., Flückiger, C., & Symonds, B. D. (2011). Alliance in individual psychotherapy. In J. C. Norcross (Ed.), *Psychotherapy Relationships that Work* (pp. 25–69). 2nd ed. New York: Oxford University Press.

Hughes, S., Timulak, L., & McElvaney, J. (2014). *Transforming emotional injury with a developmentally significant other through a series of unfinished business dialogues in clients with generalized anxiety disorder*. Annual Conference of the Society for Psychotherapy Research, Copenhagen, Denmark.

Hyde, L. W., Gorka, A., Manuck, S. B., & Hariri, A. R. (2011). Perceived social support moderates the link between threat-related amygdala reactivity and trait anxiety. *Neuropsychologia, 49*, 651–656. doi: 10.1016/j.neuropsychologia.2010.08.025.

Johnson, S. M. (2004). *Creating connection: The practice of emotionally focused couple therapy*. 2nd edition. New York: Brunner-Routledge.

Jones, W. H., Freemon, J. E., & Goswick, R. A. (1981). The persistence of loneliness: Self and other determinants. *Journal of Personality, 49*, 27–48. doi: 10.1111/j.1467-6494.1981.tb00844.x.

Keogh, C., O'Brien, C., Timulak, L. & McElvaney, J. (2011, June). *The Transformation of Emotional Pain in Emotion Focused Therapy*. 42nd Annual Conference of the International Society for Psychotherapy Research, Bern, Switzerland.

Keogh, D., Timulak, L., & McElvaney, J. (2013, November). *Treating Generalised Anxiety Disorder with Emotion Focused Therapy: A Case Study Investigation of Emotional Change Processes*. Annual Conference of Psychological Society of Ireland, Sligo.

Keyes, K. M., Eaton, N. R., Krueger, R. F., McLaughlin, K. A., Wall, M. M., Grant, B. F., & Hasin, D. S. (2012). Childhood maltreatment and the structure of common psychiatric disorders. *British Journal of Psychiatry, 200*, 107–115. doi: 10.1192/bjp.bp.111.093062.

Kiecolt-Glaser, J. K., & Newton, T. L. (2001). Marriage and health: His and hers. *Psychological Bulletin, 127*, 472. doi: 10.1037/0033-2909.127.4.472.

Klein, M. H., Mathieu, P. L., Gendlin, E. T., & Kiesler, D. J. (1969). The experiencing scale (Vol. 1). *Madison, WI: Wisconsin Psychiatric Institute.*

Kramer, U., Pascual-Leone, A., Despland, J.-N., & de Roten, Y. (in press). Emotion in an alliance rupture and resolution sequence: A theory-building case study. *Counselling and Psychotherapy Research.*

Lafrance Robinson, A., Dolhanty, J., & Greenberg, L. (2013). Emotion-focused family therapy for eating disorders in children and adolescents. *Clinical Psychology & Psychotherapy* (ahead of publication) doi: 10.1002/cpp.1861.

Leary, M. R., Twenge, J. M., & Quinlivan, E. (2006). Interpersonal rejection as a determinant of anger and aggression. *Personality and Social Psychology Review, 10*, 111–132. doi: 10.1207/s15327957pspr1002_2.

Lewis, M. (2008). The emergence of human emotions. In M. Lewis, J. M. Haviland-Jones, & L. Feldman Barrett (Eds.), *Handbook of emotions* (pp. 304–319). 3rd edition. New York: Guilford Press.

Lieberman, M. D., Eisenberger, N. I., Crockett, M. J., Tom, S. M., Pfeifer, J. H., & Way, B. M. (2007). Putting feelings into words: Affect labeling disrupts amygdala activity in response to affective stimuli. *Psychological Science, 18*, 421–428. doi: 10.1111/j.1467-9280.2007.01916.x.

Luborsky, L. & Luborsky, E. (2006). *Research and psychotherapy: The vital link.* Oxford: Jason Aronson.

MacDonald, G., Borsook, T. K., and Spielmann, S. S. (2011). Defensive avoidance of social pain via perceptions of social threat and reward. In G. MacDonald & L. A. Jensen-Campbell (Eds.), *Social pain: Neuropsychological and health implications of loss and exclusion* (pp. 141–160). Washington, DC: American Psychological Association.

MacDonald, G., & Jensen-Campbell, L. A. (Eds.). (2011). *Social pain: Neuropsychological and health implications of loss and exclusion.* Washington, DC: American Psychological Association.

Master, S. L., Eisenberger, N. I., Taylor, S. E., Naliboff, B. D., Shirinyan, D., & Lieberman, M. D. (2009). A picture's worth: Partner photographs reduce experimentally induced pain. *Psychological Science, 20*, 1316–1318.

McCranie, E. W., & Bass, J. D. (1984). Childhood family antecedents of dependency and self-criticism: Implications for depression. *Journal of Abnormal Psychology, 93*, 3. doi: 10.1037/0021-843X.93.1.3.

McNally, S., Timulak, L., & Greenberg, L. S. (2014). Transforming emotion schemes in emotion-focused therapy: A case study investigation. *Person-Centered and Experiential Psychotherapies, 13*, 128–149. doi: 10.1080/14779757.2013.871573.

Murphy, J., Timulak, L. & McElvaney, J. (June 2014). *Emotion-Focused Therapy for Generalized Anxiety Disorder: A Task Analysis of Two Chair Work with Worry.* Annual Conference of the Society for Psychotherapy Research, Copenhagen, Denmark.

Myers, K. M., Ressler, K. J., & Davis, M. (2006). Different mechanisms of fear extinction dependent on length of time since fear acquisition. *Learning & Memory, 13*, 216–223. doi: 10.1101/lm.119806.

O'Brien, K., Timulak, L., McElvaney, J. & Greenberg, L. S. (2012). *Emotion-Focused Case Conceptualisation of Generalised Anxiety Disorder: Underlying Core Emotional Pain in Clients with Generalised Anxiety Disorder*. 43rd Annual Conference of the International Society for Psychotherapy Research, Virginia Beach, USA.

Öhman, A., & Rück, C. (2007). Four Principles of Fear and Their Implications for Phobias. In J. Rottenberg & S. L. Johnson (Eds.), *Emotion and psychopathology: Bridging affective and clinical science* (pp. 167–189). Washington, DC, US: American Psychological Association.

Öhman, A., & Soares, J. J. (1994). "Unconscious anxiety": Phobic responses to masked stimuli. *Journal of Abnormal Psychology, 103*, 231–240. doi: 10.1037/0021-843X.103.2.231.

Paivio, S. C., & Greenberg, L. S. (1995). Resolving "unfinished business": Efficacy of experiential therapy using empty-chair dialogue. *Journal of Consulting and Clinical Psychology, 63*, 419–425. doi: 10.1037/0022-006X.63.3.419.

Paivio, S. C., & Pascual-Leone, A. (2010). *Emotion focused therapy for complex trauma: An integrative approach.* American Psychological Association, Washington, DC.

Panksepp, J. (2011). The neurobiology of social loss in animals: Some keys to the puzzle of psychic pain in humans. In G. MacDonald & L. A. Jensen-Campbell (Eds.), *Social pain: Neuropsychological and health implications of loss and exclusion* (pp. 11–52). Washington, DC: American Psychological Association.

Pascual-Leone, A. (2005). *Emotional processing in the therapeutic hour: Why the only way out is through.* Unpublished doctoral thesis. York University, Toronto.

Pascual-Leone, A. (2009). Emotional processing cycles in experiential therapy: "Two steps forward, one step backward". *Journal of Consulting and Clinical Psychology, 77*, 113–126. doi: 10.1037/a0014488.

Pascual-Leone, A., Gilles, P., Singh, T., & Andreescu, C. A. (2013). Problem anger in psychotherapy: An emotion-focused perspective on hate, rage, and rejecting anger. *Journal of Contemporary Psychotherapy, 43*, 83–92. doi: 10.1007/s10879-012-9214-8.

Pascual-Leone, A., & Greenberg, L. S. (2007). Emotional processing in experiential therapy: Why "the only way out is through". *Journal of Consulting and Clinical Psychology, 75*, 875–887. doi: 10.1037/0022-006X.75.6.875.

Petersen, S. E., & Posner, M. I. (2012). The attention system of the human brain: 20 years after. *Annual review of neuroscience, 35*, 73.

Pressman, S. D., Cohen, S., Miller, G. E., Barkin, A., Rabin, B. S., & Treanor, J. J. (2005). Loneliness, social network size, and immune response to influenza vaccination in college freshmen. *Health Psychology, 24*, 297. doi: 10.1037/0278-6133.24.3.297.

Quirk, G. J. (2007). Prefrontal-amygdala interactions in the regulation of fear. In J. J. Gross (Ed.), *Handbook of emotion regulation* (pp. 27–46). New York: Guilford Press.

Rennie, D. (1990). Toward a representation of the client's experience of the psychotherapy hour. In G. Lietaer, J. Rombauts & R. Van Balen (Eds.), *Client-centered and experiential psychotherapy in the nineties* (pp. 155–172). Leuven: Leuven University Press.

Rennie, D. (1994). Client's deference in psychotherapy. *Journal of Counseling Psychology, 41*, 427–437.

Rice, L. N., & Kerr, G. P. (1986). Measures of client and therapist vocal quality. In L. S. Greenberg & W. M. Pinsof (Eds.), *The psychotherapeutic process: A research handbook* (pp. 73–105). New York: Guilford Press.

Rice, L. N., & Saperia, E. P. (1984). Task analysis of the resolution of problematic reactions. In L. N. Rice & L.S. Greenberg (Eds.), *Patterns of change* (pp. 29–66). New York: Guilford Press.

Rhodes, R. H., Hill, C. E., Thompson, B. J. & Elliott, R. (1994).Client retrospective recall of resolved and unresolved misunderstanding events. *Journal of Counseling Psychology, 41*, 473–483.

Rogers, C. R. (1942). *Counseling and psychotherapy; newer concepts in practice*. Boston: Houghton Mifflin.

Rogers, C. R. (1957). The necessary and sufficient conditions of therapeutic personality change. *Journal of Consulting Psychology, 21*, 95–103. doi: 10.1037/h0045357.

Rogers, C. R. (1951). *Client-centered therapy: Its current practice, implications and theory*. Boston: Houghton Mifflin.

Rutter, M. (1985). Resilience in the face of adversity. *British Journal of Psychiatry, 147*(1), 598–611.

Safran, J. D., & Muran, J. C. (2000). *Negotiating the therapeutic alliance*. New York: Guilford Press.

Safran, J. D., Muran, J. C., & Eubanks-Carter, C. (2012). Repairing alliance ruptures. In J. C. Norcross (Ed.), *Psychotherapy Relationships that Work* (pp. 224–238). 2nd ed. New York: Oxford University Press.

Schore, A. N. (2001). Effects of a secure attachment relationship on right brain development, affect regulation, and infant mental health. *Infant Mental Health Journal, 22*, 7–66.

Shahar, B. (2013). Emotion-focused therapy for the treatment of social anxiety: An overview of the model and a case description. *Clinical Psychology & Psychotherapy.* doi: 10.1002/cpp.1853.

Timuľák, L. (1999). Humility as an important attitude in overcoming a rupture in the therapeutic relationship. *The Person-Centered Journal, 6*, 153–163.

Timulak, L. (2008). *Research in psychotherapy and counselling.* London: Sage.

Timulak, L. (2011). *Developing your counselling and psychotherapy skills and practice*. London: Sage Publications.

Timulak, L. (2014). Witnessing clients' emotional transformation: An emotion-focused therapist's experience of providing therapy. *Journal of Clinical Psychology, 70*, 741–752. doi: 10.1002/jclp.22109.

Timulak, L., Buckroyd, J., Klimas, J., Creaner, M., Wellsted, D., Bunn, F., Bradshaw, S. and Green, G. (2013). *Helpful and unhelpful aspects of eating disorders treatment involving psychological therapy.* Lutterworth: British Association for Counselling and Psychotherapy.

Timulak, L., Dillon, A., McNally, S. & Greenberg, L. S. (2012). *Transforming Shame and Loneliness in an Emotion-Focused Therapy for Depression: An Analysis of Two Successful Outcome Cases*. 43rd Annual Conference of the International Society for Psychotherapy Research, Virginia Beach, USA.

Timulak, L., & Lietaer, G. (2001). Moments of empowerment: A qualitative analysis of positively experienced episodes in brief person-centred counselling. *Counselling and Psychotherapy Research, 1*, 62–73.

Timulak, L., McElvaney, J., & O'Brien, K. (2012). *Emotion-focused therapy for GAD.* Person-Centered and Experiential Conference, Antwerp, Belgium.

Timulak, L., & Pascual-Leone, A. (2014). New Developments for Case Conceptualization in Emotion-Focused Therapy. *Clinical Psychology & Psychotherapy*. ahead-of-print. doi: 10.1002/cpp.1922.

Tronick, E. (2005). Why is connection with others so critical? The formation of dyadic states of consciousness and the expansion of individuals' states of consciousness: Coherence-governed selection and the co-creation of meaning out of messy meaning making. In J. Nadel & D. Muir (Eds.), *Emotional development: Recent research advances* (pp. 293–315). New York: Oxford University Press.

Tronick, E., Als, H., Adamson, L., Wise, S., & Brazelton, T. B. (1979). The infant's response to entrapment between contradictory messages in face-to-face interaction. *Journal of the American Academy of Child Psychiatry, 17*, 1–13. doi: 10.1016/S0002-7138(09)62273-1.

Warwar, S., & Greenberg, L. S. (1999). Client emotional arousal scale–III. Unpublished manuscript, York University, Toronto, Ontario, Canada.

Watson, J. C., Goldman, R. N., & Greenberg, L. S. (2007). *Case studies in emotion-focused treatment of depression: A comparison of good and poor outcome*. Washington, DC: American Psychological Association.

Way, B. M., & Taylor, S. E. (2011). Genetic factors in social pain. In G. MacDonald & L. A. Jensen-Campbell (Eds.), *Social pain: Neuropsychological and health implications of loss and exclusion* (pp. 95–120). Washington, DC: American Psychological Association.

Weiss, J. (1993). *How psychotherapy works?* New York: Guilford Press.

Weiss, J., & Sampson, H. (1986). *The psychoanalytic process.* New York: Guilford Press.

Welling, H., & Greenberg, L. S. (2011). *The experience of the psychotherapist: Interview with Leslie Greenberg.* Downloaded Dec. 16, 2013. http://www.psicoterapiaintegrativa.com/videos/The%20Experience%20of%20the%20Psychotherapist-Leslie%20Greenberg.pdf.

Index

acceptance and agency stage of emotional transformation 34
acknowledgment experiences 17; *see also* validation
Adamson, L. 15
adaptive anger *see* protective anger
adaptive emotions *see* compassion; protective anger; self-compassion
agency, in case conceptualisation framework 62, 74
agoraphobia 68
alliance, therapeutic 143–4
Als, H. 15
amygdala, chronic anxiety and 13
analgesic impact of caring other 4
anger: assertive 34; fear of 41; in global distress 65; negative evaluation of 41; protective (*see* protective anger); secondary (*see* rejecting anger); suppression of, as self-interruption 23
anxiety: amygdala and 13; anticipatory 24–5, 61, 62, 65, 69–70, 74, 78–9; apprehensive 11, 12, 25, 65, 69–70, 148; in case conceptualisation framework 74; chronic 13–14; core emotional pain underlying 37–8; as secondary emotional experience 7, 65; social 24–5
anxiety disorders, anticipatory fear in 69
apprehension, in case conceptualisation framework 74
assertive anger 34
attachment experiences 59
attack, traumatic 6
avoidance 25–6; acknowledgement of 37; anticipatory anxiety and 69; case conceptualisation of 61, 62, 63, 67–8, 74, 78; as contributory to global distress 68; core pain access obstructed by 110; enacting 100; fear and 20, 25, 37, 69; functions of 99, 101; identifying need obstructed by 103–4, 110; markers of 100; overcoming 99–105; problematic emotion schemes and 68; rituals and 26; of social situations 17; therapeutic approaches to 68; of triggers 36; worrying or interruption as 24, 101–2; *see also* behavioural avoidance; emotional avoidance

Barlow, D. H. 25
Baumeister, R. F. 15
behavioural avoidance 7, 20, 67–9, 78; case conceptualisation of 62, 74; overcoming 104; worry and 24, 26, 68
Borsook, T. K. 18
brain: early experiences of rejection and development of 19; 'learning' *vs.* 'surviving' brain 14, 31
Brazelton, T. B. 15
bullying 18, 42

caring, experiences of 14–15
caring behaviour, influence of genetic predispositions to benefitting from 17
caring other, calming effect of 15; *see also* other(s), salient
case conceptualisation 58–84; agency and empowerment in 74; anticipatory anxiety/apprehension in 61, 62, 69–70, 74, 78–9; avoidance in 61, 62, 63, 67–8, 74, 78; core pain in 61, 62, 63, 70–2, 74, 79–82; eight-step, of Greenberg and colleagues 58–60; emotion-focused, based on emotional transformation model 61–73; emotion schemes and 58, 59, 60, 61; global distress/secondary emotions in 61, 62, 65–6, 74–5; grieving/letting go in 74; as hypothetical

and tentative 61; rejecting anger in 74; relief in 74; for reluctant client 144; self-treatment in 66–7, 76–8; triggers/perceptions in 61, 62, 63–4, 75–6; unmet needs in 61, 62, 72–3, 74, 82–4
chair dialogue: to check impact of worrying or interrupting 101–5; to enact avoidance 100; to generate self-compassion 161; *see also* empty-chair dialogue; two-chair self-self dialogue
Chen, Z. 21
childhood, traumatic experiences in 21
children: 'learning' *vs.* 'survival' brain development in 31; overlooked 30
'clearing a space' task 87, 148–52
Coan, J. A. 15
compassion 38–43; in case conceptualisation 62, 74; core pain transformation through 126; as counterbalance to core pain 72, 86; in emotion scheme transformation 39, 43, 112–13, 139; enactment and 'letting in' of 112–13, 116; facilitation of 61; generating 117, 159; grief following 36, 44, 140; healing experiences of 39, 161, 163; in imaginary dialogues 115–25, 127, 132–3; psychoeducation about 139; in response to unmet needs 38–43; *see also* self-compassion
connection needs 11, 14–17
core pain 11, 28; case conceptualisation of 61, 62, 63, 70–2, 74, 79–82; chronic 38; differentiation of 106–7, 160–1; emotion schemes and 28, 70, 82, 109; experiencing 105–9; fear of 24; global distress obfuscating 70, 109–10; identifying 59; interconnection of emotional clusters in 20, 71–2, 82; personal narrative linked to 38; presentation of 70; as primary maladaptive emotions 28; roots of 72; secondary emotions masking 20, 26, 35–6, 109–10; staying with 28, 38, 52, 72, 97, 102, 105, 110, 141, 160; therapeutic focus on 72, 87–8; underlying depression or anxiety 37–8; from unmet needs 20; *see also* loneliness-related primary maladaptive emotions; shame-related primary maladaptive emotions; terror/fear-related primary maladaptive emotions
core pain, accessing 37–8, 86–105; case vignette 109–11; through empty-chair dialogues 89, 90–3, 94, 110; through evocative unfolding 88–9; obstruction of 109–10; overcoming avoidance in 99–105; through two-chair self-self dialogues 89, 94–9
corrective interpersonal emotional experience 53
cortisol 5, 18–19
critic chair 131
Crowley, N. 1

Damasio, A. 2, 47
Davidson, R. J. 15
depression: from chronic anxiety 14; core emotional pain underlying 37–8; as secondary emotional experience 6; self-treatment of 66
de Roten, Y. 1
Despland, J.-N. 1
development: capacity to tolerate pain and distress and 33; of emotion schemes 38
dialogues, imaginary 18, 40, 42, 64, 76, 77, 113–38; compassion in 115–25, 127, 132–3; core pain accessed through 89–99; example of 128–30; facilitation of 126–7; global distress in 115, 132; grieving in 126; protective anger in 115, 116–20, 126, 127, 132, 133, 135–7; about rejection 114–15; reparatory exchange in 128–30; resistance to 159; roles in 113–14; transformation of emotional pain in 113–38; *see also* empty-chair dialogue; two-chair self-self dialogue
Dickerson, S. S. 18
Dillon, A. 1
distress, global *see* global distress
Donzella, B. 19
DSM–5 3–4

Eisenberger, N. I. 3, 15
Elliott, R. 27, 58, 85, 86, 167
emotional avoidance 7, 20, 63; in case conceptualisation framework 62, 74; characteristics of 7; fear and 20, 25, 37, 69; forms of 67–9; through over-regulation 154–5; self-interruption as 26, 67, 155–6; self-treatment with 66, 84; treatment strategies for 153–6; unmet needs and 73; worry as 24, 25, 67–8, 78, 110
emotional clusters *see* loneliness-related primary maladaptive emotions; shame-related primary maladaptive emotions; terror/fear-related primary maladaptive emotions

emotional expression, client difficulty in 51
emotional flexibility 34
emotionally overwhelmed clients 147–53; calming 148; 'clearing a space' task for 148–52; protective anger for 152–3; self-compassion for 152
emotional pain *see* pain, emotional
emotional processing: adaptive 13; maladaptive 14, 29; within-session 34
emotional regulation, by therapist 52–3
emotional resilience 34
emotion-focused therapy i, 1
Emotion-Focused Therapy: Coaching Clients to Work through Their Feelings (Greenberg) 167
Emotion-Focused Therapy for Complex Trauma (Paivio and Pascual-Leone) 167
Emotion-Focused Therapy for Depression (Greenberg and Watson) 167
Emotion-Focused Therapy (Greenberg) 167
emotion memory structures 29
emotions: as adaptive resource and meaning system xi; client's style of processing 59; duality in working with xi
emotion schemes: activation or triggering of 20; anticipatory fear and 69–70; avoidance and 68; case conceptualisation and 58–61; compassion and protective anger in transforming 39, 43, 112–13, 139; core pains at centre of 28, 70, 82, 109; corrective emotional experiences in transforming 53; development of 38; EFT conceptualisation of 13; experiential tasks for transforming 85–6, 146; formation of 29; interconnections of 82, 144; from loneliness 17; maladaptive 14, 19, 21, 29; persistence of 17; psychotherapeutic change and 37; re-scripting of 39, 43; trauma-based 13–14
empathy 15, 50, 53, 57, 87, 105
empowerment: case conceptualisation of 62, 74; through protective anger 40, 44, 113, 126, 137
empty-chair dialogue 55, 85, 89, 90–3, 94, 110; pain differentiation using 106–7
entitlement, felt 40–1
environmental influences on suffering 5
evocative unfolding, accessing core pain through 88–9
exclusion 5–6, 17–18
exhaustion, physical 65
existential meeting, in therapeutic relationship 54–7
existential needs 28, 34
experiencer chair 131
experiential approaches to psychotherapy 58
experiential tasks *see* tasks, therapeutic

Facilitating Emotional Change (Greenberg et al.) 85, 167
fear: of anger 41; case conceptualisation of 61, 62, 69–70; of core emotional pain 24; as secondary emotional experience 7; *see also* terror/fear-related primary maladaptive emotions
felt entitlement 40–1
flexibility, emotional 34
Ford, J. D. 31

Gendlin, E. T. 148
generalised anxiety disorder 23; case vignette 78–9; emotional avoidance in 67
genetic predisposition(s): benefits from caring behaviour influenced by 17; to sensitivity to rejection 19; to suffering 5; to tolerating pain and distress 33
global distress 26–8; avoidance as contributory to 68; case conceptualisation of 61, 62, 65–6, 74–5; 'clearing a space' task for 87; clients overwhelmed by 147–53; clinical presentation of 35, 61–3, 86–7; core pain access obstructed by 70, 109–10; emotions common to 65; in imaginary dialogues 115, 132; secondary emotions present in 35; therapist's acknowledgement of 37; transformation of emotional pain and 34
Goldman, R. N. 58, 59, 85, 86, 167
Greenberg, L. S. xii, 1, 23, 27, 34, 48, 58, 59, 85, 86, 142, 167
grief/hurt stage of transformation of emotional pain 34, 44
grieving: accompanying healing experiences 113; in case conceptualisation framework 62, 74; following compassion and protective anger 36, 44, 140; in imaginary dialogues 126; during transformation of emotional pain 36
guiding instructions 105
Gunnar, M. R. 19

healing 36; spontaneous grief accompanying 113; therapist contribution to 47, 145; *see also* compassion; protective anger; self-compassion
helplessness, as secondary emotional experience 6
homework for client 139, 146
hopelessness, as secondary emotional experience 6
'hot teaching' (psychoeducation) 105, 139, 146
humanistic approaches to psychotherapy 58
humiliation: self-interruption of 23; vicious circle of 18

identity experiences 59
imaginary dialogues *see* dialogues, imaginary
incongruity, self-interruption and 23
inhibitory learning 14
injury, forms of 5–6
interpersonal situations: therapeutic relationship and 156–8; as triggers 63–4, 90
intervention, paradoxical 42, 127, 164–5

judgement, negative 5

Keogh, C. 1
Keogh, D. 1
Kramer, U. 1

learning, inhibitory 14
'learning' brain 14, 31
Learning Emotion-Focused Therapy (Elliott et al.) 85, 167
letting go 62, 74; *see also* grieving
Lieberman, M. D. 15
loneliness 14–17; in case conceptualisation framework 62; negative impact of 16; psychological and physiological correlates of 15–16
loneliness-related primary maladaptive emotions 6, 11; apprehensive fear (anxiety) of 69; avoidance strategies 36; case vignette 54–6, 76, 79–83, 141; characteristics of 71; corrective interpersonal emotional experience to address 53; early experience of 17; empathic responding to 105; implicit emotions associated with 20; interpersonal injuries leading to 29–30; negative impact of 16; negative self-attitudes and 67; triggers of 20, 71; unmet needs underlying 28, 35, 71, 73
love needs 11, 14–17

MacDonald, G. 18
McElvaney, J. 1, 23
McNally, S. 1
marital satisfaction 15
marker(s), task 68, 143; of avoidance 100; task indicated by 58, 59–60, 68, 85; for two-chair self-self dialogue 94
Master, S. L. 15
medication, avoidance through 26
memories: emotion memory structures 29; safety 14
monoamine oxidase 19
Muran, J. C. 157

Naliboff, B. D. 15
need(s): existential 28, 34; fulfilment of 2; for love and connection 11, 14–17; for safety and security 11, 12–14; unmet (*see* unmet needs); for validation 11, 17–19
neural development: early traumas and 14; 'learning' *vs.* 'survival' brain 31
Nuss, C. K. 15

O'Brien, C. 1
O'Brien, K. 1, 23
other(s), salient: analgesic impact of 4; enactments of interactions with hurtful 42; problematic self-treatments and 66; protective anger against 41–2; rejection by 114–15; support from 33; as trigger 63, 114; *see also* dialogues, imaginary
overprotection 26
oxytocin 14, 16, 17

pain, emotional 2–4, 11–32; anticipatory (secondary) anxiety and 24–5; avoidance of 25–6; capacity to tolerate 33; characteristics of 19–20; chronic 30–1; core (*see* core emotional pain); defined 2; global distress (*see* global distress); from identification with others' emotional pain 31–2; from loneliness 14–17; mainstream perspectives on 3–4; manifestations of 2–3; physical pain and 2–3, 15; responding to 4–7; roots of 29–32; self-treatment of (*see* self-treatment of emotional pain); from shame 17–19; from terror/fear experience 12–14; traumatic 30–1;

triggers of (*see* trigger(s)); undifferentiated 11; unmet needs and 5–6, 28–9
pain, physical 2–3, 15; from rejection 18; social support and 4
'pain compass' 59, 65–6
Paivio, S. C. 1, 27, 167
panic disorder 25, 68
paradoxical intervention 42, 127, 164–5
Pascual-Leone, A. 1, 27, 28, 34, 60, 61, 142, 167
physical pain *see* pain, physical
presenting problem: client's narrative about 58–9; identification of 58
protective anger 38–43; accessing 69, 165–6; in case conceptualisation 62, 74; coaching client in expression of 42; as counterbalance to core pain 40, 67, 72, 86; development/generation of 116–20, 133, 135–7, 159, 163–6; for emotionally overwhelmed clients 152–3; in emotion scheme transformation 112–13, 139; empowerment through 40, 44, 113, 126, 137; enactment and 'letting in' of 112–13; entitlement through 39, 40–1; facilitation of 39, 41, 42, 61, 110, 127, 133, 145; grief following 36, 44, 140; healing experience of 39, 161, 166; in imaginary dialogue 115, 116–20, 126, 127, 132, 133, 135–7; psychoeducation about 139; in response to unmet needs 38–43; transformation of core pain through 126; validation of 115, 117–18
psychoeducation ('hot teaching') 105, 139, 146
psychological pain *see* pain, emotional

rejecting anger 74, 115, 119, 165–6; overcoming 158–9; as stage of emotional transformation 34
rejection, experience of 17–18
relief, in case conceptualisation framework 62, 74
resignation, from chronic anxiety 14
resilience, emotional 34
Rice, L. N. 27, 58, 85, 167
rituals, avoidance of triggers through 26

sadness *see* loneliness-related primary maladaptive emotions
safety: in therapeutic relationship 49–52, 153; validation and experiences of 17
safety memories 14
safety needs 11, 12–14
Safran, J. D. 27, 157
Schaefer, H. S. 15
Sebanc, A. M. 19
secondary emotions: anticipatory anxiety 24–5, 61, 62, 65, 69–70, 74, 78–9; core pain masked by 20, 26, 35–6, 109–10; as maladaptive 27; self-interruption through 23; *see also* global distress
security needs 11, 12–14
self-assertion 163–4
self-attribution of problems 19, 22, 30
self-compassion: accessing 67, 69; development/generation of 40, 118–25, 133, 161–3; difficulties in generating 161–3; for emotionally overwhelmed clients 152; facilitating 145; forms of 104; as transformative 112
self-critic dialogue *see* two-chair self-self dialogue
self-criticism 22; enactment of 131–2; worry and 24
self-evaluation, negative 34
self-interruption 22–3, 26, 66–7; core pain access obstructed by 110; impact of 101–2; mobilisation against 103–4; self-compassion for 104–5; two-chair dialogue for 68, 155–6
self-organisation 17, 25, 29, 39; *see also* emotion schemes
self-self dialogues *see* two-chair self-self dialogue
self-soothing 16, 34
self-treatment of emotional pain 38, 61; in case conceptualisation framework 62, 66–7, 74, 76–8; case example 76–7, 109; from disappointment in self 162; enactment of 94–6; forms of 66; functions of 21, 98, 132; maladaptive 21–4; problematic (negative) 35, 66–7, 84, 94–9, 109, 130; softening of 104; as source of additional pain 35; strategies for 22–4; as trigger 64, 72, 89; two-chair dialogue for 67; *see also* self-interruption
self-worrying 23–4
serotonin 19
shame 17–19; in case conceptualisation framework 62; self-interruption of 23
shame-related primary maladaptive emotions 6, 11; anger masking 26, 158, 159; anticipatory anxiety and 24–5; apprehensive fear of 69–70; avoidance of 36, 64; case vignette 75, 79, 81–3, 98, 109, 110, 118,

134–5, 141; characteristics of 71; corrective interpersonal emotional experience to address 53; development of 19; empathic responding to 105; interpersonal injuries leading to 29; negative self-attitudes and 67; therapeutic approach to 69–70; triggers of 20–1, 71; unmet needs underlying 28, 35, 71, 73
Shirinyan, D. 15
social anxiety 24–5; anticipatory fear in 69; self-treatment of 66
social situations: avoidance of 17; loneliness and 16–17
social support, pain threshold and 4–5
somatisation 27
Spielmann, S. S. 18
strategy for therapy 85–142; accessing core pain 86–105, 109–11; case vignette 109–11; experiencing core emotional pain 105–9; identifying unmet needs 105–9; transforming core emotional pain 112–42
stressors, immediate and post-traumatic responses to 12
suffering: model of i; theory of 2; *see also* pain, emotional
support from others 33
'surviving' brain 14, 31

tasks, therapeutic: 'clearing a space' 87, 148–52; evocative unfolding 88–9; markers indicating choice of 58, 59–60, 68, 85; moment-to-moment processes within 60; with regards to unmet needs 28–9; for transforming emotion schemes 85–6, 146
Taylor, S. E. 15
terror/fear-related primary maladaptive emotions 6, 11; anticipatory anxiety *vs.* 24, 25, 69; apprehensive anxiety from 12; avoidance of 36; in case conceptualisation framework 62, 74; case vignette 79, 81–2, 83–4, 109; characteristics of 71; in transformation of emotional pain 34; from traumas 12–14; triggers of 20, 71; unmet needs underlying 35, 71
theoretical perspective *see* therapeutic relationship
therapeutic alliance 143–4
therapeutic relationship 47–57; author account of 47–9; corrective interpersonal emotional experience in 53; emotional regulation in 52–3; existential meeting in 54–7; interpersonal difficulties in 156–8; safety provision 49–52, 153; strain in 51–2
therapeutic stance 50–2
therapists in training 51
Timulak, L. 1, 23, 47, 50, 60, 61
Tout, K. 19
transformative work: embedding in overall therapy process 138–40; under time limits 145–6
trauma, terror/fear from 12–14
treatment strategy 143–66; for differentiating core pain 160–1; difficulties in generating protective anger 163–6; difficulties in generating self-compassion 161–3; for emotionally avoidant clients 153–6; for emotionally overwhelmed clients 147–53; interpersonal difficulties and 156–8; length of therapy and 143–7; for overcoming secondary anger 158–9
trigger(s) 6, 20–1, 31–2; apprehensive fear (anxiety) as fear of 69; avoidance of 36; case conceptualisation of 61, 62, 63–4, 74, 75–6; case vignette 75–6; emotion schemes activated by 20; interpersonal situations/relationships as 63–4, 90; of loneliness 20, 71; of primary terror/fear 20, 71; responses to 21–4, 66; salient other as 114; self-treatment as 64, 72, 89; of shame-related primary maladaptive emotions 71; therapeutic enactment of (*see* dialogues, imaginary); therapist's strategy with regards to 64; worry about 26
Trinity Emotion-Focused Therapy Research Group 34
Tronick, E. 15
Twenge, J. M. 15
two-chair self-self dialogue 85, 89, 94–9, 110; for emotional over-regulation 154–5; marker for 94; for self-critical processes 67; for self- interruption 68, 155–6; transformation of emotional pain in 130–8

unmet needs: articulation of 28–9, 36–8, 52, 55, 69, 82–3, 107–9, 131, 145, 160; case conceptualisation of 61, 62, 72–3, 74, 82–4; compassion and protective anger in response to 38–43; core pain and 20, 28–9; emotional avoidance and 73; emotional clusters (experiences) triggered by (*see* loneliness-related primary maladaptive emotions); shame-related primary maladaptive emotions; terror/fear-related primary maladaptive emotions; emotional pain and 5–6, 28–9, 126; identifying 105–9; obstruction by avoidance 103–4, 110; primary therapeutic task with regards to 28–9; as process 29

validation 17–19; need for 11, 17–19; of protective anger 115, 117–18; by therapist 113

Van Dulmen, M. M. 19
van Gogh, Vincent xi

Watson, J. C. 58, 85, 86, 167
Welling, H. 48
Williams, K. D. 21
Wise, S. 15
Working with Emotions in Psychotherapy (Greenberg and Paivio) 167
worry: as form of avoidance 24, 25, 67–8, 78, 110; impact of 101–2; mobilisation against 103–4; self-compassion for 104–5; about triggers 26

CPSIA information can be obtained
at www.ICGtesting.com
Printed in the USA
BVHW040220060921
616149BV00011B/417

9 781138 790186